# STUDY GUIDE

## Robert B. Harris

Indiana University – Purdue University Indianapolis

# PRINCIPLES OF
# Microeconomics

## N. Gregory Mankiw

Harvard University

**The Dryden Press**
Harcourt Brace College Publishers

Fort Worth  Philadelphia  San Diego  New York  Orlando  Austin  San Antonio
Toronto  Montreal  London  Sydney  Tokyo

*Address for orders:*
Harcourt Brace & Company
6277 Sea Harbor Drive
Orlando, Florida 32887-6777
1-800-782-4479

*Address for editorial correspondence:*
The Dryden Press
301 Commerce Street, Suite 3700
Fort Worth, Texas 76102

*Web site address:*
http://www.hbcollege.com

THE DRYDEN PRESS, DRYDEN, and the DP Logo are registered trademarks of Harcourt Brace & Company.

Printed in the United States of America

ISBN: 0-03-020194-2

9 0 1 2 3 4 5 6 202 9 8 7

The Dryden Press
Harcourt Brace College Publishers

*One must learn by doing the thing;*
*For though you think you know it*
*You have no certainty, until you try.*

*Sophocles, c. 496-406 B.C.*
*Greek playwright*
*Trachiniae*

# PREFACE

Economics is a way of thinking. It provides a tool kit for solving problems and making decisions. You may be tempted to learn economics by simply listening to lectures or relying on common sense. Don't be fooled. Economics cannot be learned by osmosis. Learning requires active participation by the student. This means solving problems and answering questions, then looking at the reasons behind both the correct and the incorrect answers.

This *Study Guide* was written to accompany N. Gregory Mankiw's *Principles of Microeconomics*. It is intended to complement the material provided in the text and your instructor's lectures. This *Guide* should help you be successful in this course.

## Objectives of the *Study Guide*

This *Guide* provides additional examples and interpretation of the economic analysis contained in the text. It also provides applications of economic analysis to a variety of economic issues and problems. While it is easier to be a passive learner—simply nodding in agreement to statements made by the instructor—working through the problems and answering the questions in this *Guide* provide a way for the student to become a more active participant in his or her education in economics. The *Guide*'s sample problems and test questions provide an alternative to waiting until an hourly examination to discover which areas need additional study.

## Organization of the *Study Guide*

Each chapter in the *Study Guide* corresponds to a chapter in Mankiw's *Principles of Microeconomics*. Each *Guide* chapter inclùdes the following sections:

- *Chapter Overview*: This section begins with a statement of purpose for the chapter and describes how it fits into the overall text. It then elaborates on the learning objectives from the text, followed by a section-by-section chapter review. The overview also includes helpful hints to guide the student's intuition in understanding the material. Many of the terms used in economics take on specialized meanings that differ from their everyday usage. To ensure that lack of knowledge of the vocabulary of economics does not interfere with understanding, the section concludes with a matching exercise for terms and definitions.

- *Problems and Short-Answer Questions*: These problems and questions provide applications and extensions of the material in the text. Working through this section provides an opportunity to review the text material and receive feedback in the form of an answer key before facing the material on a graded examination.

- *Self-Test*: This section includes True/False and Multiple-Choice Questions, along with explanations for the false True/False Questions. This section also provides useful feedback in preparation for an exam, particularly if the student analyzes the right and wrong answers.

- *Advanced Critical Thinking*: This case study applies the economic analysis from the chapter to a real-world problem.

- *Solutions*: This section provides answers to all of the problems and questions in the *Guide*, including explanations for the false True/False Questions.

## Use of the *Study Guide*

This *Guide* is intended to be a supplement to the Mankiw text. It provides an overview of the text and a variety of problems and questions to assist the student in preparing for examinations. It is not intended to replace the main text. There are several ways this *Guide* can help you master the material. Perhaps the most common way is to read through the entire chapter in the textbook then work through the *Study Guide*, identifying the areas in which you need to study further and the areas which are already mastered.

Another alternative is to read the overview section of the *Guide* immediately after reading the related section of the text, then work through practice problems and short-answer questions immediately after reading the entire chapter. In either case, the Self-Test should be taken last. Use the *Guide* as a diagnostic tool to identify sections of the text that should be re-read for additional understanding.

## Acknowledgments

I thank Greg Mankiw for writing an excellent textbook—making this *Study Guide* a joy to write. Thanks also to Anita Fallon, the development editor, for guiding me through the process by serving as editor, coordinator, coach, and general problem solver.

Numerous other reviewers contributed to the editing and revision processes, beginning with Andrew John, who worked with me to develop the organization of the Study Guide as well as reviewing the finished manuscript. Other reviewers who provided many helpful comments included: Professors C. Denise Hixson, Tim Perri, Rick Fenner, and Art Meyer.

Thanks to David Hakes, who authored the *Macroeconomics Study Guide*, for contributing Chapters 1–3 of his macro volume for inclusion in this *Guide*.

Thanks also to Terri Crews for her invaluable assistance with the revisions.

**Final Thoughts**

Economics can be tremendously exciting and rewarding as a field of study. It also can be intimidating. For it to be enjoyable, you must understand it. The material builds logically from the earliest chapters through the concluding sections. By working through the *Study Guide*, answering questions, and solving the sample problems from the beginning of the course, you can control whether the course is exciting and interesting or simply something to get through. I hope that this *Guide* will help make economics as exciting for you as it is for me.

Robert B. Harris
Indiana University–Purdue University Indianapolis
August 1997

# CONVERSION CHART FOR MANKIW'S
## *Principles of Economics* TO *Principles of Microeconomics*

# Contents

# Chapter 1: Ten Principles of Economics

## I. Chapter Overview

### A. Context and Purpose

Chapter 1 is the first chapter in a three-chapter section that serves as the introduction to the text. Chapter 1 introduces ten fundamental principles on which the study of economics is based. In a broad sense, the rest of the text is an elaboration on these ten principles. Chapter 2 will develop how economists approach problems while Chapter 3 will explain how individuals and countries gain from trade.

The purpose of Chapter 1 is to lay out ten economic principles that will serve as building blocks for the rest of the text. The ten principles can be grouped into three categories: how people make decisions, how people interact, and how the economy works as a whole. Throughout the text, references will repeatedly be made to these ten principles.

### B. Learning Objectives

In this chapter you will:

1. Learn that economics is about the allocation of scarce resources
2. Examine some of the tradeoffs that people face
3. Learn the meaning of opportunity cost
4. See how to use marginal reasoning when making decisions
5. Discuss how incentives affect people's behavior
6. Consider why trade among people or nations can be good for everyone
7. Discuss why markets are a good, but not perfect, way to allocate resources
8. Learn what determines some trends in the overall economy

After accomplishing these goals, you should be able to:

1. Define scarcity
2. Explain the classic tradeoff between "guns and butter"
3. Add up your particular opportunity cost of attending college
4. Compare the marginal costs and marginal benefits of continuing to attend school indefinitely
5. Consider how a quadrupling of your tuition payments would affect your decision to educate yourself
6. Explain why specialization and trade improve people's choices
7. Give an example of an externality
8. Explain the source of large and persistent inflation

## C. Chapter Review

### Introduction

Households and society face decisions about how to allocate scarce resources. Resources are *scarce* in that we have fewer resources than we wish. *Economics* is the study of how society manages its scarce resources. Economists study how people make decisions about buying and selling, and saving and investing. We study how people interact with one another in markets where prices are determined and quantities are exchanged. We also study the economy as a whole when we concern ourselves with total income, unemployment, and inflation.

This chapter addresses ten principles of economics. The text will refer to these principles throughout. The ten principles are grouped into three categories: how people make decisions, how people interact, and how the economy works as a whole.

### 1-1  How People Make Decisions

- *People face tradeoffs*: Economists often say, "There is no such thing as a free lunch." This means that there are always tradeoffs—to get more of something we like, we have to give up something else that we like. For example, if you spend money on dinner and a movie, you won't be able to spend it on new clothes. Socially, we face tradeoffs as a group. For example, there is the classic tradeoff between "guns and butter." That is, if we decide to spend more on national defense (guns), then we will have less to spend on social programs (butter). There is also a social tradeoff between efficiency (getting the most from our scarce resources) and equity (benefits being distributed fairly across society). Policies such as taxes and welfare make incomes more equal but these policies reduce returns to hard work, and thus, the economy doesn't produce as much. As a result, when the government tries to cut the pie into more equal pieces, the pie gets smaller.

- *The cost of something is what you give up to get it*: The *opportunity cost* of an item is what you give up to get that item. It is the true cost of the item. The opportunity cost of going to college obviously includes your tuition payment. It also includes the value of your time that you could have spent working, valued at your potential wage. It would exclude your room and board payment because you have to eat and sleep whether you are in school or not.

- *Rational people think at the margin*: Marginal changes are incremental changes to an existing plan. Rational decisionmakers only proceed with an action if the marginal benefit exceeds the marginal cost. For example, you should only go to another year of school if the benefits from that year of schooling exceed the cost of attending that year. A farmer should produce another bushel of corn only if the benefit (price received) exceeds the cost of producing it.

- *People respond to incentives*: Since rational people weigh marginal costs and benefits of activities, they will respond when costs or benefits change. For example, when the price of automobiles rises, buyers have an incentive to buy fewer cars while automobile producers have an incentive to hire more workers and produce more autos. Public policy can alter the costs or benefits of activities. For example, a luxury tax on expensive boats raises the price and discourages purchases. Some policies have unintended consequences because they alter behavior in a manner that was not predicted.

## 1-2 How People Interact

- *Trade can make everyone better off*: Trade is not a contest where one wins and one loses. Trade can make each trader better off. Trade allows each trader to specialize in what they do best, whether it be farming, building, or manufacturing, and trade their output for the output of other efficient producers. This is as true for countries as it is for individuals.

- *Markets are usually a good way to organize economic activity*: In a market economy, the decisions about what goods and services to produce, how much to produce, and who gets to consume them, are made by millions of firms and households. Firms and households, guided by self-interest, interact in the marketplace, where prices and quantities are determined. While this may appear like chaos, Adam Smith made the famous observation in the *Wealth of Nations* in 1776 that self-interested households and firms interact in markets and behave as if guided by an "invisible hand" to create desirable social outcomes. The prices generated by their competitive activity signal the value of costs and benefits to producers and consumers, whose activities unknowingly maximize the welfare of society. Alternatively, the prices dictated by central planners contain no information on costs and benefits, and therefore, these prices fail to efficiently guide economic activity. Prices also fail to efficiently guide economic activity when governments distort prices with taxes or restrict price movements with price controls.

- *Governments can sometimes improve market outcomes*: Sometimes government intervenes in the market to improve efficiency or equity. When markets fail to allocate resources efficiently, there has been *market failure*. There are many different sources of market failure. An *externality* is when the actions of one person affect the well-being of a bystander. Pollution is a standard example. *Market power* is when a single person or group can influence the price. In these cases, the government may be able to intervene and improve economic efficiency. The government may also intervene to improve equity with income taxes and welfare. Sometimes well-intentioned policy intervention has unintended consequences.

- *A country's standard of living depends on its ability to produce goods and services*: There is great variation in average incomes in different countries at a point in time and in the same country over time. These differences in incomes and standards of living are largely attributable to differences in *productivity*. Productivity is the amount of goods and services produced by each hour of a worker's time. As a result, public policy intended to improve standards of living should improve education, generate more and better tools, and improve access to current technology. Government deficits depress growth because they absorb private saving which reduces society's investment in human capital (education) and physical capital (factories).

- *Prices rise when the government prints too much money*: Inflation is an increase in the overall level of prices in the economy. High inflation is costly to the economy. Large and persistent inflation is caused by rapid growth in the quantity of money. Therefore, policymakers wishing to keep inflation low should maintain slow growth in the quantity of money.

- *Society faces a short-run tradeoff between inflation and unemployment*: A reduction in inflation tends to increase unemployment. The short-run tradeoff between inflation and unemployment is known as the *Phillips curve*. When the government decreases the quantity of money in order to lower prices, many prices are *sticky* and don't fall right away. The smaller quantity of money reduces spending on output, so sales fall, and firms lay off workers. This effect is thought to be temporary. In the short run, policymakers may be able to affect the mix of inflation and unemployment by changing government spending, taxes, and the quantity of money.

## D. Helpful Hints

1. Place yourself in the story. Throughout the text, most economic situations will be composed of economic actors—buyers and sellers, borrowers and lenders, firms and workers, and so on. When you are asked to address how any economic actor would respond to economic incentives, place yourself in the story as the buyer or the seller, the borrower or the lender, the producer or the consumer. Don't think of yourself always as the buyer (a natural tendency) or always as the seller. You will find that your role playing will usually produce the right response once you learn to think like an economist—which is the topic of the next chapter.

2. Trade is not a zero-sum game. Some people see an exchange in terms of winners and losers. Their reaction to trade is that, after the sale, if the seller is happy the buyer must be sad because the seller must have taken something from the buyer. That is, they view trade as a *zero-sum game* where what one gains the other must have lost. They fail to see that both parties to a voluntary transaction gain because each party is allowed to specialize in what it can produce most efficiently, and then trade for items

that are produced more efficiently by others. Nobody loses, because trade is voluntary. Therefore, a government policy that limits trade reduces the potential gains from trade.

3. An externality can be positive. Because the classic example of an externality is pollution, it is easy to think of an externality as a cost that lands on a bystander. However, an externality can be positive in that it can be a benefit that lands on a bystander. For example, education is often cited as a product that emits a positive externality because when your neighbor educates herself, she is likely to be more reasonable, responsible, productive, and politically astute. In short, she is a better neighbor. Positive externalities, just as much as negative externalities, may be a reason for the government to intervene to promote efficiency.

## E. Terms and Definitions

Choose a definition for each key term.

Key terms:

_____Scarcity
_____Economics
_____Efficiency
_____Equity
_____Opportunity cost
_____Marginal changes
_____Market economy
_____"Invisible hand"
_____Market failure
_____Externality
_____Market power
_____Monopoly
_____Productivity
_____Inflation
_____Phillips curve

Definitions:

1. The property of distributing output fairly among society's members
2. A situation in which the market fails to allocate resources efficiently
3. Limited resources and unlimited wants
4. The amount of goods and services produced per hour by a worker
5. The case in which there is only one seller in the market
6. The principle that self-interested market participants may unknowingly maximize the welfare of society as a whole
7. The property of society getting the most from its scarce resources

8. An economic system where interaction of households and firms in markets determine the allocation of resources
9. The short-run tradeoff between inflation and unemployment
10. When one person's actions have an impact on a bystander
11. An increase in the overall level of prices
12. Incremental adjustments to an existing plan
13. Study of how society manages its scarce resources
14. Whatever is given up to get something else
15. The ability of an individual or group to substantially influence market prices

## II. Problems and Short-Answer Questions

### A. Practice Problems

1. People respond to incentives. Governments can alter incentives and, hence, behavior with public policy. However, sometimes public policy generates unintended consequences by producing results that were not anticipated. Try to find an unintended consequence of each of the following public policies.

   a. To help the "working poor," the government raises the minimum wage to $25 per hour._____

   _____

   _____

   b. To help the homeless, the government places rent controls on apartments restricting rent to $10 per month._____

   _____

   _____

   c. To reduce the deficit and limit consumption of gasoline, the government raises the tax on gasoline by $2.00 per gallon._____

   _____

   _____

   d. To reduce the consumption of drugs, the government makes drugs illegal._____

   _____

   _____

   e. To raise the population of wolves, the government prohibits the killing of wolves._____

   _____

   f. To improve the welfare of American sugar beet growers, the government bans imports of sugar from South America._____

   _____

   _____

2. Opportunity cost is what you give up to get an item. Since there is no such thing as a free lunch, what would likely be given up to obtain each of the items listed below?

   a. Susan can work full time or go to college. She chooses college._____
   _____
   _____

   b. Susan can work full time or go to college. She chooses work._____
   _____
   _____
   _____

   c. Farmer Jones has 100 acres of land. He can plant corn, which yields 100 bushels per acre, or he can plant beans, which yield 40 bushels per acre. He chooses to plant corn._____
   _____

   d. Farmer Jones has 100 acres of land. He can plant corn, which yields 100 bushels per acre, or he can plant beans, which yield 40 bushels per acre. He chooses to plant beans._____
   _____

   e. In (a) and (b) above, and (c) and (d) above, which is the opportunity cost of which—college for work or work for college? Corn for beans or beans for corn?_____
   _____
   _____

## B. Short-Answer Questions

1. Is air scarce? Is clean air scarce?_____
   _____
   _____

2. What is the opportunity cost of saving some of your paycheck?_____
   _____
   _____

3. Why is there a tradeoff between equity and efficiency?_____
   _____
   _____

4. Water is necessary for life. Diamonds are not. Is the marginal benefit of an additional glass of water greater or lesser than an additional one carat diamond? Why?_____
_____
_____
_____

5. Your car needs to be repaired. You have already paid $500 to have the transmission fixed, but it still doesn't work properly. You can sell your car "as is" for $2000. If your car were fixed, you could sell it for $2500. Your car can be fixed with a guarantee for another $300. Should you repair your car? Why?_____
_____
_____

6. Why do you think air bags have reduced deaths from auto crashes less than we had hoped?_____
_____

7. Suppose one country is better at producing agricultural products (because they have more fertile land) while another country is better at producing manufactured goods (they have a better educational system and more engineers). If each country produced their specialty and traded, would there be more or less total output than if each country produced all of their agricultural and manufacturing needs? Why?_____
_____
_____

8. In the *Wealth of Nations* Adam Smith said, "It is not by the benevolence of the baker that you receive your bread." What do you think he meant?_____
_____
_____

9. If we save more and use it to build more physical capital, productivity will rise and we will have rising standards of living in the future. What is the opportunity cost of future growth?_____
_____

10. If the government printed twice as much money, what do you think would happen to prices and output if the economy were already producing at maximum capacity?_____
_____
_____

11. A goal for a society is to distribute resources equitably or fairly. How would you distribute resources if everyone were equally talented and worked equally hard? What if people had different talents and some people worked hard while others didn't?_____

_____

12. Who is more self-interested, the buyer or the seller?_____

_____

_____

13. Why might government deficits slow a country's growth rate? _____

_____

_____

## III. Self-Test

### A. True/False Questions

_____1.  When the government redistributes income with taxes and welfare, the economy becomes more efficient.

_____2.  When economists say, "There is no such thing as a free lunch," they mean that all economic decisions involve tradeoffs.

_____3.  Adam Smith's "invisible hand" concept describes how corporate business reaches into the pockets of consumers like an "invisible hand."

_____4.  Rational people act only when the marginal benefit of the action exceeds the marginal cost.

_____5.  The United States will benefit economically if we eliminate trade with Asian countries because we will be forced to produce more of our own cars and clothes.

_____6.  When a jet flies overhead, the noise it generates is an externality.

_____7.  A tax on liquor raises the price of liquor and provides an incentive for consumers to drink more.

_____8.  An unintended consequence of public support for higher education is that low tuition provides an incentive for many people to attend state universities even if they have no desire to learn anything.

_____9. Sue is better at cleaning and Bob is better at cooking. It will take fewer hours to eat and clean if Bob specializes in cooking and Sue specializes in cleaning than if they share the household duties evenly.

_____10. High and persistent inflation is caused by excessive growth in the quantity of money in the economy.

_____11. In the short run, a reduction in inflation tends to cause a reduction in unemployment.

_____12. An auto manufacturer should continue to produce additional autos as long as the firm is profitable, even if the cost of the additional units exceed the price received.

_____13. An individual farmer is likely to have *market power* in the market for wheat.

_____14. To a student, the opportunity cost of going to a basketball game would include the price of the ticket and the value of the time that could have been spent studying.

_____15. Workers in the United States have a relatively high standard of living because the United States has a relatively high minimum wage.

## B. Multiple-Choice Questions

1. Which of the following involve a tradeoff?
   a. buying a new car.
   b. going to college.
   c. watching a football game on Saturday afternoon.
   d. taking a nap.
   e. All of the above involve tradeoffs.

2. Tradeoffs are required because wants are unlimited and resources are
   a. efficient.
   b. economical.
   c. scarce.
   d. unlimited.
   e. marginal.

3. Economics is the study of
   a. how to fully satisfy our unlimited wants.
   b. how society manages its scarce resources.
   c. how to reduce our wants until we are satisfied.
   d. how to avoid having to make tradeoffs.
   e. how society manages its unlimited resources.

4. A rational person does not act unless
   a. the action makes money for the person.
   b. the action is ethical.
   c. the action produces marginal costs that exceed marginal benefits.
   d. the action produces marginal benefits that exceed marginal costs.
   e. none of the above.

5. Raising taxes and increasing welfare payments
   a. proves that there is such a thing as a free lunch.
   b. reduces market power.
   c. improves efficiency at the expense of equity.
   d. improves equity at the expense of efficiency.
   e. none of the above.

6. Suppose you find $20. If you choose to use the $20 to go to the football game, your opportunity cost of going to the game is
   a. nothing, because you found the money.
   b. $20 (because you could have used the $20 to buy other things).
   c. $20 (because you could have used the $20 to buy other things) plus the value of the time spent at the game.
   d. $20 (because you could have used the $20 to buy other things) plus the value of the time spent at the game, plus the cost of the soda and hot dog you consumed at the game.
   e. none of the above.

7. Foreign trade
   a. allows a country to have a greater variety of products at a lower cost than if it tried to produce everything at home.
   b. allows a country to avoid tradeoffs.
   c. makes a country more equitable.
   d. increases the scarcity of resources.
   e. none of the above.

8. Since people respond to incentives, we would expect that, if the average salary of accountants increases by 50% while the average salary of teachers increases by 20%,
   a. students will shift majors from education to accounting.
   b. students will shift majors from accounting to education.
   c. fewer students will attend college.
   d. none of the above.

9. Which of the following activities is most likely to produce an externality?
   a. A student sits at home and watches T.V.
   b. A student has a party in her dorm room.
   c. A student reads a novel for pleasure.
   d. A student eats a hamburger in the student union.

10. Which of the following products would be *least* capable of producing an externality?
    a. cigarettes.
    b. stereo equipment.
    c. inoculations against disease.
    d. education.
    e. food.

11. Which of the following situations describes the greatest *market power*?
    a. a farmer's impact on the price of corn.
    b. Saab's impact on the price of autos.
    c. Microsoft's impact on the price of desktop operating systems.
    d. a student's impact on college tuition.

12. Which of the following statements is true about a market economy?
    a. Market participants act as if guided by an "invisible hand" to produce outcomes that maximize social welfare.
    b. Taxes help prices communicate costs and benefits to producers and consumers.
    c. With a large enough computer, central planners could guide production more efficiently than markets.
    d. The strength of a market system is that it tends to distribute resources evenly across consumers.

13. Workers in the United States enjoy a high standard of living because
    a. unions in the United States keep the wage high.
    b. we have protected our industry from foreign competition.
    c. the United States has a high minimum wage.
    d. workers in the United States are highly productive.
    e. none of the above.

14. High and persistent inflation is caused by
    a. unions increasing wages too much.
    b. OPEC raising the price of oil too much.
    c. governments increasing the quantity of money too much.
    d. regulations raising the cost of production too much.

15. The Phillips curve suggests that
    a. an increase in inflation temporarily increases unemployment.
    b. a decrease in inflation temporarily increases unemployment.
    c. inflation and unemployment are unrelated in the short run.
    d. none of the above.

16. An increase in the price of beef provides information which
    a. tells consumers to buy more beef.
    b. tells consumers to buy less pork.
    c. tells producers to produce more beef.
    d. provides no information because prices in a market system are managed by planning boards.

17. You have spent $1000 building a hot dog stand based on estimates of sales of $2000. The hot dog stand is nearly completed but now you estimate total sales to be only $800. You can complete the hot dog stand for another $300. Should you complete the hot dog stand?
    a. Yes.
    b. No.
    c. There is not enough information to answer this question.

18. Referring to Question 17, your decision rule should be to complete the hot dog stand as long as the cost to complete the stand is less than
    a. $100
    b. $300
    c. $500
    d. $800
    e. none of the above.

19. Which of the following is *not* part of the opportunity cost of going on vacation?
    a. the money you could have made if you had stayed home and worked.
    b. the money you spent on food.
    c. the money you spent on airplane tickets.
    d. the money you spent on a Broadway show.

20. Productivity can be increased by
    a. raising minimum wages.
    b. raising union wages.
    c. improving the education of workers.
    d. restricting trade with foreign countries.

## IV. Advanced Critical Thinking

Suppose your university decides to lower the cost of parking on campus by reducing the price of a parking sticker from $200 per semester to $5 per semester.

1. What do you think would happen to the number of students desiring to park their cars on campus?_____
   _____

2. What do you think would happen to the amount of time it would take to find a parking place?_____
   _____

3. Thinking in terms of opportunity cost, would the lower price of a parking sticker necessarily lower the true cost of parking?_____
   _____

4. Would the opportunity cost of parking be the same for students with no outside employment and students with jobs earning $15 per hour?_____

_____

_____

_____

## V.  Solutions

### Terms and Definitions

 3  Scarcity
13 Economics
 7  Efficiency
 1  Equity
14 Opportunity cost
12 Marginal changes
 8  Market economy
 6  "Invisible hand"
 2  Market failure
10 Externality
15 Market power
 5  Monopoly
 4  Productivity
11 Inflation
 9  Phillips curve

### Practice Problems

1.  a.  Many would want to work at $25/hour but few firms would want to hire low productivity workers at this wage; therefore it would simply create unemployment.

    b.  Many renters would want to rent an apartment at $10/month, but few landlords could produce an apartment at this price, therefore this rent control would create more homelessness.

    c.  Higher gas prices would reduce the miles driven.  This would lower auto accidents, put less wear and tear on roads and cars, and reduce the demand for cars and road repairs.

    d.  This raises the price of drugs and makes selling them more profitable.  This creates more gangs and gang warfare.

    e.  Restrictions on killing wolves reduces the population of animals upon which wolves may feed—rabbits, deer, etc.

f. South American growers have difficulty repaying their bank loans to U.S. banks. They turn to more profitable crops such as coca leaves and marijuana.

2. a. She gives up income from work (and must pay tuition).

   b. She gives up a college degree and the increase in income through life that it would have brought her (but doesn't have to pay tuition).

   c. He gives up 4000 bushels of beans.

   d. He gives up 10,000 bushels of corn.

   e. Each is the opportunity cost of the other because each decision requires giving something up.

**Short-Answer Questions**

1. No, you don't have to give up anything to get it. Yes, you can't have as much as you want without giving up something to get it (pollution equipment on cars, etc.)

2. The items you could have enjoyed had you spent it (current consumption).

3. Taxes and welfare make us more equal but reduce incentives for hard work, lowering total output.

4. The marginal benefit of another glass of water is generally lower because we have so much water that one more glass is of little value. The opposite is true for diamonds.

5. Yes, because the marginal benefit of fixing the car is $2500 - $2000 = $500 and the marginal cost is $300. The original repair payment is not relevant.

6. The cost of an accident was lowered. This changed incentives so people drive faster and have more accidents.

7. There would be more total output if they specialize and trade because each is doing what it does most efficiently.

8. The baker produces the best bread possible, not out of kindness, but because it is in his best interest to do so. Self-interest can maximize social welfare.

9. We must give up consumption today.

10. Spending would double but since the quantity of output would remain the same, prices would double.

11. Fairness would require that everyone get an equal share. Fairness would require that people not get an equal share.

12. They are equally self-interested. The seller will sell to the highest bidder and the buyer will buy from the lowest offer.

13. Deficits absorb saving which reduces society's investment in capital.

## True/False Questions

1. F; the economy becomes less efficient because it decreases the incentive to work hard.
2. T
3. F; the "invisible hand" refers to how markets guide self-interested people to create desirable social outcomes.
4. T
5. F; all countries gain from voluntary trade.
6. T
7. F; higher prices reduce the quantity demanded.
8. T
9. T
10. T
11. F; a reduction in inflation tends to raise unemployment.
12. F; a manufacturer should produce as long as the marginal benefit exceeds the marginal cost.
13. F; a single farmer is too small to influence the market.
14. T
15. F; workers in the U.S. have a high standard of living because they are productive.

## Multiple-Choice Questions

1. e
2. c
3. b
4. d
5. d
6. c
7. a
8. a
9. b
10. e
11. c
12. a
13. d
14. c

15. b
16. c
17. a
18. d
19. b
20. c

**Advanced Critical Thinking**

1.  More students would wish to park on campus.

2.  It would take much longer to find a parking place.

3.  No, because we would have to factor in the value of our time spent looking for a parking place.

4.  No. Students that could be earning money working are giving up more while looking for a parking place. Therefore, their opportunity cost is higher.

# Chapter 2: Thinking Like an Economist

## I. Chapter Overview

### A. Context and Purpose

Chapter 2 is the second chapter in a three-chapter section that serves as the introduction of the text. Chapter 1 introduced ten principles of economics that will be revisited throughout the text. Chapter 2 develops how economists approach problems while Chapter 3 will explain how individuals and countries gain from trade.

The purpose of Chapter 2 is to familiarize you with how economists approach economic problems. With practice, you will learn how to approach similar problems in this dispassionate systematic way. You will see how economists employ the scientific method, the role of assumptions in model building, and the application of two specific economic models. You will also learn the important distinction between two roles economists can play: as scientists when we try to explain the economic world and as policymakers when we try to improve it.

### B. Learning Objectives

In this chapter you will:

1. See how economists apply the methods of science
2. Consider how assumptions and models can shed light on the world
3. Learn two simple models—the circular-flow and the production possibilities frontier
4. Distinguish between microeconomics and macroeconomics
5. Learn the difference between positive and normative statements
6. Examine the role of economists in making policy
7. Consider why economists sometimes disagree with one another

After accomplishing these goals, you should be able to:

1. Describe the scientific method
2. Understand the art of making useful assumptions
3. Explain the slope of a production possibilities frontier
4. Place economic issues into the categories of microeconomics or macroeconomics
5. Place economic statements into the categories of normative or positive
6. See the link between policymaking and normative statements
7. List three reasons why economists disagree

## C. Chapter Review

## Introduction

Like other fields of study, economics has its own jargon and way of thinking. It is necessary to learn the special language of economics because knowledge of the economic vocabulary will help you communicate with precision to others about economic issues. This chapter will also provide an overview of how economists look at the world.

## 2-1 The Economist as Scientist

While economists don't use test tubes or telescopes, they are scientists because they employ the *scientific method*—the dispassionate and objective development and testing of theories.

- *The scientific method: observation, theory, and more observation*: Just as in other sciences, an economist observes an event, develops a theory, and collects data to test the theory. An economist observes inflation, creates a theory that excessive growth in money causes inflation, and then collects data on money growth and inflation to see if there is a relationship. Collecting data to test economic theories is difficult, however, because economists usually cannot create data from experiments. That is, economists cannot manipulate the economy just to test a theory. Therefore, economists often use data gathered from recent economic events.

- *The role of assumptions*: Assumptions are made to make the world easier to understand. A physicist assumes an object is falling in a vacuum when measuring acceleration due to gravity. This assumption is reasonably accurate for a marble but not for a beachball. An economist may assume that prices are fixed (can't be changed) or may assume that prices are flexible (can move up or down in response to market pressures). Since prices often cannot be changed quickly (the menu in a restaurant is expensive to change) but can be changed easily over time, it is reasonable for economists to assume that prices are fixed in the short run but flexible in the long run. The art of scientific thinking is deciding which assumptions to make.

- *Economic models*: Biology teachers employ plastic models of the human body. They are simpler than the actual human body, but that is what makes them useful. Economists use economic models that are composed of diagrams and equations. Economic models are based on assumptions and are simplifications of economic reality.

- *Our first model: the circular-flow diagram*: The circular-flow diagram shows the flow of goods and services, factors of production, and monetary payments between households and firms. Households sell the factors of production such as land, labor and capital to firms, in the market for factors of production. In exchange, the households receive wages, rent, and profit. They use these dollars to buy goods and services from firms, in the market for goods and services. The firms use this revenue to pay for the factors of production, and so on. This is a simplified model of the entire economy. This version of the circular flow diagram has been simplified because it excludes international trade and the government.

- *Our second model: the production possibilities frontier*: A production possibilities frontier is a graph that shows the combinations of output the economy can possibly produce given the available factors of production and the available production technology. It is drawn assuming the economy produces only two goods. This model demonstrates the following economic principles:

  - If the economy is operating on the production possibilities frontier, it is operating *efficiently* because it is producing a mix of output that is the maximum possible from the resources available.

  - Points inside the curve are therefore *inefficient*. Points outside the curve are currently unattainable.

  - If the economy is operating on the production possibilities frontier, we can see the *tradeoffs* society faces. To produce more of one good, it must produce less of the other. The amount of one good given up when producing more of another good is the *opportunity cost* of the additional production.

  - The production possibilities frontier is bowed outward because the opportunity cost of producing more of a good increases as we near maximum production of that good. This is because we use resources better suited toward production of the other good in order to continue to expand production of the first good.

  - A technological advance in production shifts the production possibilities frontier outward. This is a demonstration of *economic growth*.

- *Microeconomics and macroeconomics*: Economics is studied on various levels. Microeconomics is the study of how households and firms make decisions and how they interact in specific markets. Macroeconomics is the study of economy-wide phenomena such as the federal deficit, the rate of unemployment, and policies to improve our standard of living. Microeconomics and macroeconomics are related because changes in the overall economy arise from decisions of millions of individuals. Although related, the methods employed in microeconomics and macroeconomics differ enough that they are often taught in separate courses.

## 2-2 The Economist as Policymaker

When economists attempt to explain the world as it is, they act as scientists. When economists attempt to improve the world, they act as policymakers. Correspondingly, *positive statements* describe the world as it is, while *normative statements* prescribe how the world ought to be. Positive statements can be confirmed or refuted with evidence. Normative statements involve values (ethics, religion, political philosophy) as well as facts.

For example, "Money growth causes inflation" is a positive statement (of a scientist). "The government ought to lower inflation" is a normative statement (of a policymaker). The two statements are related because evidence about whether money causes inflation might help us decide what tool the government should use if it chooses to lower inflation.

Economists act as policymakers to the government in many different areas. The president is advised by economists on the Council of Economic Advisers, the Department of Treasury, the Department of Labor, and the Department of Justice. Congress is advised by economists from the Congressional Budget Office and the Federal Reserve.

## 2-3 Why Economists Disagree

There are three reasons why economists have a reputation for giving conflicting advice to policymakers:

- Economists may have different scientific judgments. That is, economists may disagree about the validity of alternative positive theories about how the world works. For example, economists differ in their views of the sensitivity of household saving to changes in the after-tax return to saving.

- Economists may have different values. That is, economists may have different normative views about what policy should try to accomplish. For example, economists differ in their views of whether taxes should be used to redistribute income.

- Some economists are charlatans and cranks. Crazy economic theories and economic fads are promoted by incompetent, self-proclaimed "economists." Often these theories say what politicians and people want to hear—taxes can be lower, government spending can be higher, and so on. When these policies fail, the public thinks that the economics profession is inept. Yet qualified economists never supported these theories to begin with.

In reality, although there are legitimate disagreements among economists on many issues, there is tremendous agreement on many basic principles of economics.

## 2-4 Let's Get Going

In the next chapter, we will begin to apply the ideas and methods of economics. As you begin to think like an economist, you will use a variety of skills—mathematics, history, politics, philosophy—with the objectivity of a scientist.

### D. Helpful Hints

1.  Opportunity costs are usually not constant along a production possibilities frontier. Notice that the production possibilities frontier shown in the following graph is bowed outward. It shows the production tradeoffs for an economy that produces only paper and pencils.

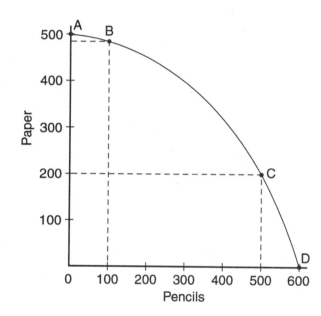

If we start at the point where the economy is using all of its resources to produce paper, producing 100 units of pencils only requires a tradeoff or an opportunity cost of 25 units of paper (point A to point B). This is because when we move resources from paper to pencil production, we first move those resources best suited for pencil production and poorly suited for paper production. Therefore, pencil production increases with very little decrease in paper production. However, if the economy were operating at point C, the opportunity cost of an additional 100 pencils (point C to D) is 200 units of paper. This is because we now move resources toward pencil production that were extremely well suited for paper production and are poorly suited for pencil production. Therefore, as we produce more and more of any particular good, the opportunity cost per unit tends to rise because resources are specialized. That is, resources are not equally well suited for producing each output.

The argument above applies when moving either direction on the production possibilities frontier. For example, if we start at point D (maximum production of pencils) a small reduction in pencil production (100 units) releases enough resources to increase production of paper by a large amount (200 units). However, moving from point B to point A only increases paper production by 25 units.

2. A production possibilities frontier only shows the choices available—not which point of production is best. A common mistake made by students when using production possibilities frontiers is to look at a production possibilities frontier and suggest that a point somewhere near the middle "looks best." Students make this subjective judgment because the middle point appears to provide the biggest total number of units of production of the two goods. However, ask yourself the following question: Using the production possibilities frontier in the previous graph, what production point would be best if paper were worth $10 per sheet and pencils were worth 1 cent per dozen? We would move our resources toward paper production. What if paper were worth 1 cent per sheet and pencils were worth $50 each? We would move our resources toward pencil production. Clearly, what we actually choose to produce depends on the price of each good. Therefore, a production possibilities frontier only provides the choices available; it alone cannot determine which choice is best.

3. Economic disagreement is interesting but economic consensus is more important. Economists have a reputation for disagreeing with one another because we tend to highlight our differences. While our disagreements are interesting to us, the matters on which we agree are more important to you. There are a great number of economic principles for which there is near unanimous support from the economics profession. The aim of this text is to concentrate on the areas of agreement within the profession as opposed to the areas of disagreement.

## E. Terms and Definitions

Choose a definition for each key term.

Key terms:

_____Scientific method
_____Economic models
_____Circular-flow diagram
_____Factors of production
_____Production possibilities frontier
_____Opportunity cost
_____Efficiency
_____Microeconomics
_____Macroeconomics
_____Positive statements
_____Normative statements

Definitions:

1. Inputs such as land, labor, and capital
2. The study of economy-wide phenomena
3. Objective development and testing of theories

4. Whatever is given up to get something else
5. Prescription for how the world ought to be
6. Getting maximum output from the resources available
7. Descriptions of the world as it is
8. Simplifications of reality based on assumptions
9. A graph that shows the combinations of output the economy can possibly produce given the available factors of production and the available production technology
10. The study of how households and firms make decisions and how they interact in markets
11. A diagram of the economy that shows the flow of goods and services, factors of production, and monetary payments between households and firms

## II. Problems and Short-Answer Questions

### A. Practice Problems

1. Identify the parts of the circular-flow diagram immediately involved in the following transactions.

   a. Mary buys a car from General Motors for $20,000._____

   _____

   _____

   _____

   _____

   b. General Motors pays Joe $5000/month for work on the assembly line.

   _____

   _____

   _____

   _____

   c. Joe gets a $15 hair cut._____

   _____

   _____

   _____

   _____

   d. Mary receives $10,000 of dividends on her General Motors stock.

   _____

   _____

   _____

   _____

2. The following table provides information about the production possibilities frontier of Athletic Country.

| Bats | Rackets |
|------|---------|
| 0 | 420 |
| 100 | 400 |
| 200 | 360 |
| 300 | 300 |
| 400 | 200 |
| 500 | 0 |

a. Plot and connect these points to create Athletic Country's production possibilities frontier.

b. If Athletic Country currently produces 100 bats and 400 rackets, what is the opportunity cost of an additional 100 bats?_____

c. If Athletic Country currently produces 300 bats and 300 rackets, what is the opportunity cost of an additional 100 bats?_____

d. Why does the additional production of 100 bats in part (c) cause a greater tradeoff than the additional production of 100 bats in part (b)?_____

e. Suppose Athletic Country is currently producing 200 bats and 200 rackets. How many additional bats could they produce without giving up any rackets? How many additional rackets could they produce without giving up any bats?_____

_____

_____

f. Is the production of 200 bats and 200 rackets efficient? Explain._____

_____

_____

3. The following production possibilities frontier shows the available tradeoffs between consumption goods and capital goods. Suppose two countries face the identical production possibilities frontier shown below.

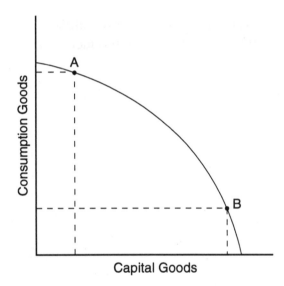

a. Suppose Party Country chooses to produce at point A while Parsimonious Country chooses to produce at point B. Which country will experience more growth in the future? Why?_____

_____

_____

b. In this model, what is the opportunity cost of future growth?_____

_____

c. Demonstrate the impact of growth on a production possibilities frontier such as the one shown above. Would the production possibilities frontier for Parsimonious Country shift more or less than that for Party Country? Why?_____

_____

d. Show the shift in the production possibilities curve if there was an increase in technology that only affected the production of capital goods.

e. Does the shift in part (d) above imply that all additional production must be in the form of capital goods? Why?_____

_____

**B. Short-Answer Questions**

1. Describe the scientific method._____

_____

2. What is the role of assumptions in any science?_____

_____

3. Is a more realistic model always better?_____
_____
_____

4. Why does a production possibilities frontier have a negative slope (slope down and to the right)?_____
_____
_____

5. Why is the production possibilities frontier bowed outward? _____
_____
_____

6. What are the two subfields within economics?  Which is more likely to be a building block of the other?  Why?_____
_____
_____
_____

7. When an economist makes a normative statement, are they more likely to be acting as a scientist or a policymaker?  Why?_____
_____
_____
_____

8. Which statements are testable:  positive statements or normative statements? Why?_____
_____

9. Name three reasons why economists disagree._____
_____
_____

10. Name two economic propositions on which more than 90% of economists agree._____
_____
_____

## III. Self-Test

### A. True/False Questions

_____ 1.   Economic models must mirror reality or they are of no value.

_____ 2.   Assumptions make the world easier to understand because they simplify reality and focus our attention.

_____ 3.   It is reasonable to assume that the world is composed of only one person when modeling international trade.

_____ 4.   When people act as scientists, they must try to be objective.

_____ 5.   If an economy is operating on its production possibilities frontier, it must be using its resources efficiently.

_____ 6.   If an economy is operating on its production possibilities frontier, it must produce less of one good if it produces more of another.

_____ 7.   Points outside the production possibilities frontier are attainable but inefficient.

_____ 8.   If an economy were experiencing substantial unemployment, the economy is producing inside the production possibilities frontier.

_____ 9.   The production possibilities frontier is bowed outward because the tradeoffs between the production of any two goods are constant.

_____ 10.  An advance in production technology would cause the production possibilities curve to shift outward.

_____ 11.  Macroeconomics is concerned with the study of how households and firms make decisions and how they interact in specific markets.

_____ 12.  The statement, "An increase in inflation tends to cause unemployment to fall in the short run," is normative.

_____ 13.  When economists make positive statements, they are more likely to be acting as scientists.

_____ 14.  Normative statements can be refuted with evidence.

_____ 15.  Economists may appear to disagree more than they actually do because many crazy economic theories are supported only by unqualified charlatans or cranks.

## B. Multiple-Choice Questions

1. The scientific method requires that
   a. the scientist use test tubes and have a clean lab.
   b. the scientist be objective.
   c. the scientist use precision equipment.
   d. only incorrect theories are tested.
   e. only correct theories are tested.

2. Which of the following is most likely to produce scientific evidence about a theory?
   a. An economist employed by the AFL/CIO doing research on the impact of trade restrictions.
   b. A radio talk show host collecting data on how capital markets respond to taxation.
   c. A tenured economist employed at a leading university analyzing the impact of bank regulations on rural lending.
   d. A lawyer employed by General Motors addressing the impact of air bags on passenger safety.

3. Which of the following statements regarding the circular-flow diagram is true?
   a. The factors of production are owned by households.
   b. If Susan works for IBM and receives a paycheck, the transaction takes place in the market for goods and services.
   c. If IBM sells a computer, the transaction takes place in the market for factors of production.
   d. The factors of production are owned by firms.
   e. None of the above.

4. In which of the following cases is the assumption most reasonable?
   a. To estimate the speed at which a beachball falls, a physicist assumes that it falls in a vacuum.
   b. To address the impact of money growth on inflation, an economist assumes that money is strictly coins.
   c. To address the impact of taxes on income distribution, an economist assumes that everyone earns the same income.
   d. To address the benefits of trade, an economist assumes that there are two people and two goods.

5. Economic models are
   a. created to duplicate reality.
   b. built with assumptions.
   c. usually made of wood and plastic.
   d. useless if they are simple.

6. Which of the following is not a factor of production?
   a. land
   b. labor
   c. capital
   d. money
   e. all of the above

7. Points on the production possibilities frontier are
   a. efficient.
   b. inefficient.
   c. unattainable.
   d. normative.
   e. none of the above

8. Which of the following will not shift a country's production possibilities frontier outward?
   a. an increase in the capital stock
   b. an advance in technology
   c. a reduction in unemployment
   d. an increase in the labor force

9. Economic growth is depicted by
   a. a movement along a production possibilities frontier toward capital goods.
   b. a shift in the production possibilities frontier outward.
   c. a shift in the production possibilities frontier inward.
   d. a movement from inside the curve toward the curve.

Use the following graph to answer questions 10-13.

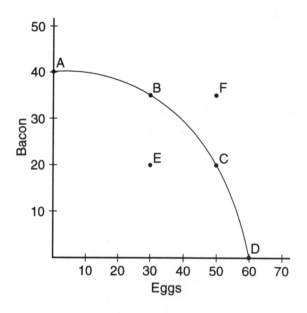

10. If the economy is operating at point C, the opportunity cost of producing an additional 15 units of bacon is
    a. 10 units of eggs.
    b. 20 units of eggs.
    c. 30 units of eggs.
    d. 40 units of eggs.
    e. 50 units of eggs.

11. If the economy were operating at point E
    a. the opportunity cost of 20 additional units of eggs is 10 units of bacon.
    b. the opportunity cost of 20 additional units of eggs is 20 units of bacon.
    c. the opportunity cost of 20 additional units of eggs is 30 units of bacon.
    d. 20 additional units of eggs can be produced with no impact on bacon production.

12. Point F represents
    a. a combination of production that can be reached if we reduce the production of eggs by 20 units.
    b. a combination of production that is inefficient because there are unemployed resources.
    c. a combination of production that can be reached if there is a sufficient advance in technology.
    d. none of the above.

13. As we move from point A to point D
    a. the opportunity cost of eggs in terms of bacon is constant.
    b. the opportunity cost of eggs in terms of bacon falls.
    c. the opportunity cost of eggs in terms of bacon rises.
    d. the economy becomes more efficient.
    e. the economy becomes less efficient.

14. Which of the following issues is related to microeconomics?
    a. the impact of money on inflation
    b. the impact of technology on economic growth
    c. the impact of the deficit on saving
    d. the impact of oil prices on auto production

15. Which of the following statements about microeconomics and macroeconomics is *not* true?
    a. The study of very large industries is a topic within macroeconomics.
    b. Macroeconomics is concerned with economy-wide phenomena.
    c. Microeconomics is a building block for macroeconomics.
    d. Microeconomics and macroeconomics cannot be entirely separated.

16. Which of the following statements is normative?
    a. Printing too much money causes inflation.
    b. People work harder if the wage is higher.
    c. The unemployment rate should be lower.
    d. Large government deficits cause an economy to grow more slowly.

17. In making which of the following statements is an economist acting more like a scientist?
    a. A reduction in unemployment benefits will reduce the unemployment rate.
    b. The unemployment rate should be reduced because unemployment robs individuals of their dignity.
    c. The rate of inflation should be reduced because it robs the elderly of their savings.
    d. The state should increase subsidies to universities because the future of our country depends on education.

18. Positive statements are
    a. microeconomic.
    b. macroeconomic.
    c. statements of prescription that involve value judgments.
    d. statements of description that can be tested.

19. Suppose two economists are arguing about policies that deal with unemployment. One economist says, "The government should fight unemployment because it is the greatest social evil." The other economists responds, "Hogwash. Inflation is the greatest social evil." These economists
    a. disagree because they have different scientific judgments.
    b. disagree because they have different values.
    c. disagree because at least one of them is a charlatan or a crank.
    d. really don't disagree at all. It just looks that way.

20. Suppose two economists are arguing about policies that deal with unemployment. One economist says, "The government could lower unemployment by one percentage point if it would just increase government spending by 50 billion dollars." The other economist responds, "Hogwash. If the government spent an additional 50 billion dollars, it would reduce unemployment by only one tenth of one percent, and that effect would only be temporary!" These economists
    a. disagree because they have different scientific judgments.
    b. disagree because they have different values.
    c. disagree because at least one of them is a charlatan or a crank.
    d. really don't disagree at all. It just looks that way.

## IV. Advanced Critical Thinking

You are watching the McNeil News Hour on public television. The first focus section is a discussion of the pros and cons of free trade (lack of obstructions to international trade). For balance, there are two economists present—one in support of free trade and one opposed. Your roommate says, "Those economists have no idea what's going on. They can't agree on anything. One says free trade makes us rich. The other says it will drive us into poverty. If the experts don't know, how is the average person ever going to know whether free trade is best?"

1. Can you give your roommate any insight into why economists might disagree on this issue?_____
   _____
   _____
   _____

2. Suppose you discover that 93% of economists believe that free trade is generally best (which is the greatest agreement on any single issue). Could you now give a more precise answer as to why economists might disagree on this issue?
   _____
   _____
   _____

3. What if you later discovered that the economist opposed to free trade worked for a labor union. Would that help you explain why there appears to be a difference of opinion on this issue?_____
   _____
   _____
   _____

## V. Solutions

### Terms and Definitions

 _3_ Scientific method
 _8_ Economic models
 _11_ Circular-flow diagram
 _1_ Factors of production
 _9_ Production possibilities frontier
 _4_ Opportunity cost
 _6_ Efficiency
 _10_ Microeconomics
 _2_ Macroeconomics
 _7_ Positive Statements
 _5_ Normative Statements

**Practice Problems**

1. a. $20,000 of spending from households to market for goods and services. Car moves from market for goods and services to household. $20,000 of revenue from market for goods and services to firms while car moves from firm to market for goods and services.

   b. $5000 of wages from firms to market for factors of production. Inputs move from market for factors of production to firms. Labor moves from households to market for factors of production while $5000 income moves from market for factors to households.

   c. $15 of spending from households to market for goods and services. Service moves from market for goods and services to household. Service moves from firms to market for goods and services in return for $15 revenue.

   d. $10,000 of profit from firms to market for factors of production. Inputs move from market for factors of production to firms. Capital services move from households to market for factors of production in return for $10,000 income.

2. a.

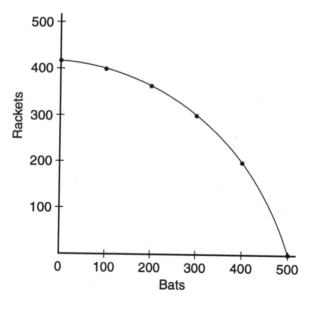

   b. 40 rackets.

   c. 100 rackets.

   d. Because as we produce more bats, the resources best suited for making bats are already being used. Therefore it takes even more resources to produce 100 bats and greater reductions in racket production.

e.  200 bats.  160 rackets.

f.  No.  Resources were not used efficiently if production can be increased with no opportunity cost.

3.  a.  Parsimonious country.  Capital (plant and equipment) is a factor of production and producing more of it now will increase future production.

b.  Fewer consumption goods are produced now.

c.

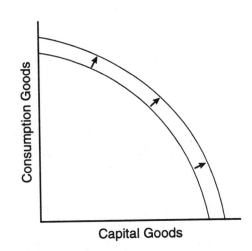

The production possibilities curve will shift more for Parsimonious Country because they have experienced a greater increase in factors of production (capital).

d.

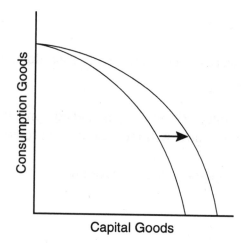

Capital Goods

    e.  No, the outward shift improves choices available for both consumption and capital goods.

## Short-Answer Questions

1. The dispassionate development and testing of theory by observing, testing, and observing again.

2. To simplify reality so that we can focus our thinking on what is actually important.

3. Not necessarily. Realistic models are more complex. They may be confusing and they may fail to focus on what is important.

4. Because if an economy is operating efficiently, production choices have opportunity costs. If we want more of one thing, we must have less of another.

5. Because resources are specialized and, thus, are not equally well suited for producing different outputs.

6. Microeconomics and macroeconomics. Microeconomics is more of a building block of macro because when we address macro issues (say unemployment) we have to consider how individuals respond to work incentives such as wages and welfare.

7. As a policymaker because normative statements are prescriptions about what ought to be and are somewhat based on value judgments.

8. Positive statements are statements of fact and are refutable by examining evidence.

9. Economists may have different scientific judgments. Economists may have different values. Some economists are charlatans and cranks.

10. A ceiling on rents reduces the quantity and quality of housing available. Tariffs and import quotas usually reduce general economic welfare.

## True/False Questions

1. F; economic models are simplifications of reality.
2. T
3. F; there must be at least two individuals for trade.
4. T
5. T
6. T
7. F; points outside the production possibilities frontier cannot yet be attained.
8. T
9. F; it is bowed outward because the tradeoffs are not constant.
10. T
11. F; macroeconomics is the study of economy-wide phenomena.
12. F; this statement is positive.
13. T
14. F; normative statements cannot be refuted.
15. T

## Multiple-Choice Questions

1. b
2. c
3. a
4. d
5. b
6. d
7. a
8. c
9. b
10. b
11. d
12. c
13. c
14. d
15. a
16. c
17. a
18. d
19. b
20. a

### Advanced Critical Thinking

1. Economists may have different scientific judgments. Economists may have different values. Some economists are charlatans and cranks. There may not really be any real disagreement.

2. Those opposed to free trade are likely to have different values or to be charlatans and cranks. There is not much disagreement on this issue within the mainstream economics profession.

3. Yes. It suggests that impediments to international trade may benefit some groups (unionized labor) but these impediments are unlikely to benefit the public in general. Supporters of these policies are promoting their own interests.

## VI. Appendix

### Practice Problems

1. The following ordered pairs of price and quantity demanded describe Joe's demand for cups of gourmet coffee:

| Price per cup of coffee | Quantity demanded of coffee |
|---|---|
| $5 | 2 cups |
| $4 | 4 cups |
| $3 | 6 cups |
| $2 | 8 cups |
| $1 | 10 cups |

a. Plot and connect the ordered pairs on the graph provided below.

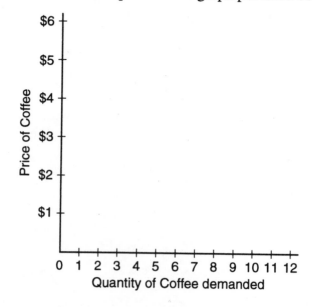

b. What is the slope of Joe's demand curve for coffee in the price range of $5 and $4?_____

c. What is the slope of Joe's demand curve for coffee in the price range of $2 and $1?_____

d. Are the price of coffee and Joe's quantity demanded of coffee positively correlated or negatively correlated? How can you tell?_____

_____

_____

e. If the price of coffee moves from $2 per cup to $4 per cup, what happens to the quantity demanded? Is this a movement along a curve or a shift in the curve?

_____

_____

f. Suppose Joe's income doubles from $20,000 per year to $40,000 per year. Now the following ordered pairs describe Joe's demand for gourmet coffee. Plot these ordered pairs on the graph provided in part (a) above.

| Price per cup of coffee | Quantity demanded of coffee |
|---|---|
| $5 | 4 cups |
| $4 | 6 cups |
| $3 | 8 cups |
| $2 | 10 cups |
| $1 | 12 cups |

g. Did the doubling of Joe's income cause a movement along his demand curve or a shift in his demand curve? Why? _____

_____

_____

2. An alien lands on earth and observes the following: On mornings when people carry umbrellas, it tends to rain later in the day. The alien concludes that umbrellas cause rain.

a. What error has the alien committed?_____

b. What role did *expectations* play in the alien's error?

_____

_____

c. If rain is truly caused by humidity, temperature, wind currents, and so on, what additional type of error has the alien committed when it decided that umbrellas cause rain?_____

**True/False Questions**

_____ 1. When graphing in the coordinate system, the x-coordinate tells us the horizontal location while the y-coordinate tells us the vertical location of the point.

_____ 2. When a line slopes upward in the x,y-coordinate system, the two variables measured on each axis are positively correlated.

_____ 3. Price and quantity demanded for most goods are positively related.

_____ 4. If three variables are related, one of them must be held constant when graphing the other two in the x,y coordinate system.

_____ 5. If three variables are related, a change in the variable not represented on the x,y coordinate system will cause a movement along the curve drawn in the x,y coordinate system.

_____ 6. The slope of a line is equal to the change in y divided by the change in x along the line.

_____ 7. When a line has negative slope, the two variables measured on each axis are positively correlated.

_____ 8. There is a positive correlation between lying down and death. If we conclude from this evidence that it is unsafe to lie down, we have an *omitted variable* problem because critically ill people tend to lie down.

_____ 9. Reverse causality means that while we think A causes B, B may actually cause A.

_____ 10. Since people carry umbrellas to work in the morning and it rains later in the afternoon, carrying umbrellas must cause rain.

# VII. Solutions for Appendix

## Practice Problems

1.  a.

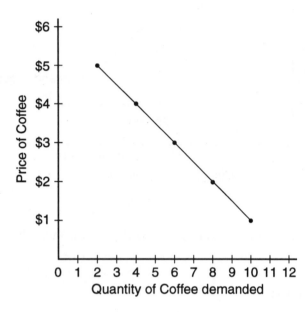

   b.  -1/2

   c.  -1/2

   d.  Negatively correlated.  Because an increase in price is associated with a decrease in quantity demanded.  That is, the demand curve slopes negatively.

   e.  Decrease by 4 cups.  Movement along curve.

f.

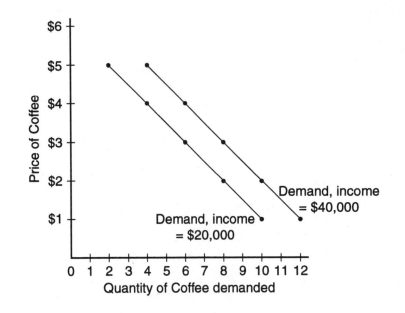

g. Shift in curve because a variable changed (income) which is not measured on either axis.

2. a. Reverse causality.

b. Since rain can be predicted, people's expectation of rain causes them to carry umbrellas *before* it rains, making it appear as if umbrellas cause rain.

c. Omitted variables.

**True/False Questions**

1. T
2. T
3. F; they are negatively correlated.
4. T
5. F; a change in a variable not represented on the graph will cause a shift in the curve.
6. T
7. F; negative slope implies negative correlation.
8. T
9. T
10. F; this is an example of reverse causation.

# Chapter 3: Interdependence and the Gains from Trade

## I. Chapter Overview

### A. Context and Purpose

Chapter 3 is the third chapter in the three-chapter section that serves as the introduction of the text. The first chapter introduced ten fundamental principles of economics. The second chapter developed how economists approach problems. This chapter shows how people and countries gain from trade (which is one of the ten principles discussed in Chapter 1).

The purpose of Chapter 3 is to demonstrate how everyone can gain from trade. Trade allows people to specialize in the production of things for which they have a comparative advantage and then trade for things other people produce. Because of specialization, total output rises and through trade we are all able to share in the bounty. This is as true for countries as it is for individuals. Since everyone can gain from trade, restrictions on trade tend to reduce welfare.

### B. Learning Objectives

In this chapter you will:

1. Consider how everyone can benefit when people trade with one another
2. Learn the meaning of absolute advantage and comparative advantage
3. See how comparative advantage explains the gains from trade
4. Apply the theory of comparative advantage to everyday life and national policy

After accomplishing these goals, you should be able to:

1. Show how total production rises when individuals specialize in the production of goods for which they have a comparative advantage
2. Explain why all people have a comparative advantage even if they have no absolute advantage
3. Demonstrate the link between comparative advantage and opportunity cost
4. Explain why people who are good at everything still tend to specialize

### C. Chapter Review

**Introduction**

Each of us consumes products every day that were produced in a number of different countries. Complex products contain components that were produced in many different countries so these products have no single country of origin. Those who produce are neither generous nor ordered by government to produce. People produce because they wish to trade and get something in return. Hence, trade makes us interdependent.

## 3-1 A Parable for the Modern Economy

Imagine a simple economy. There are two people—a cattle rancher and a potato farmer. There are two goods—meat and potatoes.

- If each can produce only one product (the rancher can produce only meat and the farmer potatoes) they will trade just to increase the variety of products they consume. Each benefits because of increased variety.

- If each can produce both goods, but each is more efficient than the other at producing one good, then each will specialize in what he or she does best (again the rancher produces meat and the farmer produces potatoes), total output will rise, and they will trade. Trade allows each to benefit because trade allows for specialization, and specialization increases the total production available to share.

- If one producer is better than the other at producing *both* meat and potatoes, there are the same advantages to trade but it is more difficult to see. Again, trade allows each to benefit because trade allows for specialization, and specialization increases the total production available to share. To understand the source of the gains from trade when one producer is better at producing both products, we must understand the concept of comparative advantage.

## 3-2 The Principle of Comparative Advantage

To understand *comparative advantage*, we begin with the concept of *absolute advantage*. Absolute advantage compares the quantity of inputs required to produce a good. The producer that requires fewer resources (say fewer hours worked) to produce a good is said to have an absolute advantage in the production of that good. That is, the most efficient producer (the one with the highest productivity) has an absolute advantage.

While absolute advantage compares the actual cost of production for each producer, *comparative advantage* compares *opportunity costs* of production for each producer. The producer with the lower opportunity cost of production is said to have a comparative advantage. Regardless of absolute advantage, if producers have *different opportunity costs* of production for each good, each should specialize in the production of the good for which their opportunity cost of production is lower. That is, each producer should produce the item for which they have a comparative advantage. They can then trade some of their output for the other good. Trade makes both producers better off because trade allows for specialization, and specialization increases the total production available to be shared.

The decision to specialize and the resulting gains from trade are based on comparative advantage, not absolute advantage. Although a single producer can have an absolute advantage in the production of both goods, he/she cannot have a comparative advantage in the production of both goods because a low opportunity cost of producing one good implies a high opportunity cost of producing the other good.

In summary, trade allows producers to exploit the differences in their opportunity costs of production. Each specializes in the production of the good for which they have the lower opportunity cost of production and, thus, a comparative advantage. This increases total production which makes the economic pie larger. Everyone can benefit. The additional production generated by specialization is the gain from trade.

## 3-3 Applications of Comparative Advantage

The principle of comparative advantage applies to individuals as well as countries.

Recall, absolute advantage does not determine specialization in production. For example, Michael Jordan may have an absolute advantage in basketball and lawn mowing. However, because he can earn $5000/hour playing basketball, he is better off paying someone to mow his lawn (even if they do it more slowly than he) as long as he can get someone to do it for less than $5000/hour. This is because the opportunity cost of an hour of mowing for Michael Jordan is $5000. Michael Jordan will likely specialize in basketball and trade for other services. He does this because he has a comparative advantage in basketball and a comparative disadvantage in lawn mowing even though he has an absolute advantage in both.

Trade between countries is subject to the same principle of comparative advantage. Goods produced abroad and sold domestically are called imports. Goods produced domestically and sold abroad are called exports. Even if the United States has an absolute advantage in the production of both cars and food, it should specialize in the production of the item for which it has a comparative advantage. Since the opportunity cost of food is low in the United States (better land) and high in Japan, the United States should produce more food and export it to Japan in exchange for imports of autos from Japan. While the U.S. gains from trade, the impact of trade on U.S. auto workers is different from the impact of trade on U.S. farmers.

Adam Smith in his 1776 book, *An Inquiry into the Nature and Causes of the Wealth of Nations*, and David Ricardo in his 1817 book, *Principles of Political Economy and Taxation*, both recognized the gains from trade through specialization and the principle of comparative advantage. Current arguments for free trade are still based on their work.

## D. Helpful Hints

1. A step by step example of comparative advantage. What follows is an example which will demonstrate most of the concepts discussed in Chapter 3. It will give you a pattern to follow when answering questions at the end of the chapter in your text and for the problems that follow in this Study Guide.

Suppose we have the following information about the productivity of industry in Japan and Korea. The data are the units of output per hour of work.

|        | steel | televisions |
|--------|-------|-------------|
| Japan  | 6     | 3           |
| Korea  | 8     | 2           |

A Japanese worker can produce 6 units of steel or 3 units of TVs per hour. A Korean worker can produce 8 units of steel or 2 units of TVs per hour.

We can plot the production possibilities frontier for each country assuming each country has only one worker and the worker works only one hour. To plot the frontier, plot the end points and connect them with a line. For example, Japan can produce 6 units of steel with its worker or 3 units of televisions. It can also allocate one half hour to the production of each and get 3 units steel and 1 1/2 TVs. Any other proportion of the hour can be allocated to the two productive activities. The production possibilities frontier is linear in these cases because the labor resource can be moved from the production of one good to the other at a constant rate. We can do the same for Korea. Without trade, the production possibilities frontier is the consumption possibilities frontier, too.

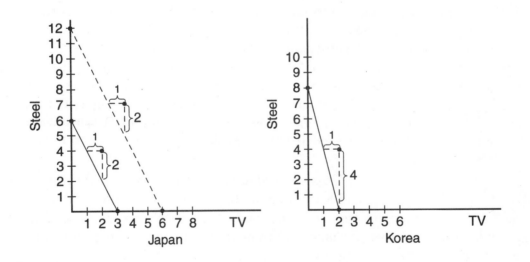

*Comparative advantage* determines specialization and trade. The opportunity cost of a TV in Japan is 2 units of steel which is shown by the slope of the production possibilities frontier in the previous graph. Alternatively, the opportunity cost of one unit of steel in Japan is 1/2 of a TV. In Korea, the opportunity cost of a TV is 4 units of steel and the cost of a unit of steel is 1/4 of a TV. Since the opportunity cost of a TV is lower in Japan, Japan has a comparative advantage in TV production and should specialize in TVs. Since the opportunity cost of steel is lower in Korea, Korea has a comparative advantage in steel production and should specialize in steel.

What is the range of prices at which each country would be willing to exchange? If Japan specializes in TV production and produces 3 televisions, it would be willing to trade TVs for steel as long as the price of steel is below 1/2 TV per unit of steel because that was the Japanese price for a unit of steel prior to trade. Korea would be willing to specialize in steel production and trade for TVs as long as the price of a TV is less than 4 units of steel because that was the Korean price of a TV prior to trade. In short, the final price must be between the original tradeoffs each faced in the absence of trade. One TV will cost between 2 and 4 of units of steel. One unit of steel will cost between 1/2 and 1/4 of a TV.

2. Trade allows countries to consume outside their original production possibilities frontier. Suppose that Japan and Korea settle on a trading price of 3 units of steel for 1 TV (or 1/3 of a TV for 1 unit of steel). (I am giving you this price. There is nothing in the problem that would let you calculate the final trading price. You can only calculate the range in which it must lie.) This price is halfway between the two prices that each faces in the absence of trade. The range for the trading price is 4 units of steel for 1 TV to 2 units of steel for 1 TV.

If Japan specializes in TV production, produces 3 televisions, and exports 1 TV for 3 units of steel, Japan will be able to consume 2 TVs and 3 units of steel. If we plot this point (2 TVs and 3 steel) on Japan's graph, we see that it lies outside its production possibilities frontier. If Korea specializes, produces 8 units of steel, and exports 3 units for 1 TV, Korea will be able to consume 5 units of steel and 1 TV. If we plot this point (5 steel and 1 TV) on Korea's graph, we see that it also lies outside its production possibilities frontier.

This is the gain from trade. Trade allows countries (and people) to specialize. Specialization increases world output. After trading, countries consume outside their individual production possibilities frontiers. In this way, trade is like an improvement in technology. It allows countries to move beyond their current production possibilities frontiers.

3. Only comparative advantage matters—absolute advantage is irrelevant. In the previous example, Japan had an absolute advantage in the production of TVs because it could produce 3 per hour while Korea could only produce 2. Korea had an absolute advantage in the production of steel because it could produce 8 units per hour compared to 6 for Japan.

To demonstrate that comparative advantage, not absolute advantage, determines specialization and trade, we alter the previous example so that Japan has an absolute advantage in the production of both goods. To this end, suppose Japan becomes twice as productive as in the previous table. That is, a worker can now produce 12 units of steel or 6 TVs per hour.

| | steel | televisions |
|---|---|---|
| Japan | 12 | 6 |
| Korea | 8 | 2 |

Now Japan has an absolute advantage in the production of both goods. Japan's new production possibilities frontier is the dashed line in the previous graph. Will this change the analysis? Not at all. The opportunity cost of each good within Japan is the same—2 units of steel per TV or 1/2 TV per unit of steel (and Korea is unaffected). For this reason, Japan still has the identical comparative advantage as before and it will specialize in TV production while Korea will specialize in steel. However, since productivity has doubled in Japan, its entire set of choices has improved and, thus, its material welfare has improved.

## E. Terms and Definitions

Choose a definition for each key term.

Key terms:

_____Absolute advantage
_____Comparative advantage
_____Gains from trade
_____Opportunity cost
_____Imports
_____Exports

Definitions:

1. Whatever is given up to obtain some item
2. The comparison among producers of a good based on their opportunity cost
3. Goods produced domestically and sold abroad
4. Goods produced abroad and sold domestically
5. The comparison among producers of a good based on their productivity
6. The increase in total production due to specialization allowed by trade

## II. Problems and Short-Answer Questions

### A. Practice Problems

1. Angela is a college student. She takes a full load of classes and has only 5 hours per week for her hobby. Angela is artistic and can make 2 clay pots per hour or 4 coffee mugs per hour.

   a. Draw Angela's production possibilities frontier for pots and mugs.

   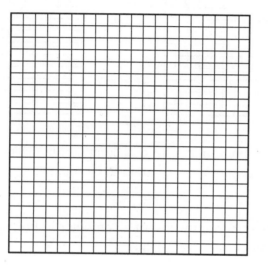

   b. What is Angela's opportunity cost of one pot? 10 pots? _____
   _____

   c. What is Angela's opportunity cost of one mug? 10 mugs? _____
   _____

   d. Why is her production possibilities frontier a straight line instead of bowed out like those presented in Chapter 2?_____
   _____

2. Suppose a worker in Germany can produce 15 computers or 5 tons of grain per month. Suppose a worker in Poland can produce 4 computers or 4 tons of grain per month. For simplicity, assume that each country has only one worker.

   a. Fill out the following table:

   |         | computers | grain |
   |---------|-----------|-------|
   | Germany |           |       |
   | Poland  |           |       |

b. Graph the production possibilities frontier for each country.

c. What is the opportunity cost of a computer in Germany? What is the opportunity cost of a ton of grain in Germany?_____

_____

d. What is the opportunity cost of a computer in Poland? What is the opportunity cost of a ton of grain in Poland?_____

_____

e. Which country has the absolute advantage in producing computers? Grain?_____

_____

f. Which country has the comparative advantage in producing computers? Grain?_____

_____

_____

_____

g. Each country should tend toward specialization in the production of which good? Why?_____

_____

_____

_____

h. What are the range of prices for computers and grain for which both countries would benefit?_____

_____

_____

i. Suppose Germany and Poland settle on a price of 2 computers for 1 ton of grain or 1/2 ton of grain for a computer. Suppose each country specializes in production and they trade 4 computers for 2 tons of grain. Plot the final consumption points on the graphs you made in part (b) above. Are these countries consuming inside or outside of their production possibilities frontier?_____

_____

j. Suppose the productivity of a worker in Poland doubles so that a worker can produce 8 computers or 8 tons of grain per month. Which country has the absolute advantage in producing computers? Grain?_____

_____

_____

k. After the doubling of productivity in Poland, which country has a comparative advantage in producing computers? Grain? Has the comparative advantage changed? Has the material welfare of either country changed?_____

_____

_____

_____

_____

l. How would your analysis change if you assumed, more realistically, that each country had 10 million workers?_____

_____

_____

_____

3. Suppose a worker in the United States can produce 4 cars or 20 computers per month while a worker in Russia can produce 1 car or 5 computers per month. Again, for simplicity, assume each country has only one worker.

a. Fill out the following table:

|  | cars | computers |
|---|---|---|
| United States |  |  |
| Russia |  |  |

b. Which country has the absolute advantage in the production of cars? Computers?_____

_____

_____

c. Which country has the comparative advantage in the production of cars? Computers?_____

_____

_____

_____

d. Are there any gains to be made from trade?  Why?_____

_____

_____

e. Does your answer in (d) above help you pinpoint a source for gains from trade?_____

_____

_____

f. What might make two countries have different opportunity costs of production? (Use your imagination.  This was not directly discussed in Chapter 3.)_____

_____

_____

_____

## B. Short-Answer Questions

1. Why do people choose to become interdependent as opposed to self-sufficient?

_____

_____

_____

2. Why is comparative advantage important in determining trade instead of absolute advantage?_____

_____

_____

3. What are the gains from trade?_____

_____

_____

4. Why is a restriction of trade likely to reduce material welfare?_____

_____

_____

5. Suppose a lawyer that earns $200 per hour can also type at 200 words per minute. Should the lawyer hire a secretary who can only types 50 words per minute? Why?_____

_____

_____

6. Evaluate this statement: A technologically advanced country, which is better than its neighbor at producing everything, would be better off if it closed its borders to trade because the less productive country is a burden to the advanced country.

_____

_____

_____

_____

## III. Self-Test

### A. True/False Questions

_____ 1. If Japan has an absolute advantage in the production of an item, it must also have a comparative advantage in the production of that item.

_____ 2. Comparative advantage, not absolute advantage, determines the decision to specialize in production.

_____ 3. Absolute advantage is a comparison based on productivity.

_____ 4. Self-sufficiency is the best way to increase one's material welfare.

_____ 5. Comparative advantage is a comparison based on opportunity cost.

_____ 6. If a producer is self-sufficient, the production possibilities frontier is also the consumption possibilities frontier.

_____ 7. If a country's workers can produce 5 hamburgers per hour or 10 bags of French fries per hour, absent trade, the price of 1 bag of fries is 2 hamburgers.

_____ 8. If producers have different opportunity costs of production, trade will allow them to consume outside their production possibilities frontiers.

_____ 9. If trade benefits one country, its trading partner must be worse off due to trade.

_____10. Talented people that are the best at everything have a comparative advantage in the production of everything.

_____11. The gains from trade can be measured by the increase in total production that comes from specialization.

_____12. When a country removes a specific import restriction, it always benefits every worker in that country.

_____13. If Germany's productivity doubles for everything it produces, this will not alter its prior pattern of specialization because it has not altered its comparative advantage.

_____14. If an advanced country has an absolute advantage in the production of everything, it will benefit if it eliminates trade with less developed countries and becomes completely self-sufficient.

_____15. If gains from trade are based solely on comparative advantage, and if all countries have the same opportunity costs of production, then there are no gains from trade.

## B. Multiple-Choice Questions

1. If a nation has an absolute advantage in the production of a good,
   a. it can produce that good at a lower opportunity cost than its trading partner.
   b. it can produce that good using fewer resources than its trading partner.
   c. it can benefit by restricting imports of that good.
   d. it will specialize in the production of that good and export it.
   e. none of the above

2. If a nation has a comparative advantage in the production of a good,
   a. it can produce that good at a lower opportunity cost than its trading partner.
   b. it can produce that good using fewer resources than its trading partner.
   c. it can benefit by restricting imports of that good.
   d. it must be the only country with the ability to produce that good.
   e. none of the above

3. Which of the following statements about trade is true?
   a. Unrestricted international trade benefits every person in a country equally.
   b. People who are skilled at all activities cannot benefit from trade.
   c. Trade can benefit everyone in society because it allows people to specialize in activities in which they have an absolute advantage.
   d. Trade can benefit everyone in society because it allows people to specialize in activities in which they have a comparative advantage.

4.  According to the principle of comparative advantage,
    a.  countries with a comparative advantage in the production of every good need not specialize.
    b.  countries should specialize in the production of goods which they enjoy consuming more than other countries.
    c.  countries should specialize in the production of goods for which they use fewer resources in production than their trading partners.
    d.  countries should specialize in the production of goods for which they have a lower opportunity cost of production than their trading partners.

5.  Which of the following statements is true?
    a.  Self-sufficiency is the road to prosperity for most countries.
    b.  A self-sufficient country consumes outside their production possibilities frontier.
    c.  A self-sufficient country can, at best, consume on its production possibilities frontier.
    d.  Only countries with an absolute advantage in the production of every good should strive to be self-sufficient.

6.  Suppose a country's workers can produce 4 watches per hour or 12 rings per hour. If there is no trade,
    a.  the domestic price of 1 ring is 3 watches.
    b.  the domestic price of 1 ring is 1/3 of a watch.
    c.  the domestic price of 1 ring is 4 watches.
    d.  the domestic price of 1 ring is 1/4 of a watch.
    e.  the domestic price of 1 ring is 12 watches.

7.  Suppose a country's workers can produce 4 watches per hour or 12 rings per hour. If there is no trade,
    a.  the opportunity cost of 1 watch is 3 rings.
    b.  the opportunity cost of 1 watch is 1/3 of a ring.
    c.  the opportunity cost of 1 watch is 4 rings.
    d.  the opportunity cost of 1 watch is 1/4 of a ring.
    e.  the opportunity cost of 1 watch is 12 rings.

The following table shows the units of output a worker can produce per month in Australia and Korea. Use this table for questions 8-15.

|           | Food | Electronics |
|-----------|------|-------------|
| Australia | 20   | 5           |
| Korea     | 8    | 4           |

8. Which of the following statements about absolute advantage is true?
   a. Australia has an absolute advantage in the production of food while Korea has an absolute advantage in the production of electronics.
   b. Korea has an absolute advantage in the production of food while Australia has an absolute advantage in the production of electronics.
   c. Australia has an absolute advantage in the production of both food and electronics.
   d. Korea has an absolute advantage in the production of both food and electronics.

9. The opportunity cost of 1 unit of electronics in Australia is
   a. 5 units of food.
   b. 1/5 of a unit of food.
   c. 4 units of food.
   d. 1/4 of a unit of food.

10. The opportunity cost of 1 unit of electronics in Korea is
    a. 2 units of food.
    b. 1/2 of a unit of food.
    c. 4 units of food.
    d. 1/4 units of food.

11. The opportunity cost of 1 unit of food in Australia is
    a. 5 units of electronics.
    b. 1/5 of a unit of electronics.
    c. 4 units of electronics.
    d. 1/4 of a unit of electronics.

12. The opportunity cost of 1 unit of food in Korea is
    a. 2 units of electronics.
    b. 1/2 of a unit of electronics.
    c. 4 units of electronics.
    d. 1/4 of a unit of electronics.

13. Which of the following statements about comparative advantage is true?
    a. Australia has a comparative advantage in the production of food while Korea has a comparative advantage in the production of electronics.
    b. Korea has a comparative advantage in the production of food while Australia has a comparative advantage in the production of electronics.
    c. Australia has a comparative advantage in the production of both food and electronics.
    d. Korea has a comparative advantage in the production of both food and electronics.
    e. There is no comparative advantage for either country because the opportunity cost of producing each good is the same in each country.

14. Korea should
    a. specialize in food production, export food, and import electronics.
    b. specialize in electronics production, export electronics, and import food.
    c. produce both goods because neither country has a comparative advantage.
    d. produce neither good because it has an absolute disadvantage in the production of both goods.

15. Prices of electronics can be stated in terms of units of food. What is the range of prices of electronics for which both countries could gain from trade?
    a. The price must be greater than 1/5 of a unit of food but less than 1/4 of a unit of food.
    b. The price must be greater than 4 units of food but less than 5 units of food.
    c. The price must be greater than 1/4 of a unit of food but less than 1/2 of a unit of food.
    d. The price must be greater than 2 units of food but less than 4 units of food.

16. Suppose the world consists of two countries—the U.S. and Mexico. Further, suppose there are only two goods—food and clothing. Which of the following statements is true?
    a. If the U.S. has an absolute advantage in the production of food, then Mexico must have an absolute advantage in the production of clothing.
    b. If the U.S. has a comparative advantage in the production of food, then Mexico must have a comparative advantage in the production of clothing.
    c. If the U.S. has a comparative advantage in the production of food, it must also have a comparative advantage in the production of clothing.
    d. If the U.S. has a comparative advantage in the production of food, Mexico might also have a comparative advantage in the production of food.
    e. none of the above.

Use the following production possibilities frontiers to answer questions 17-19.
Assume each country has the same number of workers, say 20 million, and that each axis is measured in metric tons per month.

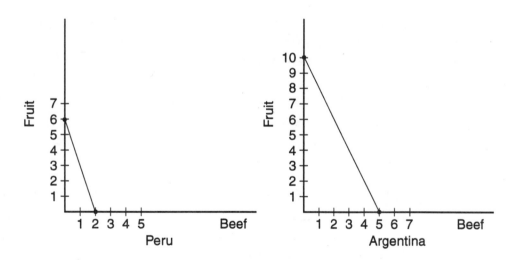

Peru

Argentina

17. Argentina has a comparative advantage in the production of
    a. both fruit and beef.
    b. fruit.
    c. beef.
    d. neither fruit nor beef.

18. Peru will export
    a. both fruit and beef.
    b. fruit.
    c. beef.
    d. neither fruit nor beef.

19. The opportunity cost of producing a metric ton of beef in Peru is
    a. 1/3 ton of fruit.
    b. 1 ton of fruit.
    c. 2 tons of fruit.
    d. 3 tons of fruit.
    e. 6 tons of fruit.

20. Joe is a tax accountant. He receives $100 per hour doing tax returns. He can type 10,000 characters per hour into spreadsheets. He can hire an assistant who types 2500 characters per hour into spreadsheets. Which of the following statements is true?
    a. Joe should not hire an assistant because the assistant cannot type as fast as he.
    b. Joe should hire the assistant as long as he pays the assistant less than $100 per hour.
    c. Joe should hire the assistant as long as he pays the assistant less than $25 per hour.
    d. none of the above

## IV. Advanced Critical Thinking

You are watching an election debate on television. A candidate says, "We need to stop the flow of foreign automobiles into our country. If we limit the importation of autos, our domestic auto production will rise and the United States will be better off."

1. Is it likely that the *United States* will be better off if it limits auto imports? Explain._____
   _____
   _____

2. Will anyone in the United States be better off if it limits auto imports? Explain._____
   _____
   _____

3. In the real world, does every person in the country gain when restrictions on imports are reduced? Explain._____

_____

_____

## V. Solutions

### Terms and Definitions

_5_ Absolute advantage
_2_ Comparative advantage
_6_ Gains from trade
_1_ Opportunity cost
_4_ Imports
_3_ Exports

### Practice Problems

1. a.

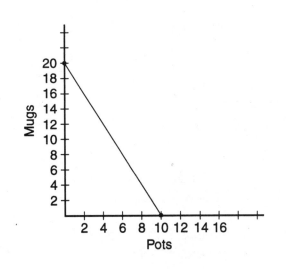

  b. 2 mugs.  20 mugs.

  c. 1/2 pot.  5 pots.

  d. Because here resources can be moved from the production of one good to another at a constant rate.

2. a.

| | computers | grain |
|---|---|---|
| Germany | 15 | 5 |
| Poland | 4 | 4 |

b.

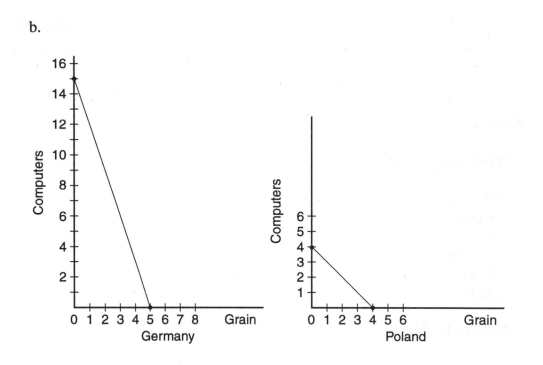

Germany

Poland

c.  1/3 ton grain.  3 computers.

d.  1 ton grain.  1 computer.

e.  Germany because one worker can produce 15 compared to 4.  Germany because one worker can produce 5 compared to 4.

f.  Germany because a computer has the opportunity cost of only 1/3 ton of grain compared to 1 ton of grain in Poland. Poland because a ton of grain has the opportunity cost of only 1 computer compared to 3 computers in Germany.

g.  Germany should produce computers while Poland should produce grain because the opportunity cost of computers is lower in Germany and the opportunity cost of grain is lower in Poland.  That is, each has a comparative advantage in those goods.

h.  Grain must cost less than 3 computers to Germany.  Computers must cost less than 1 ton of grain to Poland.

i.

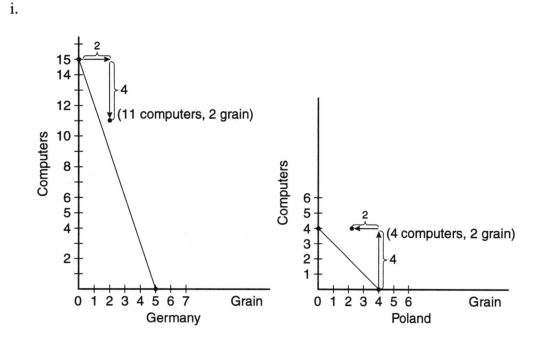

They are consuming outside their production possibilities frontier.

j.  Germany because one worker can produce 15 compared to 8. Poland because one worker can produce 8 compared to 5.

k.  Germany has comparative advantage in computers. Poland has comparative advantage in grain. No change in comparative advantage. Poland is better off, however, because it now has a larger set of choices.

l.  It would not change absolute advantage or comparative advantage. It would change the scale in the previous two graphs by a factor of 10 million.

3.  a.

|  | cars | computers |
|---|---|---|
| United States | 4 | 20 |
| Russia | 1 | 5 |

b.  United States because one worker can produce 4 compared to 1. The United States because one worker can produce 20 compared to 5.

c.  In both, the opportunity cost of 1 car is 5 computers. In both, the opportunity cost of 1 computer is 1/5 of a car. Therefore, neither has a comparative advantage in either good.

d.  No. Each can get the same tradeoff between goods domestically.

e.  Yes. There need to be differences in opportunity costs of producing goods across countries for there to be gains from trade.

f. Resources or technology might be different across countries. That is, workers could be differently educated, land could be of different quality, or the available technology might be different.

## Short-Answer Questions

1. Because a consumer gets a greater variety of goods at a much lower cost than he could produce by himself. That is, there are gains from trade.

2. What is important in trade is how a country's costs without trade differ from each other. This is determined by the relative opportunity costs across countries.

3. The additional output that comes from countries with different opportunity costs of production specializing in the production of the item for which they have the lower domestic opportunity cost.

4. Because it forces people to produce at a higher cost than they pay when they trade.

5. Yes, as long as the secretary earns less than $50/hour, the lawyer is ahead.

6. This is not true. All countries can gain from trade if their opportunity costs of production differ. Even the least productive country will have a comparative advantage at producing something, and it can trade this good to the advanced country for less than the advanced country's opportunity cost.

## True/False Questions

1. F; absolute advantage compares the quantities of inputs used in production while comparative advantage compares the opportunity costs.
2. T
3. T
4. F; restricting trade eliminates gains from trade.
5. T
6. T
7. F; the price of 1 bag of fries is 1/2 of a hamburger.
8. T
9. F; voluntary trade benefits both traders.
10. F; a low opportunity cost of producing one good implies a high opportunity cost of producing the other good.
11. T
12. F; it may harm those involved in that industry.
13. T
14. F; voluntary trade benefits all traders.
15. T

## Multiple-Choice Questions

1.  b
2.  a
3.  d
4.  d
5.  c
6.  b
7.  a
8.  c
9.  c
10. a
11. d
12. b
13. a
14. b
15. d
16. b
17. c
18. b
19. d
20. c

## Advanced Critical Thinking

1.  No. If the U.S. imports autos, it is because the opportunity cost of producing them elsewhere is lower than in the United States.

2.  Yes. Those associated with the domestic auto industry—stockholders of domestic auto producers and auto workers.

3.  No. When we reduce restrictions on imports, the *country* gains from the increased trade but individuals in the affected domestic industry may lose.

# Chapter 4: The Market Forces of Supply and Demand

## I. Chapter Overview

### A. Context and Purpose

Earlier chapters provided an overview of the "economic way of thinking," in order to explain the operation of a mixed market economy such as that of the United States. Chapter 4 describes the components of a market economy, providing a foundation for the discussion of consumer and producer behavior in the chapters that follow.

One of the cornerstones of a market economy is the interaction of supply and demand. Unfortunately, these terms are not well understood: A parrot can be taught to squawk "supply and demand" without any knowledge of the concepts. You can read the newspapers on any given day and find examples of the misuse of supply and demand. The terms take on a very specific meaning in economics that differs from their everyday use. This chapter explains what an economist means by supply and demand and shows how they interact to determine prices and quantities of goods and services. It also shows how various factors that change either supply or demand ultimately lead to changes in market prices and quantities.

### B. Learning Objectives

In this chapter you will:

1. Learn what a competitive market is.
2. Examine what determines the demand for a good in a competitive market.
3. Examine what determines the supply of a good in a competitive market.
4. See how supply and demand together set the price of a good and the quantity sold.
5. Consider the key role of prices in allocating scarce resources in market economies.

After accomplishing these goals, you should be able to:

1. Define and give an example of a competitive market.
2. a. Explain the Law of Demand and the resulting negative slope of the demand curve for a good or service.
   b. Identify the factors that may cause the demand curve to shift.
   c. Distinguish a *change in demand* (rightward or leftward shift of the whole demand curve) from a *change in quantity demanded* (movement up or down the existing curve).

3.  a.  Explain the Law of Supply and the resulting positive slope of the supply curve for a good or service.
    b.  Identify the factors that may cause the supply curve to shift, recognizing that buyers and sellers are different people responding to different incentives.
    c.  Distinguish a *change in supply* (rightward or leftward shift of the whole supply curve) from a *change in quantity supplied* (movement up or down the existing curve).
4.  Combine supply and demand curves to determine equilibrium (market-clearing) price and quantity in a market and predict the effect on equilibrium price and quantity of a change in any of the factors that affect supply or demand.
5.  Explain the central role of prices in allocating resources in a market economy, relating that role to the fundamental questions (what, how, and for whom) that must be answered in any society.

## C. Chapter Review

### 4-1 Markets and Competition

Supply and demand refer to the behavior of sellers and buyers, who are different groups of people responding to different economic incentives, as they interact in markets for goods and services. Markets can be local, regional, national, or even global, contrary to the traditional notion of a market as a physical location. Markets can take many forms, depending upon the degree of competition among sellers. At one extreme, a perfectly competitive market is one in which no single buyer or seller can influence price. At the other extreme, a monopolistic market contains a single seller.

### 4-2 Demand

Demand refers to the amounts of a good or service that buyers are willing and able to buy at various prices, holding constant all of the other factors that affect how much consumers are willing to buy. That is, demand is the relationship between price and the quantity that people will buy. Consumers respond to economic incentives: They tend to buy less of a good or service as the price rises. This negative relationship between price and quantity demanded is known as the Law of Demand. When shown graphically, this relationship becomes the demand curve. The other factors that we hold constant in deriving a demand curve include the following:

- Income
- Prices of related goods
- Tastes
- Expectations
- Number of buyers

A change in any of these factors is likely to cause *demand* to change, that is, shift the whole demand curve to the right or the left. Notice that the one factor not included in this list is the price of the good itself. Even though a change in price causes a change in *quantity demanded*, it does not change the entire relationship between price and quantity, as represented by a *demand curve*.

### 4-3 Supply

Supply refers to the amounts of a good or service that sellers are willing and able to sell at various prices, holding all other factors constant. It is the relationship between price and the quantity supplied. Sellers respond to economic incentives. They increase their willingness to sell as the price rises. This *direct* relationship between price and quantity supplied is known as the *law of supply*. The supply curve is the graphical representation of this relationship, representing *willingness to sell* (not physical inventories that are available). The other factors that we hold constant in deriving a supply curve include the following:

- Input prices
- Technology
- Expectations
- Number of sellers

Essentially, the supply curve holds constant any of the factors that affect the cost of producing and selling another unit of output. If those costs increase, the willingness to sell at any given price decreases, so the supply curve shifts to the left. If costs decrease, then the supply curve shifts to the right.

### 4-4 Supply and Demand Together

Neither supply nor demand by itself can determine the price or the quantity of a good or service in a market. Supply and demand are like two blades of a pair of scissors; both are required to make the system work. When shown graphically, supply and demand curves intersect at a unique price and quantity known as the *equilibrium price* and *equilibrium quantity*. The equilibrium (or market-clearing) price is the only price at which the sellers' willingness to sell exactly equals the buyers' willingness to buy. If the market price is above the equilibrium price, quantity supplied will exceed quantity demanded by an amount known as *excess supply*, which is the same thing as a *surplus*. If the market price is below the equilibrium price, quantity demanded will exceed quantity supplied by an amount known as *excess demand*, or a *shortage*.

A change in *demand* (unlike a change in *quantity demanded* due to a change in price) means that the demand curve has shifted, due to a change in one of the underlying factors. If demand increases (shifts to the right), this tends to increase equilibrium quantity and price, causing sellers to increase their quantity supplied as they move along the (unchanging) supply curve. If demand decreases (shifts to the left), the reverse occurs: Equilibrium quantity and price both decrease, and quantity supplied decreases.

Similarly, a change in supply means that the supply curve has shifted, so that sellers' willingness to sell has changed at every price. If supply increases (shifts to the right), equilibrium quantity will rise and price will drop, causing buyers to increase their quantity demanded as they move along the (unchanging) demand curve. If supply decreases (shifts to the left), equilibrium quantity decreases, but price increases, and quantity demanded decreases.

If both curves shift in the same direction, the outcome depends on which curve shifts relatively more. For example, if both supply and demand increase, we know that equilibrium quantity must also rise, but price could go either up or down, depending on the relative changes in supply and demand. If supply increases relatively more than demand, this will tend to drive price down, but if demand increases more than supply, the additional willingness to buy will drive price up.

## 4-5 Conclusion: How Prices Allocate Resources

In any economic system, scarce resources have to be allocated among competing uses. Society must decide what goods and services to produce, how to produce them, and for whom they are to be produced. In a market economy, prices are the signals that guide the allocation of resources among competing uses. Rising prices serve both to ration increasingly scarce resources and to stimulate additional production when desired by society. Falling prices indicate the reverse, namely that it may be appropriate to shift resources to a higher valued use elsewhere. Prices allow decentralized decisionmaking by thousands of buyers and sellers acting independently without any central planning.

## D. Helpful Hints

1. *Supply means willingness to sell.* In everyday usage, supply often refers to physical stocks of a product or resource, in the form of inventories available for sale. In economics, however, **supply** means ***willingness to sell***. For example, the newspapers often report changes in global petroleum supplies, when really they mean inventories or petroleum reserves. The supply of petroleum is the willingness to sell those reserves, not the petroleum itself.

2. *Demand means willingness to buy.* Demand is not simply consumer wants. Demand represents wants backed up by dollars and our willingness to spend them.

3. *A market is a collection of buyers and sellers.* Markets are not physical locations; rather they are the interaction of buyers and sellers. Such interaction can occur at a physical location: for example, an auction may represent a separate market. However, buyers and sellers can interact on a national or even global level, particularly as electronic communications grow. Money markets, for example, involve buyers and sellers around the world.

4. *"Demand" is the entire schedule or curve.* Demand refers to the whole demand schedule or demand curve, not just a point on the curve. It represents all of the price-quantity combinations that are acceptable to consumers. Because of this, we

do not refer to increased sales due to a price cut as an increase in *demand*. There is, of course, an increase in the *quantity demanded*, but this is not an increase (or shift to the right) in demand itself.

5. *"Quantity Demanded" is a point on the demand curve*. When there is a change in price, quantity demanded changes, but demand itself does not change. Quantity demanded is synonomous with consumption, or sales, or quantity sold.

6. *"Supply" is the entire schedule or curve*. Supply refers to the whole supply schedule or supply curve, not just a point on the curve. For supply to shift, the underlying factors that we hold constant in plotting a supply curve must change. Changing the price simply means that we plot a new point on the existing supply curve, representing a new quantity. Of course an increase in price encourages suppliers to sell more; however, we call this response to higher price an increase in *quantity supplied*, rather than an increase (or shift) in *supply*.

7. *"Quantity Supplied" is a point on the supply curve*. When there is a change in price, the quantity supplied changes, even though the supply curve itself does not shift. The quantity supplied at a particular price is the amount that sellers are willing to sell at that price.

## E. Terms and Definitions

Choose a definition for each key term.

Key Terms:

_____Law of Demand
_____Demand
_____Quantity demanded
_____Excess demand
_____Law of Supply
_____Supply
_____Quantity supplied
_____Excess supply
_____Market
_____Equilibrium price
_____Equilibrium quantity
_____Competitive market
_____Monopolistic competition
_____Oligopoly

Definitions:

1. The observation that sellers tend to offer more for sale at a higher price and less for sale at a lower price.
2. In any market, the price at which quantity supplied equals quantity demanded; the price corresponding to the intersection of supply and demand.
3. A market with only a few sellers that do not always compete aggressively.
4. The quantity on the demand curve corresponding to a particular price.
5. The quantity that is sold in any market at the equilibrium price; the quantity corresponding to the intersection of supply and demand.
6. A surplus, equal to quantity supplied minus quantity demanded, at a supply price higher than equilibrium.
7. Any place or arrangement in which buyers and sellers make exchanges and where similar goods and services tend to have similar prices.
8. The amounts of a good or service that people are willing and able to buy at various prices, holding constant factors other than price.
9. The observation that buyers tend to buy more at a lower price and less at a higher price.
10. The quantity on the supply curve corresponding to a particular price supplied.
11. A market in which there are numerous buyers and sellers, each of which is a price taker who is too small to influence the market price.
12. The amounts of a good or service that sellers are willing and able to sell at various prices, holding constant factors other than price.
13. A shortage, equal to quantity demanded minus quantity supplied, at a price below equilibrium.
14. A market with many sellers offering slightly different products; each seller has some control over price.

## II. Problems and Short-Answer Questions

### A. Practice Problems

The supply and demand schedules below show hypothetical prices and quantities in the market for corn. The initial quantity supplied is shown by $Q_s$, and the quantity demanded is $Q_d$.

### The Market for Corn
(in millions of bushels)

| Price | $Q_d$ | $Q_s$ | $Q_s'$ |
|-------|-------|-------|--------|
| $6.00 | 220 | 400 | ____ |
| $5.50 | 240 | 360 | ____ |
| $5.00 | 260 | 320 | ____ |
| $4.50 | 280 | 280 | ____ |
| $4.00 | 300 | 240 | ____ |
| $3.50 | 320 | 200 | ____ |
| $3.00 | 340 | 160 | ____ |

1. Plot the supply and demand curves for the initial supply and demand, $Q_s$ and $Q_d$, on the graph that follows the questions.

   a. The equilibrium price of corn is $_____.

   b. The equilibrium quantity of corn is _____ million bushels.

   c. At a price of $3.00/bushel, there would be a (shortage, surplus) _____ of _____ million bushels, and the price would tend to (fall, rise)_____.

   d. At a price of $5.00/bushel, there would be a (shortage, surplus) _____ of _____ million bushels, and the price would tend to (fall, rise)_____.

2. Suppose that the supply of corn increased by 60 million bushels at every price. Show the new supply schedule as $Q_s'$ on the previous table.

   a. The new equilibrium price of corn is $_____.

   b. The new equilibrium quantity of corn is _____ million bushels.

   c. Has the demand for corn changed as a result of this change in supply? Explain briefly._____
   _____
   _____

3. Give an example of a factor that could have caused such an increase in the supply of corn, and explain briefly.
   _____
   _____

4. Notice that the increase in supply has resulted in a lower price and a higher quantity. Does this violate the Law of Supply, which states that the quantity of a good supplied increases as its price increases, all else equal? Explain briefly.
   _____
   _____
   _____

The Market for Corn

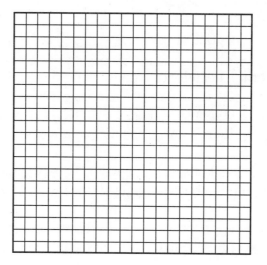

## B. Short-Answer Questions

1. The problem in the preceding section included a demand schedule for corn. What would you expect to happen to the demand schedule for corn if consumers' income rose, and corn is a normal good? What if corn is an inferior good? Explain briefly.

_____

_____

_____

_____

2. Explain why the price of a complement or a substitute can alter the demand for a good, even though the price of the good itself does not shift the demand.

_____

_____

_____

_____

# III. Self-Test

## A. True/False Questions

_____1.   A decrease in the price of soft drinks will increase their demand (shift the curve to the right).

_____2.   The supply of petroleum is fixed, because there is only a finite amount in the ground.

_____3.   At the equilibrium price, the amount that sellers are willing to provide is just equal to the amount that buyers are willing to buy.

_____4.   An improvement in technology tends to reduce the supply (shift it to the left).

_____5.   An increase in raw materials prices tends to reduce the supply (shift it to the left).

_____6.   If sellers expect prices to rise in the future, this could cause prices to rise today by encouraging sellers to reduce their current supply in anticipation of a price hike.

_____7.   A market refers to a physical location in which buyers and sellers interact.

_____8.   A price below equilibrium results in excess supply.

_____9.   Excess demand tends to drive price up until the market reaches equilibrium price and quantity.

_____10.  An increase in supply tends to increase equilibrium price and quantity.

_____11.  An equal increase in both supply and demand tends to increase equilibrium price and quantity.

_____12.  An increase in supply accompanied by a proportionate decrease in demand tends to decrease equilibrium price while leaving equilibrium quantity unchanged.

_____13.  The market supply curve is the vertical summation of all the individual supply curves.

_____14.  Assuming that pizza and beer are complements, a decrease in the price of pizza would increase the demand for beer.

_____15.  If pizza and hamburgers are substitutes, a decrease in the price of pizza would increase the demand for hamburgers.

## B. Multiple-Choice Questions

1.  Which of the following would not increase the demand (shift the curve to the right) for beer?
    a. A new FDA study concludes that beer cures colds and skin disorders.
    b. A price war results in beer selling for $.05/bottle.
    c. Bars begin giving away spicy snacks to their customers.
    d. The price of a substitute, hard liquor, rises.
    e. There is an increase in the drinking-age population.

2. If buyers believe that the price of automobile antifreeze will rise soon, due to an increase in the price of ethylene glycol, which is used to make antifreeze, the most likely immediate result will be:
   a. a decrease (shift to the left) in the demand for antifreeze, due to a change in tastes.
   b. a decrease (shift to the left) in the demand for antifreeze, due to a shift to substitutes.
   c. an increase in the quantity demanded, due to the change in supply.
   d. an increase (shift to the right) in the demand for antifreeze, due to a change in expectations.
   e. no change in demand; only supply will change.

3. If a new technological breakthrough in genetic engineering makes it possible to grow twice as much corn per acre as had been possible in the past, the most likely result will be:
   a. a decrease (shift to the left) in the supply of corn, due to the increased costs associated with the new technology.
   b. an increase (shift to the right) in the supply of corn, due to the reduced cost of production.
   c. an increase in the demand for corn, due to the greatly reduced price.
   d. an increase in quantity supplied, due to the increased willingness to sell corn.
   e. a shift from corn production to wheat production, using all of the extra land not needed for corn production.

4. A college student made the following statement to a friend at a college sporting event: "This football stadium is a good example of how unrealistic economics is: my economics professor claims that according to a so-called 'Law of Supply', supply varies directly with price, yet anybody can look around and see that the supply is fixed at 80,000 seats, no matter what the price is!" What was wrong with his statement?
   a. This is simply an exception to the Law of Supply; it doesn't mean that it isn't relevant for most cases.
   b. Supply isn't fixed at 80,000 seats; it is *quantity supplied* that is fixed.
   c. Supply isn't the same thing as the physical stock of a good or service that is available; rather, supply is *willingness to sell*.
   d. *Supply* doesn't vary directly with price, it is *quantity supplied* that varies with price.
   e. Both c and d are correct.

Use the following graph to answer questions 5-8:

The Market for Personal Size Pizzas

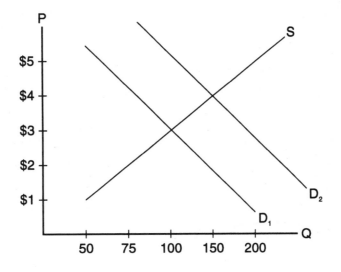

5. On the graph above, the initial equilibrium price and quantity are:
   a.  P=$2.00; Q=75
   b.  P=$2.00; Q=150
   c.  P=$3.00; Q=100
   d.  P=$4.00; Q=75
   e.  P=$4.00; Q=150

6. Which of the following would cause the demand for pizzas to shift to the right among college students?
   a.  an increase in federal financial aid to college students
   b.  half-price pizzas for anybody with a college ID
   c.  an increase in the price of a complement, beer
   d.  a decrease in the price of a substitute, hamburgers
   e.  a drop in the number of students attending college

7. After an increase in demand, the new equilibrium price and quantity are:
   a.  P=$2.00; Q=75
   b.  P=$2.00; Q=150
   c.  P=$3.00; Q=100
   d.  P=$4.00; Q=75
   e.  P=$4.00; Q=150

8. The increase in demand would cause supply to:
   a.  decrease (shift to the left).
   b.  increase (shift to the right).
   c.  first increase, then decrease over time.
   d.  either rise or fall, depending on the magnitude of the change in demand.
   e.  neither rise nor fall, although quantity supplied would increase.

Use the following graph to answer questions 9-12:

The Market for Hand-Held Calculators

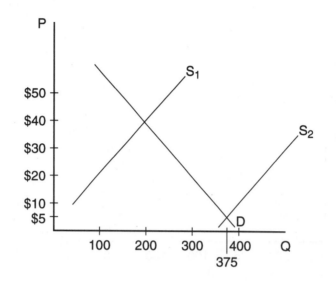

9. On the graph above, the initial equilibrium price and quantity are:
   a. P=$5; Q=375
   b. P=$10; Q=350
   c. P=$20; Q=100
   d. P=$30; Q=250
   e. P=$40; Q=200

10. Of the following, the factor that would cause an increase (shift to the right) in supply is:
   a. improved technology.
   b. lower labor productivity.
   c. increased prices of substitutes.
   d. increased demand.
   e. higher price.

11. As a result of the increase in supply, the new equilibrium price and quantity are:
   a. P=$5; Q=375
   b. P=$10; Q=350
   c. P=$20; Q=100
   d. P=$30; Q=250
   e. P=$40; Q=200

12. Suppose that the demand for calculators rose even more than the supply had increased. The net effect of the two increases would be the following change in equilibrium price and quantity:
   a. an increase in quantity but a slight decrease in price.
   b. increases in both quantity and price.
   c. decreases in both quantity and price.
   d. an increase in price but a decrease in quantity.
   e. an increase in price but an indeterminate effect on quantity.

13. Supply curves represent
    a. willingness to sell.
    b. physical stocks.
    c. inventories.
    d. willingness to buy.
    e. total production.

14. The supply curve for a good or service shows the sellers'
    a. target price.
    b. minimum acceptable price.
    c. maximum acceptable price.
    d. average acceptable price.
    e. inventories of finished products.

15. If equilibrium quantity rises but equilibrium price remains unchanged, the cause is:
    a. an increase in both supply and demand.
    b. an increase in demand and decrease in supply.
    c. a decrease in demand and increase in supply.
    d. a decrease in both demand and supply.
    e. an increase in demand in a market subject to a price ceiling.

16. If equilibrium price rises but equilibrium quantity remains unchanged, the cause is:
    a. an increase in both supply and demand.
    b. an increase in demand and decrease in supply.
    c. a decrease in demand and increase in supply.
    d. a decrease in both demand and supply.
    e. an increase in demand in a market subject to a price ceiling.

17. If equilibrium quantity and price rise, the cause is:
    a. an increase in demand without a change in supply.
    b. an increase in demand and decrease in supply.
    c. a decrease in demand and increase in supply.
    d. a decrease in both demand and supply.
    e. an increase in demand in a market subject to a price ceiling.

18. A freeze that destroys half of the coffee crop in South America would likely raise the price of coffee,
    a. reducing the demand for coffee and increasing the demand for tea.
    b. reducing the quantity demanded for coffee and increasing the demand for tea.
    c. reducing the demand for both coffee and tea.
    d. reducing the quantity demanded for both coffee and tea.
    e. reducing the demand for coffee and increasing the supply of coffee.

19. An inferior good is one for which demand:
    a. rises as income rises.
    b. falls as income rises.
    c. is unrelated to income.
    d. is low because of the low quality of the good.
    e. is high because the good must be replaced often.

20. Bars frequently offer "free" food during Happy Hour, because:
    a. they feel charitable.
    b. they get discounts on food from wholesalers.
    c. they can increase the demand for drinks this way, because food and drinks are complementary goods.
    d. food and drinks are substitute goods, so lowering the price of food increases the demand for drinks.
    e. they don't always behave rationally.

## IV. Advanced Critical Thinking

Consider the following editorial that appeared in following a freeze that destroyed much of the coffee crop in the late 1970s:

> *Coffee prices, it seems, are coming down again, after hitting a record high of $4.42 last year. An Agriculture Department economist, who had predicted $5-a-pound coffee this year, says he "underestimated the power of the U.S. consumer movement." Perhaps, or maybe, as with so many economists these days, he simply forgot his freshman economics, which has nothing to do with "movements." The coffee market is behaving the way the basic textbooks say a market behaves: Prices go up, demand falls, and prices come down.*
> —The Wall Street Journal, November 30, 1977

1. Suppose that coffee had started out at an equilibrium price of $1.00/pound prior to the freeze.
    a. Show graphically the initial equilibrium, labeling supply and demand as $S_1$ and $D_1$, respectively. Use $Q_1$ to identify the original equilibrium quantity.

    b. Show graphically the effect of a freeze that destroys much of the coffee crop, labeling the new supply as $S_2$ and the new equilibrium quantity as $Q_2$. The new equilibrium price is $4.42.)

    c. Did you shown a change in demand in your answer to part b? Why or why not?
    _____
    _____

d. Based on your analysis in parts (a–c), critique the *Wall Street Journal* editorial. What's wrong with their analysis?_____

_____

_____

_____

## V. Solutions

### Terms and Definitions

| | |
|---|---|
| 9 | Law of Demand |
| 8 | Demand |
| 4 | Quantity demanded |
| 13 | Excess demand |
| 1 | Law of Supply |
| 12 | Supply |
| 10 | Quantity supplied |
| 6 | Excess supply |
| 7 | Market |
| 2 | Equilibrium price |
| 5 | Equilibrium quantity |
| 11 | Competitive market |
| 14 | Monopolistic competition |
| 3 | Oligopoly |

### Practice Problems

1a.  $4.50

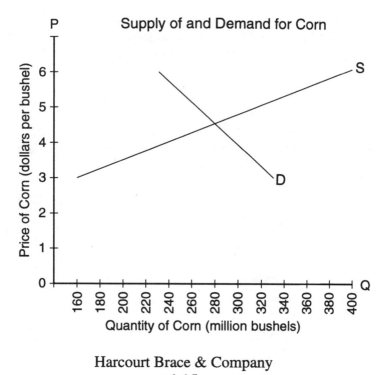

1b. 280
1c. shortage, 180, rise
1d. surplus, 60, fall

2a. $4.00
2b. 300
2c. Demand has not changed. Supply increased, moving the equilibrium along the existing demand curve to a higher quantity and lower price.

3. Any of the factors that lower cost of production could shift the supply to the right, indicating increased willingness to sell at each price. For example, improvements in technology that increase productivity would lower cost and increase the supply.

4. No, this does not violate the Law of Supply. The Law of Supply holds other factors, such as technology, constant. This represents a new supply curve, with an increased *willlingness to sell*, corresponding to increased productivity. Both the old and new supply curves follow the Law of Supply: As long as those other factors are constant, sellers will tend to be willing to sell more only at a higher price.

**Short-Answer Questions**

1. An increase in consumer income increases the demand for normal goods and decreases the demand for inferior goods. This result would hold for corn just as it does for other goods.

2. Prices of other goods are held constant in deriving a demand curve, even though they can affect consumption. When they change, the demand also changes (shifts right or left). The price of the good itself does not shift the demand, however, because price is already built into our definition of demand. Demand for a good includes all of the quantities that consumers are willing to buy at various prices of the good, holding other factors constant.

**True/False Questions**

1. F; quantity demanded, not demand, will increase.
2. F; the physical stock of petroleum in the ground is fixed, but the supply is willingness to sell, which is not fixed.
3. T
4. F; technology tends to *increase* the supply (shift it to the right) by increasing productivity; that is, increasing output per unit of input.
5. T
6. T
7. F; a market need not be in a specific physical location; buyers and sellers can interact without being in the same location.

8. F; price below equilibrium results in excess demand, as buyers try to buy more than sellers are willing to sell at the low price.
9. T
10. F; increased supply moves the equilibrium to the right along the demand curve, resulting in a higher quantity and lower price.
11. F; an increase in both supply and demand will increase equilibrium quantity, but the effect on price depends on which curve shifts more; if they shift equally, price remains unchanged.
12. T
13. F; market supply is the horizontal summation of the individual supply curves; for each price, it represents the sum of all of the individual quantities supplied.
14. T
15. F; a decrease in the price of a good tends to decrease the demand for its substitutes.

## Multiple-Choice Questions

| | | | |
|---|---|---|---|
| 1. b | 6. a | 11. a | 16. b |
| 2. d | 7. e | 12. b | 17. a |
| 3. b | 8. e | 13. a | 18. b |
| 4. e | 9. e | 14. b | 19. b |
| 5. c | 10. a | 15. a | 20. c |

## Advanced Critical Thinking

1a. The original equilibrium should be at a price of $1.00, with the quantity simply labeled $Q_1$.
1b. The new equilibrium should be at a price of $4.42 and a quantity of $Q_2$, after a leftward shift in supply and a movement along the (unchanged) demand curve. Equilibrium price is higher and quantity is lower.
1c. Demand did not change; only the quantity demanded changed as the supply shifted left, moving along the existing demand curve. There were no changes in the factors that are held constant in deriving a demand curve.
1d. The newspaper's analysis was flawed. They confused (shifts in) demand with simple changes in quantity demanded in response to a price change. For the price to fall, one of the factors (other than price) affecting either supply or demand must have changed.

# Chapter 5:  Elasticity and Its Application

## I. Chapter Overview

### A.  Context and Purpose

Chapters 4-6 introduce the basics of a market economy, beginning with an overview of supply and demand as its cornerstones and concluding with a look at the role of government.

This chapter extends the discussion of supply and demand that was introduced in the previous chapter, exploring consumer and producer responsiveness to changes in market conditions such as price.  To measure this responsiveness, economists use the term *elasticity*.  For example, consumers' relative responsiveness to changes in price as they move along the demand curve is known as price elasticity of demand.  When consumers (or producers) are relatively more responsive to changes in price, their demand (or supply) is considered to be more elastic, just as a rubber band that is very elastic is highly responsive or stretchy.  Knowledge of consumers' elasticity is useful for sellers, who need to know how price changes will affect sales and total revenues, as well as government officials, who need to know how changes in taxes or other public policies will affect behavior.

### B.  Learning Objectives

In this chapter you will:

1.  Learn the meaning of elasticity of demand.
2.  Examine what determines the elasticity of demand.
3.  Learn the meaning of the elasticity of supply.
4.  Examine what determines elasticity of supply.
5.  Apply the concept of elasticity in three very different markets.

After accomplishing these goals, you should be able to:

1.  Calculate price elasticity of demand and interpret the results, including the effects on total revenue when price changes, and distinguish elasticity from slope.
2.  List and explain the effects of the factors that determine the elasticity of demand.
3.  Calculate price elasticity of supply and interpret the results.
4.  List and explain the effects of the factors that determine the elasticity of supply.
5.  Use the concepts of supply and demand elasticity to explain the effects of supply or demand changes in various market on price, quantity, and total revenues.

## C. Chapter Review

### 5-1 The Elasticity of Demand

The price elasticity of demand refers to consumer responsiveness to changes in price, as shown below:

Elasticity of Demand = % Change in Quantity Demanded / % Change in Price

Demand is said to be elastic if the % change in quantity demanded exceeds the % change in price; that is, when the ratio is greater than one (ignoring the minus sign). Demand is inelastic if the %change in quantity demanded is less than the % change in price, (the ratio is less than one). If the % change in quantity equals the % change in price, the elasticity is unitary.

Several factors determine the price elasticity of demand:

- **Necessities vs. luxuries**: the less essential a good or service is perceived to be, the more elastic is the demand, all else equal.
- **Availability of close substitutes**: goods with close substitutes tend to have more elastic demand.
- **Definition of the market**: a narrow definition of the product tends to result in more elastic demand, because of the availability of close substitutes.
- **Time horizon**: the longer the time period, the greater the elasticity, as consumers have more time to adapt and find substitutes.

Price elasticity of demand is particularly significant because of its implications for total revenue when price changes. Because Total Revenue = Price x Quantity, sellers desiring to increase total revenue should raise price only if demand is inelastic, so that the drop in quantity demanded will be relatively smaller than the increase in price. Otherwise, if demand is elastic, a price hike will result in a relatively larger drop in quantity demanded, and Price x Quantity, or Total Revenue, will decline. If demand is unitary, then a price hike will be exactly offset by a drop in quantity, and total revenue will remain unchanged.

Another type of demand elasticity is income elasticity, which measures the responsiveness of demand to changes in income, as follows:

Income Elasticity = % Change in Quantity Demanded / % Change in Income

A good with a positive income elasticity is known as a normal good; in this case, as income rises, demand rises. A good with a negative income elasticity is an inferior good; in this case, as income rises, demand falls. Some goods may even shift from one category to another as we move from one income bracket to another. Consider the case of public higher education. For most people, it is a normal good (income elasticity > 0).

However, for people in the higher income brackets, the demand for public higher education actually declines as income rises, because they shift from public to more expensive private colleges and universities. For those high-income consumers, public higher education is an inferior good (income elasticity < 0).

## 5-2 The Elasticity of Supply

Price elasticity of supply refers to the responsiveness of quantity supplied to changes in price, as shown below:

Elasticity of Supply = % Change in Quantity Supplied / % Change in Price

When this ratio is greater than one, supply is elastic. When the ratio is less than one, supply is inelastic. When the percentage changes in quantity supplied and price are equal, the ratio is one, and supply elasticity is unitary.

## 5-3  Three Applications of Supply, Demand, and Elasticity

- **Agriculture**. Dramatic increases in agricultural productivity over the years have increased supply (shifted the supply curve to the right), driving down the prices of foodstuffs. Inelastic demand for agricultural products has resulted in relatively small increases in quantity demanded. An ironic result of the productivity explosion in agriculture was that farmers received lower revenues and incomes.

- **OPEC**. In the early 1970s, the Organization of Petroleum Exporting Countries (OPEC) was able to restrict supply and raise petroleum prices drastically. Inelastic demand helped make this policy successful in the short run. However, in the long run, both buyers and sellers are more able to adapt. Greater elasticity of demand and supply over time meant that OPEC could not maintain the higher prices.

- **Illegal Drugs**. A major tool in the war on drugs has been interdiction, or attempts to cut off the supply.  The basic tools of economic analysis suggest that this should not be too surprising. Interdiction reduces the supply of drugs, which results in higher prices. However, the demand for drugs by addicts is highly inelastic; therefore, higher prices lead to increased total revenues. Fewer drugs are being sold for a higher price. The net effect is that addicts must spend more to support their habits, which may lead to increased incidence of crime as addicts steal more to support their habits.  It is for this reason that public policy has turned increasingly to policies such as drug education programs designed to decrease the demand for illegal drugs.

## D.  Helpful Hints

1. *Elasticity means responsiveness.* In its most general sense, elasticity is responsiveness, whether we are talking about rubber bands or people.  In

economics, we use various types of elasticity to measure people's responsiveness to changes in economic factors such as price or income. The price elasticity of demand is particularly important because it provides immediate information about the effect of a change in price upon total consumer spending on the product. To the seller, this spending represents revenue. If consumer demand is highly elastic, or responsive to price, sellers can raise total revenue by cutting price. Even though price falls, the increased quantity demanded (and sold) more than makes up for the drop in price, as the dollar value of consumer spending (and revenue for the seller) rises. On the other hand, if demand is inelastic, cutting price will not generate enough additional sales to compensate, and total revenue will fall.

2. *Elasticity is not the same thing as slope.* Slope is constant along a straight-line demand curve, but price elasticity of demand varies with the point on the curve. This should be apparent if you keep in mind that slope is the steepness of the curve, which does not change along a straight-line demand curve, but the elasticity is the ratio of the relative changes in quantity and price, which depends on the starting point. Clearly a $1.00 change in price is a bigger percentage change when the initial price is $1.00 than when it starts at $1000.00!

## E. Terms and Definitions

Choose a definition for each key term.

Key terms:

_____Elasticity
_____Price elasticity of demand
_____Total revenue
_____Income elasticity of demand
_____Price elasticity of supply
_____Normal good
_____Inferior good

Definitions:

1. Total consumer spending for a product; Price x Quantity demanded.
2. Responsiveness to a change in an economic factor such as price or income.
3. Any good for which an increase in income leads to decreased demand; characterized by a negative income elasticity.
4. The percentage change in quantity demanded that results from a given percentage change in price; percentage change in quantity/percentage change in price.
5. The percentage change in quantity supplied that results from a given percentage change in price; percentage change in quantity/percentage change in price.
6. The percentage change in quantity demanded that results from a given percentage chance in income; percentage change in quantity/percentage change in income.

7. Any good for which an increase in income leads to increased demand; characterized by a positive income elasticity.

## II. Problems and Short-Answer Questions

### A. Practice Problems

1. The City Zoo is losing money. The City Council is unwilling to contribute any tax dollars to support the zoo, asserting that the administration should simply raise prices in order to balance its budget. The price of admission is currently $4.00/person, with average daily attendance of 600 people. The City Council argues that the zoo needs to raise only one additional dollar per visitor to break even (the zoo is currently losing about $600/day). The zoo management has hired you to estimate the demand for admissions to the zoo and recommend a pricing policy.

   The demand schedule that you have estimated is shown below:

### Demand for Zoo Admissions

| Price | Quantity of Tickets Demanded/Day | Total Revenue | % Change in Price | % Change in Quantity | Elasticity |
|-------|----------------------------------|---------------|-------------------|----------------------|------------|
| $ 0   | 1200 | _____ | | | |
| $1.00 | 1050 | _____ | _____ | _____ | _____ |
| $2.00 | 900  | _____ | _____ | _____ | _____ |
| $3.00 | 750  | _____ | _____ | _____ | _____ |
| $4.00 | 600  | _____ | _____ | _____ | _____ |
| $5.00 | 450  | _____ | _____ | _____ | _____ |
| $6.00 | 300  | _____ | _____ | _____ | _____ |
| $7.00 | 150  | _____ | _____ | _____ | _____ |
| $8.00 | 0    | _____ | _____ | _____ | _____ |

   a. Fill in the blanks in the preceding table. (Use the midpoint method to calculate the percentage changes and elasticity).

b. What is your recommendation regarding pricing, given the zoo's budget crisis? Should they change the price from the current $4.00? Justify your position, based upon your estimate of the elasticity of demand. _____

_____

_____

_____

_____

_____

2. Consider the demand curve for sofas shown below. Use the midpoint method to calculate elasticity in the questions that follow.

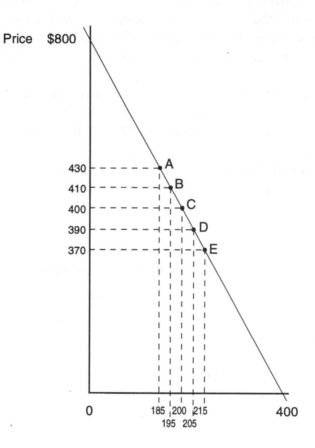

a.  What is the slope of the demand curve for sofas? _____

b.  What is the elasticity between points A and B? _____

c.  What is the elasticity between B and D? _____

d.  What is the elasticity between D and E? _____

e.  In general, what happens to elasticity as quantity increases along a straight-line demand curve?  Which part of the demand curve is elastic?  Which part is inelastic?  Explain._____

_____

_____

_____

_____


## B.  Short-Answer Questions

1.  How could a good such as a new mid-priced car be both an inferior good and a normal good?_____

_____

_____

_____

_____


## III.  Self-Test

### A.  True/False Questions

_____1.    The demand for Amoco gasoline is more elastic than the demand for gasoline in general.

_____2.    A seller facing an elastic demand curve will experience a drop in total revenue if he raises price.

_____3.    The longer the time period, the more elastic is the demand for a good or service, all else equal.

_____4.    A normal good is one for which the income elasticity is greater than one.

_____5.    A good perceived by the consumer to be a necessity will tend to have an elastic demand.

_____6.    For a good with a price elasticity of demand of 0.8, an increase in price will cause total consumer spending on the good to rise.

_____7.    Elasticity tends to be constant along a straight-line demand curve.

_____8.    The major problem facing agriculture in the U.S. today is the slow pace in implementing necessary technological changes in the production and distribution of food.

_____9. Basic supply and demand analysis shows clearly that drug interdiction designed to cut the supply of illegal drugs is our best hope to win the war on drugs.

_____10. A major reason why OPEC has been unable to maintain high energy prices over a long period of time is that buyers can find more substitutes in response to high oil prices in the long run.

_____11. An inferior good is a good characterized by a very low demand.

_____12. The price elasticity of supply is likely to be greater for motor vehicles in general than it is for a specialized market, such as sport utility vehicles.

_____13. The most likely effect of a global drought would be to lower farm incomes.

_____14. If the price elasticity of demand is unitary, then a change in price will leave total revenue unaffected.

_____15. If price elasticity of demand is zero, then any price change will also have a zero effect on total revenue.

## B. Multiple-Choice Questions

1. All else equal, the price elasticity of demand tends to be higher:
   a. the more substitutes there are for the good or service.
   b. the shorter the time period involved.
   c. the more consumers perceive the good to be a necessity.
   d. the more broadly defined the market is.
   e. the less important the product is in consumers' budgets.

2. A seller desiring to increase total revenue should:
   a. raise price only if demand is elastic.
   b. raise price only if demand is inelastic.
   c. lower price if demand is inelastic.
   d. lower price if demand has unitary elasticity.
   e. make pricing decisions based on elasticity of supply, not demand.

3. Senator Jones wants to reduce cigarette smoking by increasing tobacco taxes. It will probably take a fairly large tobacco tax to make much of a difference, because:
   a. price is irrelevant for consumers.
   b. demand for cigarettes is totally inelastic.
   c. demand for cigarettes is relatively inelastic.
   d. supply of tobacco is relatively inelastic.
   e. supply of tobacco is relatively elastic.

4. As income rises during economic upturns, consumption of potatoes declines, yet as income falls during economic downturns, consumption of potatoes rises. The most likely explanation is:
   a. changing tastes for potatoes.
   b. negative income elasticity of demand.
   c. very low price elasticity of demand.
   d. very high price elasticity of supply.
   e. high income elasticity of demand.

5. The price elasticity of demand is the:
   a. percentage change in price/percentage change in quantity demanded.
   b. change in price/change in quantity demanded.
   c. change in demand/change in price.
   d. percentage change in price/percentage change in income.
   e. percentage change in quantity demanded/percentage change in price.

6. Which of the following is most likely to have a high income elasticity of demand?
   a. fancy restaurant meals.
   b. lunches at fast food restaurants.
   c. brown bag lunches from home.
   d. apples.
   e. sardines.

7. If people always spend 25% of their incomes on housing, then the income elasticity of demand for housing is:
   a. 0.25.
   b. 1.00.
   c. 2.50.
   d. 25.0.
   e. indeterminate.

8. The demand for food is generally:
   a. income inelastic and price elastic.
   b. income elastic and price inelastic.
   c. both income and price elastic.
   d. both income and price inelastic.
   e. elastic in the short run, but inelastic in the long run.

Use the following information to answer questions 9 and 10. The city is considering a fare hike for its city bus service. At the current fare of $0.50, daily ridership is 1000 people. The city estimates that if it raises fares to $1.00, ridership will decline to 600.

9.  Using the midpoint method of calculating elasticity, the price elasticity of demand is:
    a.  0.
    b.  0.75.
    c.  1.00.
    d.  6.00.
    e.  800.

10. If the city wants to raise more revenue from its bus system, it should:
    a.  raise the price to $1.00.
    b.  keep the price at $0.50 and wait for demand to increase.
    c.  first lower the price to attract riders, then gradually increase price.
    d.  first raise price to get revenues, then lower price after the buses are paid off.
    e.  offer discount coupons to attract ridership.

11. A strict drug interdiction policy that reduces the supply of illegal drugs is most likely to:
    a.  reduce drug consumption but increase drug-related crime.
    b.  reduce both drug consumption and drug-related crime.
    c.  increase both drug consumption and drug-related crime.
    d.  increase drug consumption but reduce drug-related crime.
    e.  reduce drug consumption but leave drug-related crime unchanged.

12. An inferior good is a product for which:
    a.  quality is below average.
    b.  price elasticity of demand is very low.
    c.  income elasticity is negative.
    d.  demand increases slowly as income increases.
    e.  supply is inelastic.

13. If the price elasticity of demand is 0.5, then a 20% price hike will lead to a:
    a.  5% drop in quantity demanded.
    b.  10% drop in quantity demanded.
    c.  20% drop in quantity demanded.
    d.  40% drop in quantity demanded.
    e.  100% drop in quantity demanded.

14. If a 10% price hike leads to a 30% increase in quantity supplied, then the:
    a.  price elasticity of demand is 0.33.
    b.  price elasticity of supply is 0.33.
    c.  price elasticity of demand is 3.0.
    d.  price elasticity of supply is 3.0.
    e.  income elasticity is 30.0.

15. Of the following, the main reason why OPEC has been unable to keep oil prices high is that:
    a. demand tends to become more elastic in the long run.
    b. supply tends to be more inelastic in the long run.
    c. government regulations have prevented it.
    d. massive new petroleum discoveries have increased the supply.
    e. consumer boycotts have driven the price down.

16. Price elasticity of supply tends to be higher:
    a. the longer the time period.
    b. the easier it is for more new firms to enter the industry.
    c. the more adaptable the firms can be to changing market conditions.
    d. for manufactured goods than for antiques.
    e. for all of the above.

17. Bill buys one six-pack of beer each week, regardless of price (he drinks it on Saturday night). Which of the following statements is correct?
    a. price elasticity of demand is 0.
    b. price elasticity of demand is 1.
    c. price elasticity of demand is 6.
    d. price elasticity of supply is greater than 1.
    e. none of the above.

18. A horizontal demand curve has a price elasticity of:
    a. zero.
    b. between zero and one.
    c. one.
    d. between one and infinity.
    e. infinity.

19. A vertical supply curve has a price elasticity of:
    a. zero.
    b. between zero and one.
    c. one.
    d. between one and infinity.
    e. infinity.

20. A straight-line (constant-slope) demand curve has an elasticity that:
    a. remains constant along its length.
    b. increases as quantity demanded increases along its length.
    c. decreases as quantity demanded increases along its length.
    d. first increases then decreases as quantity demanded increases.
    e. none of the above.

## IV. Advanced Critical Thinking

        Antiquated Airlines of America (AAA) must decide on a pricing policy for flights between Pittsburgh and Columbus. It has two types of travelers, business and leisure passengers, whose demand curves are $D_B$ and $D_L$, respectively.

| BUSINESS TRAVELERS | | LEISURE TRAVELERS | |
|---|---|---|---|
| $D_B$ | | $D_L$ | |
| Price | Quantity Demanded | Price | Quantity Demanded |
| $400 | 200 | $400 | 0 |
| 300 | 300 | 300 | 100 |
| 200 | 0 | 200 | 300 |
| 100 | 500 | 100 | 500 |

1.  If their goal is to maximize total revenue, and they have enough seats to satisfy all of the demand, what price should they charge business travelers? What about leisure travelers? Explain. Do airlines actually behave this way? How can they charge two different prices for essentially the same product (how do they separate the two markets)? _____

    _____

    _____

    _____

    _____

    _____

    _____

    _____

2.  Can you think of any other examples of real-world price discrimination—charging different prices to different people for the same product—based on differences in the price elasticity of demand between two (or more) groups of consumers?

    _____

    _____

    _____

    _____

## V. Solutions

### Terms and Definitions

_____2_____Elasticity
_____4_____Price elasticity of demand
_____1_____Total revenue

_____6_____Income elasticity of demand
_____5_____Price elasticity of supply
_____7_____Normal good
_____3_____Inferior good

## Practice Problems

1 a.

| Price | Quantity of Tickets Demanded/day | Total Revenue | % Change in Price | %Change in Quantity | Elasticity |
|---|---|---|---|---|---|
| $ 0 | 1200 | 0 | | | |
| $1.00 | 1050 | $1050 | 200 | 13 | 0.07 |
| $2.00 | 900 | $1800 | 67 | 15 | 0.22 |
| $3.00 | 750 | $2250 | 40 | 18 | 0.45 |
| $4.00 | 600 | $2400 | 29 | 22 | 0.76 |
| $5.00 | 450 | $2250 | 22 | 29 | 1.32 |
| $6.00 | 300 | $1800 | 18 | 40 | 2.22 |
| $7.00 | 150 | $1050 | 15 | 67 | 4.47 |
| $8.00 | 0 | 0 | 13 | 200 | 15.38 |

b. They should leave the price as it is. The demand is price elastic upwards, so the if the zoo increased price, quantity demanded would fall more than enough to compensate for the increase, and total revenue would actually fall. The zoo is already gathering as much total revenue as it can, given its attractiveness to consumers; if it is to pay for itself, either costs must be cut, its attractiveness must be increased, or both.

2 a. -2.0 (Remember: Slope = rise/run = Δprice/Δquantity, for any two points on this straight-line or constant slope demand curve. Even the end points will work: 800/400 = 2)

b. 1.1 (Δquantity/quantity ÷ Δprice/price = 10/190 ÷ 20/420)

c. 1.0 (Δquantity/quantity ÷ Δprice/price = 10/200 ÷ 20/400)

d. 0.9 ($\Delta$quantity/quantity $\div \Delta$price/price= 10/210 $\div$ 20/380)

e. Elasticity falls as quantity increases along the straight-line demand curve. The upper part of the demand curve is always elastic, and the lower part is always inelastic. To see how this happens, consider points A, B, C, and D along the demand curve in the previous figure. Even though price and quantity change by constant amounts, the percentage changes also depend on the *levels* of price and quantity, which vary as we move along the demand curve. All straight-line demand curves behave this way: As price declines and quantity increases (down the demand curve), the elasticity declines, and as price increases and quantity declines (up the demand curve), elasticity increases.

## Short-Answer Questions

1. Goods are not likely to have constant income elasticities over all income ranges. Many products are normal goods initially, but as income rises, they often become inferior goods as people switch to more upscale products. For example, a mid-priced automobile tends to have a fairly high income elasticity for most people, but above some income level, the income elasticity actually becomes negative, as people substitute more expensive automobiles for the mid-price models. Even a luxury model could be an inferior good for some very high-income consumers.

## True/False Questions

1. T
2. T
3. T
4. F; a normal good has an income elasticity greater than zero.
5. F; necessities tend to have inelastic demand curves.
6. T
7. F; slope is constant but elasticity varies along a straight-line demand curve.
8. F; the major problem is inelastic demand, so that increased supply lowers total revenues.
9. F; because of highly inelastic demand, cutting supply is not very effective in the short run.
10. T
11. F; an inferior good is any good with a negative income elasticity.
12. F; elasticity tends to be greater, the more narrowly defined is the market.
13. F; by reducing supply and raising price in the face of inelastic demand, a drought would actually raise total consumer spending on food (total revenue) and farm income.
14. T
15. F; if elasticity is less than one (including zero), then total revenue will move in the same direction as price. If elasticity is zero, then quantity does not change, and total revenue will change in proportion to the change in price.

## Multiple-Choice Questions

| | | | |
|---|---|---|---|
| 1. a | 6. a | 11. a | 16. e |
| 2. b | 7. b | 12. c | 17. a |
| 3. c | 8. d | 13. b | 18. e |
| 4. b | 9. b | 14. d | 19. a |
| 5. e | 10. a | 15. a | 20. c |

## Advanced Critical Thinking

1. Sell business travelers 300 tickets at $300 each, for total revenues of $900. Sell leisure travelers 300 tickets at $200 each, for total revenues of $600 from leisure travelers. This will maximize revenues from both groups. Of course the airline should make sure that it has enough seats first, so that it doesn't sell seats for $200 that it could have sold for $300 to business travelers. Airlines separate the leisure and business markets through restrictions such as advance purchase and Saturday night layover requirements that business travelers generally are unwilling to meet. Leisure travelers, whose demand tends to be relatively elastic, are generally more willing than business travelers to accept such restrictions in order to get a low fare.

2. Any example of a product that is sold for different prices to different groups of people would work here, as long as the price differentials are not due to differences in cost of production. For example, senior citizen or student discounts for movie tickets or restaurants are used to lower the price for those people with higher elasticity of demand without cutting the price for everyone. Another example is "early-bird" specials that restaurants use to cut the price for those who are willing to eat at a less popular time.

# Chapter 6: Supply, Demand, and Government Policies

## I. Chapter Overview

### A. Context and Purpose

The previous two chapters introduced the basics of supply and demand, including market equilibrium, factors shifting the curves, and elasticity. The next section will develop more fully the supply/demand model in order to investigate the implications for social welfare.

To provide a transition into the extended supply/demand discussion, this chapter extends the analysis of supply and demand to include the role of government in a mixed market economy. In exploring the role of government, Chapter 6 considers the effects of price controls such as minimum-wage laws. It also deals with questions of tax incidence; that is, who actually pays various taxes.

### B. Learning Objectives

In this chapter you will:

1. Examine the effects of government policies that put a ceiling on prices.
2. Examine the effects of government policies that put a floor under prices.
3. Consider how a tax on a good affects the price of the good and the quantity sold.
4. Learn that taxes levied on buyers and taxes levied on sellers are equivalent.
5. See how the burden of a tax is split between buyers and sellers.

After accomplishing these goals, you should be able to:

1. Show graphically the shortage that occurs from a market subject to a price ceiling below equilibrium and explain why a price ceiling above equilibrium has no effect.
2. Show graphically the surplus that occurs from a market subject to a price floor above equilibrium and explain why a price floor below equilibrium has no effect.
3. Demonstrate that a tax on buyers shifts the demand curve and that a tax on sellers shifts the supply curve.
4. Explain that a tax places a wedge between buyers and sellers, shifting the *relative* positions of the supply and demand curves, regardless of whether the tax is on the buyer or the seller.
5. Show graphically the shift in supply or demand that results from the imposition of a tax and identify the effect on equilibrium price and quantity.

## C. Chapter Review

### 6-1 Controls on Prices

#### • Price Ceilings

In a competitive market, a price that is below equilibrium causes shortages, because quantity demanded exceeds quantity supplied. The resulting shortage tends to drive up price to equilibrium, eliminating the shortage. That is, price serves as a rationing device. When government steps in to hold the price below equilibrium, it also prevents price from serving its function as a rationing device. As a result, the shortage continues, requiring a rationing mechanism other than price. Of course, if the government sets a price ceiling that is higher than the equilibrium price, it will have no effect. For example, a ceiling price of $5.00/gallon for gasoline in the United States would have no effect, because it is well above the market equilibrium price.

#### • Price Floors

Just as a price ceilings can cause a shortage, a price floor or government-imposed minimum price above the equilibrium price will cause a surplus. A price above equilibrium reduces quantity demanded and increases quantity supplied (relative to equilibrium), resulting in a surplus. Normally, however, competition would drive price down until the surplus was eliminated. When government keeps the price artificially high, competition cannot perform this function, and the surplus continues as long as price is above equilibrium. Of course, a price floor below equilibrium has no effect: A price floor of $.10/gallon for milk would have no effect in the United States today, because the price of milk is already far above that level.

### 6-2 Taxes

It is not always clear who actually pays a given tax, because supply and/or demand tend to adjust in response to changes in taxes. To identify who actually bears the burden of a tax, we need to consider *tax incidence* after buyers and sellers adapt their behavior to the tax.

#### • Taxes on Buyers

When a tax is levied on the buyer of a good or service, this raises the effective price to the buyer without affecting the seller's price. Because the tax makes buying the product less attractive, it lowers the quantity demanded at every price. That is, it shifts the demand curve to the left, lowering the equilibrium price. The lower price means that sellers are also made worse off by the tax. In short, sellers are forced to bear part of the cost of the tax in the form of a lower price. How much of the tax is shifted to the seller is determined by the market; specifically, by the relative elasticities of supply and demand. For example, if supply is totally inelastic (with a vertical supply curve), sellers will continue to supply the same quantity, regardless of price. Therefore, buyers can shift the whole tax to sellers, who do not adapt their behavior in response to the lower price. If supply is totally elastic (horizontal), price does not change when there is a tax on buyers. As a result, the buyers must bear the entire burden of the tax.

## • Taxes on Sellers

Just as taxes on buyers shift the demand curve, so do taxes on sellers shift the supply curve to the left by raising the seller's cost by the amount of the tax. Because this decrease in supply drives up price, part of the tax is shifted to the buyer in the form of a higher price. How much is shifted depends on the relative elasticities of supply and demand. Consider the case of totally inelastic demand (a vertical demand curve): buyers will buy the same quantity regardless of price. As a result, sellers can pass along the entire tax to the consumer without losing any sales. At the other extreme, if demand is totally elastic (a horizontal demand curve), sellers cannot pass along any of the tax without losing all of their sales.

The actual burden of a tax, or the *tax incidence*, is determined by the relatively elasticities of supply and demand. If demand elasticity is higher than supply elasticity, then the buyers are more adaptable and will avoid most of the tax. If supply elasticity is higher than demand elasticity, then sellers can avoid most of the tax. If either curve is totally inelastic, then that group will pay the entire tax.

## D. Helpful Hints

1. *Price ceilings and floors matter only if they are binding.* Remember that not all price ceilings and floors cause disturbances in markets. A price ceiling causes shortages only if it is *below* the equilibrium price (and is enforced). A ceiling, or maximum price, that is above the equilibrium price cannot prevent the market from reaching equilibrium. Similarly, a price floor causes surpluses only if it is *above* the equilibrium price and it is enforced. A price floor set below the equilibrium price will not prevent the market from reaching equilibrium. A price ceiling...

2. *Taxes cause vertical shifts.* Even though we normally look at supply and demand shifts in terms of left and right, it is useful in the case of tax incidence to look at the vertical shifts. A tax on buyers causes a vertical shift down in the demand curve that is just equal to the tax. For quantity demanded to stay the same, price must fall by the full amount of the tax that the buyer must pay. A tax on sellers causes a vertical shift up the price axis in the supply curve just equal to the tax. For quantity supplied to stay the same, price must increase by the full amount of the tax that the seller must pay.

3. *Taxes on buyers and taxes on sellers are equivalent.* Consider the case of a tax imposed in a market in which neither supply nor demand is totally elastic or totally inelastic. Although a tax on buyers shifts the demand curve, and a tax on sellers

shifts the supply curve, the end result of either tax is reduced quantity sold, a higher price paid by buyers, and a lower price received by sellers. The difference between the prices paid and received is the tax, which introduces a wedge between buyers and sellers. Politically, it sometimes makes sense to switch a tax from buyers to sellers, or vice versa, but economically, it makes no sense: the result is the same. For example, Social Security taxes by law are split evenly between workers and employers, but the tax incidence is determined by the market, after supply and demand shift and wages adjust.

## E. Terms and Definitions

Choose a definition for each key term.

Key terms:

_____Price ceiling
_____Price floor
_____Tax incidence
_____Tax wedge

Definitions:

1. A legal minimum on the price of a good.
2. The ultimate burden of a tax, after supply and demand adjust to the tax.
3. A legal maximum on the price of a good.
4. The effect of a tax on a good or service that lowers the price received by sellers relative to the price paid by buyers. This gap is the tax wedge.


## II. Problems and Short-Answer Questions

### A. Practice Problems

Use the table to answer the questions below. Note that $Q_D$ is the initial quantity demanded and $Q_S$ is the initial quantity supplied:

## The Market for Widgets

| Price | $Q_D$ | $Q_S$ | $Q_S'$ | $Q_D'$ |
|-------|-------|-------|--------|--------|
| $1.00 | 1000 | 0 | 0 | 800 |
| $1.50 | 900 | 100 | 0 | 700 |
| $2.00 | 800 | 200 | 0 | 600 |
| $2.50 | 700 | 300 | 100 | 500 |
| $3.00 | 600 | 400 | 200 | 400 |
| $3.50 | 500 | 500 | 300 | 300 |
| $4.00 | 400 | 600 | 400 | 200 |
| $4.50 | 300 | 700 | 500 | 100 |
| $5.00 | 200 | 800 | 600 | 0 |

1. What are the initial equilibrium price and quantity? ___$P_1$= $_____ ; $Q_1$=_____

2. Suppose that the government imposes a new $1.00/unit tax on the sellers of widgets. The tax shifts the supply schedule from the original $Q_S$ to the new $Q_S'$.

   a. The new equilibrium price and quantity are: ___$P_2$=$_____ ; $Q_2$=_____ .
   b. How much of the $1.00 tax is borne by the seller? _____
   c. How much of the tax is borne by the buyer? _____
   d. Show graphically the old and new equilibria, labeling the original supply as S and the new supply as $S_1$. Label clearly the vertical shift in supply and the change in price and quantity as a result of the tax.

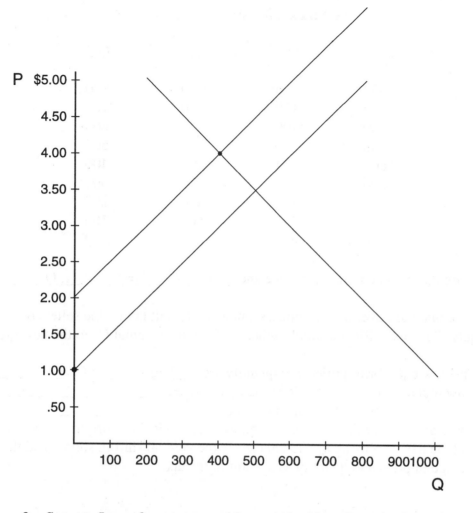

P $5.00
4.50
4.00
3.50
3.00
2.50
2.00
1.50
1.00
.50

100  200  300  400  500  600  700  800  9001000

Q

3. Senator Jones from a state with several widget factories has proposed a new piece of legislation that would change the widget tax. Her bill would switch the tax from the seller to the buyer, under the rationale that the widget makers are losing money and cannot afford to pay the tax. If the bill passes Congress, supply will shift back from $Q_S'$ to $Q_S$, and demand will shift from $Q_D$ to $Q_D'$.

    a. The new equilibrium price and quantity are:  __P3=$_____ ; Q3=_____.
    b. How much of the $1.00 tax is borne by the seller?_____?
    c. How much of the tax is borne by the buyer?_____?
    d. Did the new legislation help the sellers? Why or why not?_____
    _____
    _____
    _____

    e. Show graphically the original (pretax) equilibrium and the new equilibrium, labeling the original demand as D and the new demand as $D_1$. Label clearly the vertical shift in demand and the change in price and quantity as a result of the tax.

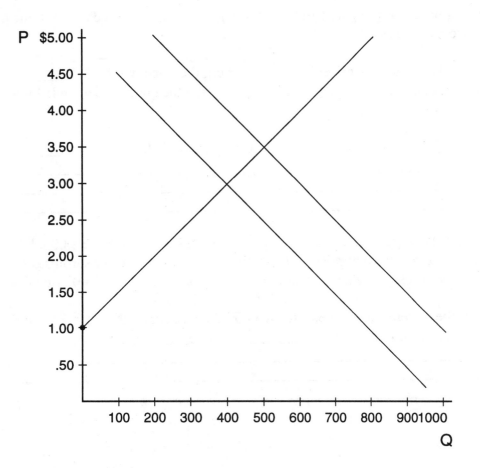

P $5.00

4.50

4.00

3.50

3.00

2.50

2.00

1.50

1.00

.50

100  200  300  400  500  600  700  800  900 1000

Q

4. Congress has voted to abolish the widget tax, so price and quantity have returned to the original equilibrium. To help the widget makers in her state, Senator Jones has proposed legislation that would enact a price floor of $4.00 in the market for widgets.

a. As a result of her legislation, the price will be $_____, quantity supplied will be $Q_S$ =_____, quantity demanded will be $Q_D$ =_____, and there will be a  (shortage/surplus/neither)  of _____. The actual quantity sold will be _____.

b. Who is helped and who is hurt by the price floors? _____
_____
_____
_____

c. If the price floor had been enacted while the $1.00 tax on sellers was already in effect, what would have happened to price and quantity? Would there have been a shortage or surplus? _____
_____
_____
_____

5. Suppose that pressure from consumer groups leads to a reduction in the price floor from $4.00 to $3.00.

   a. With the new price floor (and no tax), the price will be $_____, quantity supplied will be $Q_S =$ _____, and the quantity demanded will be $Q_D$ = _____.

   b. What is the effect of the new price floor at $3.00? Explain. _____
   _____
   _____
   _____

   c. Show graphically the effects of a price floor of $4.00 and $3.00, labeling clearly the equilibrium price and quantity and any shortages or surpluses that result in each case. Label the $4.00 price floor as $P_{F1}$ and the $3.00 price floor as $P_{F2}$.

6. If the government had enacted a $3.00 price ceiling rather than a price floor, the result would have been: _____
   _____
   _____
   _____

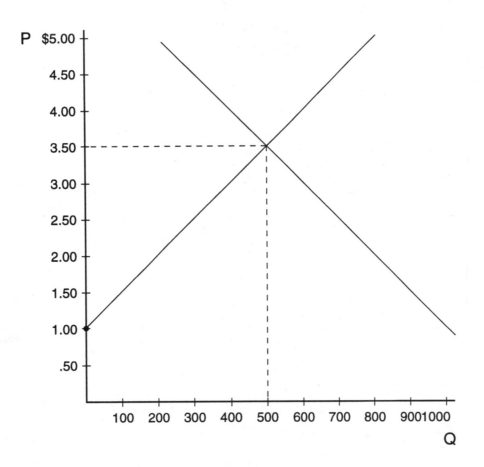

## Short-Answer Questions

1. In 1997, the social security tax rate was 7.65% on employers and 7.65% on employees, for a total payroll tax of 15.3%. Conflicting pieces of legislation before Congress would change the statutory or legal burden of the tax for a variety of alleged efficiency and equity reasons. One group would like to place the entire tax on employees, in order to provide an incentive for employers to create more jobs. An opposing group would like to place the entire tax on employers, in order to help workers who are facing a reduced standard of living.

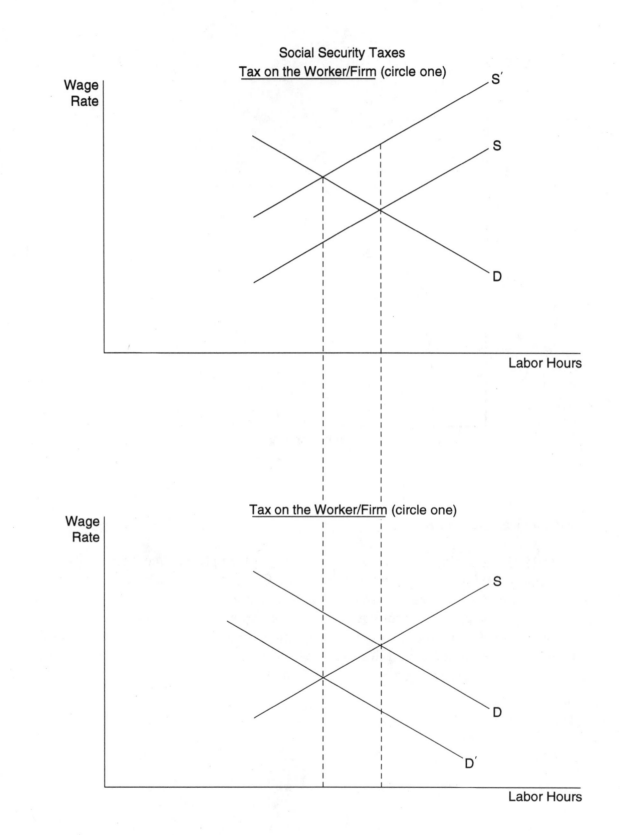

Social Security Taxes
Tax on the Worker/Firm (circle one)

Tax on the Worker/Firm (circle one)

a. Show graphically the effects of the two proposals. Identify which curve shifts in each case (labor supply or demand for labor) by circling the appropriate response (worker or firm) in the subtitle above each diagram. On both diagrams, label the original wage as $w_e$ and the equilibrium quantity of labor hired as $L_e$. Label the wage actually received by the workers (after the tax) as $w_w$. Label the wage actually paid (after a tax) by the firms as $w_f$. Label the resulting tax wedge between supply and demand. Show the effect on employment (number of hours of labor hired) as $L_1$.

b. What will happen to wages if the tax is levied against the employers? What if the tax is levied against the employees? What about employment (compare the results of the two proposals in terms of the effect on equilibrium hours worked)?

_____
_____
_____
_____

c. Who are the winners and who are the losers (if any) if either of these proposals is enacted? Explain. _____

_____
_____
_____

2. Suppose that next year crude oil prices skyrocket because of a crisis in the Middle East. As a result, gasoline prices rise by 50%. Congress caves in to political pressure and places a six-month price ceiling on gasoline at the previous year's levels.

a. What will be the effect on quantity demanded of rolling back gasoline prices? Explain how this could happen. _____

_____
_____
_____

b. What will be the effect on quantity supplied of rolling back gasoline prices? Explain. _____

_____
_____
_____

c. What would be the overall effect of this price ceiling? _____

_____
_____
_____

## III. Self-Test

### A. True/False Questions

_____1.　A price ceiling above equilibrium tends to cause shortages.

_____2.　A price floor above equilibrium tends to cause surpluses.

_____3.　A tax levied on buyers of a good or service shifts the demand curve to the right.

_____4.　A tax levied on sellers of a good or service shifts the supply curve to the left.

_____5.　A $1.00/unit tax on sellers generally will raise price by $1.00.

_____6.　A $5.00/unit tax on buyers generally will lower the equilibrium price by less than $5.00.

_____7.　Regardless of who is the legal taxpayer, the entire tax bill is shifted to consumers in the form of higher prices.

_____8.　A $1.00/unit tax on sellers is economically equivalent to a $1.00/unit tax on buyers, except that the tax on sellers is more equitable for low-income buyers.

_____9.　A $.50/pack cigarette tax, levied against the seller, is likely to be paid mostly by the seller.

_____10.　Economists are generally opposed to price controls, unless the controls are needed to improve equity.

_____11.　Tax incidence refers to the legal burden of tax.

_____12.　Rent controls are likely to cause shortages of housing, particularly in the short run.

_____13.　The incidence of the Social Security tax is determined by Congress.

_____14.　Rent controls are least likely to cause shortages of housing if the supply of housing is inelastic.

_____15.　The burden of a tax always falls on the side of the market with the smaller price elasticity.

### B. Multiple-Choice Questions

1. A $500 per automobile pollution tax on the manufacturers will shift the:
   a. demand curve down by $500.
   b. demand curve up by $500.
   c. supply curve up by $500.
   d. supply curve down by $500.
   e. supply and demand curves down by $500.

2. A tax is most likely to be paid by the seller when the:
   a. demand is elastic and supply is inelastic.
   b. demand is inelastic and supply is elastic.
   c. tax is levied on the seller.
   d. supply and demand are elastic.
   e. supply and demand are inelastic.

3.  A binding price ceiling causes
    a.  shortages.
    b.  quantity supplied greater than quantity demanded.
    c.  competition among buyers, driving price up to equilibrium.
    d.  excess supply.
    e.  all of the above.

4.  A price floor below the equilibrium price causes:
    a.  shortages.
    b.  surpluses.
    c.  excess demand.
    d.  excess supply.
    e.  none of the above.

5.  A tax will be split equally between buyers and sellers when:
    a.  the government splits the tax equally between buyers and sellers.
    b.  supply and demand are equal.
    c.  supply and demand have equal elasticities.
    d.  supply has an infinite elasticity and demand has a zero elasticity.
    e.  none of the above.

6.  A $1 recycling fee imposed by the government on the buyer whenever a new tire is
    sold will move the:
    a.  demand curve down by $1.00.
    b.  demand curve up by $1.00.
    c.  supply curve up by $1.00.
    d.  supply curve down by $1.00.
    e.  none of the above.

7.  A binding minimum wage:
    a.  raises the quantity of labor supplied.
    b.  reduces the quantity of labor demanded.
    c.  causes surpluses of labor.
    d.  causes unemployment.
    e.  all of the above.

8.  A tax on buyers is:
    a.  equivalent to a tax on sellers.
    b.  likely to be harder on the poor than a tax on sellers.
    c.  harder to shift than a tax on sellers.
    d.  easier to shift than a tax on sellers.
    e.  none of the above.

9. When we say that a tax introduces a wedge in a market, we mean that the tax:
   a. wedges money away from buyers.
   b. wedges money away from sellers.
   c. creates a wedge between the new and old equilibrium prices.
   d. introduces a wedge between the price paid by the buyer and that received by the seller.
   e. none of the above.

10. The most likely effect of price ceilings holding the price of gasoline down to $.75/gallon would be:
    a. more affordable gasoline for the general public.
    b. increased quantity supplied, to take advantage of the additional demand.
    c. decreased quantity demanded.
    d. increased exploration by oil companies trying to find cheaper oil reserves.
    e. long lines at the gasoline pumps.

11. All else equal, a binding price ceiling will cause greater shortages if:
    a. both supply and demand are inelastic.
    b. both supply and demand are elastic.
    c. supply is elastic, but demand is inelastic.
    d. supply is inelastic, but demand is elastic.
    e. none of the above: a price ceiling won't cause a shortage.

12. A good way to distinguish shortage from scarcity is that:
    a. we can eliminate a shortage by raising price, but scarcity cannot be eliminated.
    b. shortages result from price controls, but scarcity results from sellers holding back output.
    c. shortage means that we can't have all that we want at a zero price; scarcity means that we can't have all we want at any price.
    d. at a high enough price, there is no scarcity, but shortages continue to exist even at high prices.
    e. none of the above: scarcity and shortage mean essentially the same thing.

13. Which of the following statements is true of surpluses?
    a. A surplus results whenever price is held above equilibrium.
    b. In markets that are allowed to adjust, surpluses tend to be eliminated by competition among sellers.
    c. Surpluses result from binding price floors.
    d. A surplus is calculated as quantity supplied less quantity demanded.
    e. All of the above are true.

14. Shortages result whenever:
    a. wants are unlimited and resources are limited.
    b. wants are limited and resources are unlimited.
    c. price is held above equilibrium.
    d. price is held below equilibrium.
    e. quantity supplied exceeds quantity demanded.

15. All else equal, a binding price floor will cause less of a surplus if:
    a. both supply and demand are inelastic.
    b. both supply and demand are elastic.
    c. supply is elastic, but demand is inelastic.
    d. supply is inelastic, but demand is elastic.
    e. none of the above: A price floor won't cause a surplus.

## IV. Advanced Critical Thinking

Participants at a recent economics seminar in San Francisco pointed out to the speaker that there is a basic flaw in the logic of microeconomics, which is built upon the concept of scarcity. They observed that housing is not really scarce in San Francisco, even though a very modest apartment can rent for well over $1000. According to these critics, it is simply landlords' greed that prevents everyone from having affordable housing. They provided statistics showing that the numbers of dwellings and the number of families were roughly equal, which they felt provided proof that there is not a scarcity of housing. Consequently, they argued for rent controls as a solution to the housing crisis in San Francisco. What's wrong with this way of thinking? Is it valid to argue that scarcity does not exist just by counting the number of houses? Are houses freely available at a zero price? Suppose that rent controls forced the rent on a $1000 apartment down to $100. What would happen to new construction? To maintenance on existing apartments? What would happen to the quantity demanded? Write an economist's response to these critics of mainstream economics._____

_____
_____
_____
_____
_____
_____

## V. Solutions

### Terms and Definitions

__3__ Price ceiling
__1__ Price floor

___2___Tax incidence
___4___Tax wedge

## Practice Problems

1.  $P_1$= \$3.50;   $Q_1$= 500

2.  a.  <u>$P_2$=\$4.00;   $Q_2$=400.</u>
    b.  <u>\$0.50</u>
    c.  <u>\$0.50</u>
    d.

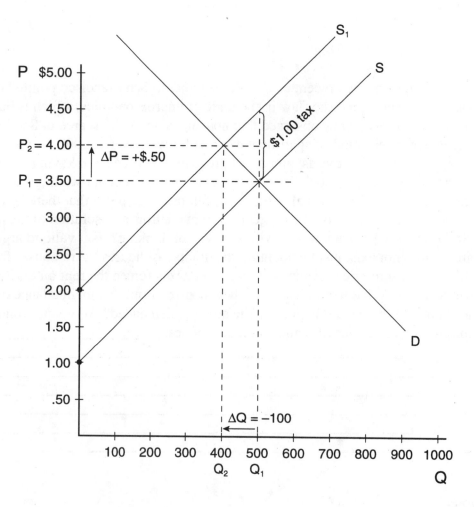

3. a. <u>$P_3=\$3.00$; $Q_3=400$.</u>
   b. <u>$\$0.50$</u>
   c. <u>$\$0.50$</u>
   d. No, the change in the legal burden did not help either the buyers or the sellers. The actual tax incidence after the market adjusts is identical. With either version of the tax, the quantity is 400 and buyers end up paying a total of $4.00 per widget, with sellers receiving only $3.00. The $1.00 gap is the tax that goes to the government. The only thing that changes is who actually writes the check to the government.
   e.

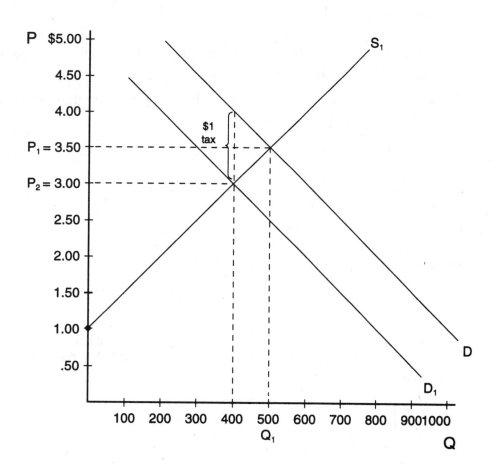

4.  a.  As a result of her legislation, the price will be P= $4.00, quantity supplied will be   $Q_S$ =600, quantity demanded will be $Q_D$ = 400, and there will be a  (surplus) of  200 . The actual quantity sold will be 400.

    b.  Consumers are hurt by the price floor, because they must pay an additional $0.50/widget.  Some sellers benefit by receiving higher prices for their product, but others are made worse off because they cannot find a market for all that they produce at $4.00.

    c.  With a $1.00 tax on sellers, the price already would have been at $4.00, so the floor would have had no effect on either price or quantity.  It simply would have mandated a price that already existed.  The price would stay at $4.00 and the quantity at 400.  The market would clear, so there would be neither a shortage nor a surplus.

5.  a.  With the new price floor, the price will be $3.50, quantity supplied will be $Q_S$= 500, and the quantity demanded will be $Q_D$ =500.

    b.  The new price floor is below the equilibrium price; therefore, it will have no effect on either price or quantity.

    c.

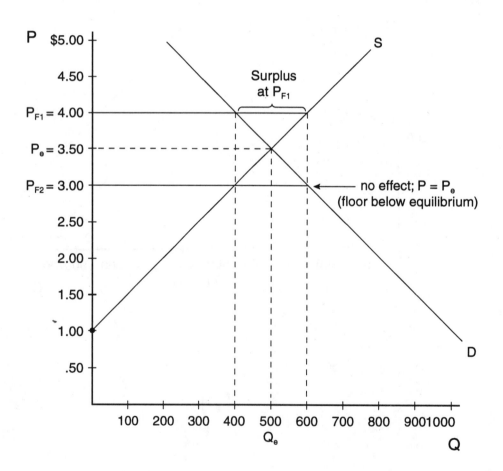

6. A shortage, or excess demand, of 200 units, because quantity demanded at $3.00 is 600, which is greater than the quantity supplied of 400.

## B. Short-Answer Questions

1. a. (See the following graph)

   b. Neither the employers nor the employees gain or lose as a result of a change in the legal burden of the Social Security tax. The actual tax incidence depends on the relative elasticities of the supply of and demand for labor. A payroll tax like Social Security is a tax on the labor market. How the tax burden actually is allocated between workers and employers is determined by the market rather than by government. Of course, there may be political winners or losers. Politicians who supported one of these proposals would gain or lose, depending upon the popularity of the proposal.

2. a. When government rolls back gasoline prices, one result is an increase in quantity demanded. Buyers who would have car pooled or cut back on leisure driving or taken mass transit will not make the effort when the price of gasoline is reduced. People respond to economic incentives.

   b. Sellers will respond to the lower gasoline prices by cutting back on the production of gasoline. To some extent, they will switch from gasoline production to other petroleum products. They will also cut back on petroleum production until the price goes back up by capping existing wells. If they expect the lower prices to continue, they will even cut back on exploration for new oil reserves.

   c. The result would be a shortage of gasoline, evidenced by long lines at gasoline stations. Buyers would try to get around the controls by offering bribes under the table to sellers. Because price will no longer work to ration scarce gasoline, the government may enact a rationing system to deal with the shortage. Otherwise, long waits may serve as the rationing device for gasoline.

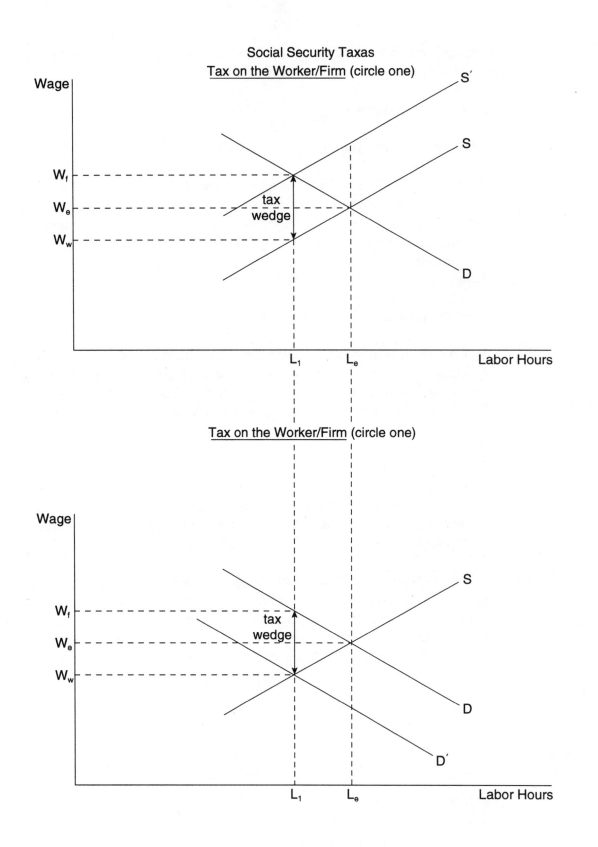

Social Security Taxas
Tax on the Worker/Firm (circle one)

Tax on the Worker/Firm (circle one)

## True/False Questions

1. F; a ceiling (maximum price) above equilibrium has no effect, because the market will reach equilibrium before it reaches the legal maximum price.
2. T
3. F; a tax on buyers reduces their willingness to buy (the quantity demanded) at each price; which means that demand falls (shifts to the left).
4. T
5. F; normally demand has some non-zero elasticity that prevents sellers from passing the entire tax along to the buyer; price will normally go up, but by less than $1.00.
6. T
7. F; taxes are shifted relatively more to the side of the market with the lower elasticity.
8. F; the two taxes are equivalent, even in terms of equity.
9. F; given that the demand for cigarettes is highly inelastic, the tax is likely to be paid primarily by the buyers.
10. F; economists are generally opposed to price controls; most prefer other means to improve equity.
11. F; tax incidence refers to the ultimate burden of the tax, after the market responds.
12. F; rent controls cause increasing shortages in the long run, after landlords have time to adjust by letting buildings depreciate and not building new housing units.
13. F; the incidence of the Social Security tax is determined by the relative elasticities of labor supply and demand in the labor market.
14. T
15. T

## Multiple-Choice Questions

| | | | | | |
|---|---|---|---|---|---|
| 1. | c | 6. | a | 11. | b |
| 2. | a | 7. | e | 12. | a |
| 3. | a | 8. | a | 13. | e |
| 4. | e | 9. | d | 14. | d |
| 5. | c | 10. | e | 15. | a |

## Advanced Critical Thinking

Scarcity means that we cannot have everything we want at a zero price. People respond to economic incentives. If rent controls reduce the price of housing below the equilibrium level, quantity demanded will rise as people respond. Some buyers will choose to move into more spacious or luxurious housing; others may choose to move out of the family home and live on their own. All else equal, more people also will want to move into the area if housing is cheaper. On the supply side, however, nothing has happened to make more housing available to meet the demand. On the contrary, the seller (landlord) has an incentive to supply less housing. It may be tempting to think of the supply of housing as fixed; however, this view is not correct. Consider the extreme case: Is it realistic to think that at a zero price, housing would still be available? Of course not! Particularly in the long run, the market will respond to below-equilibrium rents by building fewer housing units and allowing existing housing to deteriorate without repair or replacement. The stock of housing will shrink as quantity supplied responds to the lower price. It will benefit those buyers who are lucky enough to get housing at a reduced price. However, it will hurt those buyers who cannot get housing, even though they were willing to pay a higher price. It will also hurt sellers in general. The old saying is true: There really are no free lunches (or apartments).

# Chapter 7:  Consumers, Producers, and the Efficiency of Markets

## I. Chapter Overview

### A. Context and Purpose

Earlier chapters provided an overview of supply and demand as a way to set prices and determine how much to produce.  This chapter looks at the question of whether or not supply and demand produce an outcome that is desirable from the standpoint of society.  That is, does the market give us the maximum possible social well-being?  The following two chapters will apply these results to policy questions regarding taxation and trade with other countries.  In an economic sense, do we really know what's good for us?  This section of three chapters will help to find the answers.

### B. Learning Objectives

In this chapter you will:

1.  Examine the link between buyers' willingness to pay for a good and the demand curve.
2.  Learn how to define and measure consumer surplus.
3.  Examine the link between sellers' costs of producing a good and the supply curve.
4.  Learn how to define and measure producer surplus.
5.  See that the equilibrium of supply and demand maximizes total surplus in a market.

After accomplishing these goals, you should be able to:

1.  Demonstrate that the market demand curve is a horizontal summation of all buyers' willingness to buy a good.
2.  Explain that consumer surplus is the additional benefit to the consumer beyond the price paid, and that it exists because of the downward sloping demand curve.
3.  Show that the supply is the horizontal summation of all the sellers' willingness to sell a good, and that the minimum acceptable price is just equal to the opportunity cost of producing and selling another unit.
4.  Explain that producer surplus is the excess received by the seller beyond the cost of production when the seller just breaks even on the last unit produced; it results because of the upward-sloping supply curve.
5.  Demonstrate graphically and explain why the competitive equilibrium of supply and demand maximizes the combined producer and consumer surplus.

## C. Chapter Review

Does the market provide the socially optimal quantities of goods and services? This chapter investigates that question, using the tools of *welfare economics*, which is the study of how society's allocation of resources affects economic well-being. As explained in the following two sections, the net social gain from providing a good or service is the sum of the consumer surplus from buying the product and the producer surplus from selling the product.

### 7-1  Consumer Surplus

Part of the social gain from producing at the competitive equilibrium is *consumer surplus*, which is the amount that a buyer is willing to pay for a good minus the amount actually paid. That is, consumer surplus is the additional amount that the buyer would have willingly paid to get the product beyond the market price that he or she actually paid. Because the demand curve measures willingness to pay, the area under the demand curve but above the market price represents consumer surplus. Sellers of course would like to capture that surplus by charging higher prices to buyers who are willing to pay more, while charging lower prices to those who are less willing to pay. This is known as price discrimination. Given that in the absence of price discrimination, the market price reflects the willingness to pay of the marginal buyer, the following conditions must be met *for consumers to receive a surplus*:

- *Demand is downward sloping*: This is because additional units are worth less to the consumer than the units that came before.

- *Perfect price discrimination is not possible*; otherwise, sellers could charge every buyer a different price that reflects each buyer's willingness to pay, which would eliminate any surplus for the consumers.

As an example, suppose that you are looking for cheap transportation—you will pay up to $3000 for a reliable used car that gets decent mileage. Luckily for you, reliable, if not beautiful, cars are available for $2000. If you buy at the market price of $2000, you will gain a consumer surplus of $1000 ($3000 - $2000).

### 7-2  Producer Surplus

The mirror image of consumer surplus is *producer surplus*, which is the amount a seller is paid, minus the cost of production. That is, producer surplus is the excess that the seller receives beyond his or her opportunity cost of providing the good or service. *Producer surplus exists when*:

- *Supply is positively sloped*, suggesting that sellers respond to economic incentives by supplying more at a higher price than at a lower price.

- *The market price reflects the willingness to sell of the marginal seller*, so that everyone but the marginal seller earns a surplus at the single market price.

As an example, suppose that you are interested in selling your old car in order to buy a newer one. You are willing to unload it for $500, but luckily for you, the market values the car at $2000. If you sell it, you will earn a producer surplus of $1500 ($2000 - $500). The price was determined by the interaction of the marginal buyer and seller, each of whom valued the car at $2000.

## 7-3 Market Efficiency

In the previous two sections, we saw that both buyers and sellers can benefit by accepting the market price. Voluntary exchange occurs only if it benefits both parties. In the example with the used car that the market valued at $2000, both the buyer and the seller gained. The buyer who would have paid $3000 gained a consumer surplus of $1000, and the seller who would have sold for as little as $500 gained a producer surplus of $1500. The total surplus therefore is the sum of the consumer and producer surpluses, or $2500 ($1000 + $1500). This total surplus represents a net gain to society from the voluntary exchange between the buyer and seller. In fact, the market price could have been any price between $500 and $3000 and both buyer and seller would have agreed to the deal, resulting in the same total surplus, or net social gain, of $2500! For example, suppose that the buyer had been able to get the seller to accept only $500. Then the producer surplus would have been $0, but the consumer surplus would have been $2500 ($3000 - $500). Even when the gains are unevenly distributed between buyers and sellers, the total is still the same. We may not be able to agree about which price is most equitable, but we can agree that the market outcome is *efficient*, meaning that the allocation of resources maximizes total surplus. *Equity*—the fairness of the distribution of well-being among the various buyers and sellers—requires normative judgments that go beyond positive economics.

In summary, *competitive markets* tend to:

- *Allocate the output of goods to the buyers who value them the most.*

- *Allocate production to the sellers who can produce them at the lowest opportunity cost.*

- *Produce the quantity of goods that maximizes the sum of consumer and producer surplus.*

## 7-4 Conclusion: Market Efficiency and Market Failure

When markets work efficiently, they maximize total social well-being. However, *market failure* may occur when *market power* allows some of the buyers or sellers to control price to some extent, or when there are *externalities*—costs or benefits that affect social welfare but are not considered by buyers or sellers because they are borne by someone else.

## D. Helpful Hints

1. *A change in price alone simply reallocates the total surplus between consumers and producers.* It is very tempting to argue that price is directly responsible for differences in social welfare. For example, when sellers take advantage of inelastic demand to raise price, this directly lowers social welfare. Only if the quantity sold changes does the total surplus change. The used car example demonstrates that the total surplus can remain the same even when consumer surplus is either maximized or eliminated, as long as there is an offsetting change in producer surplus. We may feel that a certain outcome is unfair, but that is a separate question from the efficiency resulting from maximizing total welfare.

2. *Remember that exchanges are voluntary.* Market exchanges make both the buyer and the seller better off because nobody is forced to trade if they don't want to. The more voluntary exchanges that occur, the more gains from trade there are.

## E. Terms and Definitions

Choose a definition for each key term.

Key terms:

_____Welfare economics
_____Willingness to pay
_____Consumer Surplus
_____Cost
_____Producer Surplus
_____Efficiency
_____Equity
_____Market Power
_____Externalities
_____Market Failure

Definitions:

1. In economics, cost means opportunity cost.
2. The inability of the market to provide efficient allocation of resources, for example because of market power or externalities.
3. A state in which an allocation of resources maximizes total surplus (consumer plus producer surplus).

4. The maximum price that a buyer will pay for a given quantity of a good; a measure of the value that the buyer put on the good.
5. The study of how the allocation of resources affects economic well-being, or social welfare.
6. The amount a seller is paid minus the cost of production.
7. The amount that a buyer is willing to pay for a good minus the amount the buyer actually pays for it.
8. Costs or benefits of an action that are not taken into account by the buyers or sellers, even though they affect social welfare.
9. The fairness of a distribution of economic well-being among members of society.
10. The ability of some buyers or sellers to control prices.


## II. Problems and Short-Answer Questions

### A. Practice Problems

1. There are five consumers looking for a particular used car in Farmville, Virginia. Betsy is willing to pay $6000, Kathy would pay $5000, Fred would pay $4000, Gwen would pay $3000, and Camille would pay $2000. There are also five local dealers with cars that would satisfy the consumers: Bill's Beautiful Bargains has a car that cost Bill $6000, Al's Autos has one for which his opportunity cost was $5000, Cal's Classic Cars has one that cost $4000, Tim's Transportation has one that cost $3000, and Buy-A Bomb has one that it is willing to sell for $2000. (Assume that all of the used cars are identical, except for the price charged.)

   a. Plot the supply and demand diagrams for the used cars in the space below:

   b. If the market moves to a single equilibrium price, how many autos will be sold, and at what price? Will this maximize efficiency? Explain._____
   _____
   _____
   _____
   _____

c.  Label the consumer and producer surplus on your diagram. What is the dollar value of the consumer surplus? the producer surplus? the total surplus? Explain how you calculated them. _____

_____

_____

_____

_____

d.  It appears that each consumer could find a seller that would sell at a price that would coincide with the consumer's willingness to pay, if each buyer negotiated separately with a seller that matched his or her willingness to buy. For example, Bill is not very competitive, with a minimum price of $6000, but there is one buyer—Betsy—who would pay that much. Of course, for this to work, buyers and sellers would have to be unaware of the better options available elsewhere; otherwise, Betsy for example, could do better buying from a lower-cost seller. Would it be more or less efficient for the buyers and sellers to be matched according to their willingness to buy and sell? (Hint: What would happen to total surplus, compared to the competitive solution?)_____

_____

_____

_____

_____

_____

2. a.  Explain how the free market maximizes total surplus. What assumptions are required for this result to occur? _____

_____

_____

_____

b.  What happens to total surplus if production goes beyond the equilibrium? Explain._____

_____

_____

c.  What happens to total surplus if production stops short of equilibrium? Explain.

_____

_____

_____

## B. Short-Answer Questions

1. Contrast the efficiency and equity goals in economic policymaking. How do they differ? _____

_____

_____

_____

_____

_____

## III. Self-Test

### A. True/False Questions

_____1.  Welfare economics is the study of government income redistribution programs such as Food Stamps and AFDC.

_____2.  Consumer surplus is the difference between consumers' willingness to pay and the demand curve.

_____3.  Producer surplus refers to unsold inventories, due to a market price above equilibrium.

_____4.  When free markets work effectively, they maximize the sum of consumer and producer surplus.

_____5.  An efficient allocation of resources is one that maximizes the fairness of the outcome.

_____6.  The sum of consumer and producer surplus is a measure of the economic well-being of a society.

_____7.  Equity and efficiency are two economic goals that typically go together— usually an efficient outcome is an equitable outcome.

_____8.  Free markets do not work efficiently in the presence of externalities.

_____9.  Adam Smith believed that society's well-being was maximized by careful regulation of markets by a benevolent government.

_____10.  The major advantage of using supply and demand to allocate resources is the inherent fairness of the outcome.

_____11.  The demand curve measures the quantity of a good or service that a consumer wants.

_____12.  The equilibrium price is the willingness to pay of the average buyer.

_____13.  The equilibrium price is the willingness to sell of the marginal seller.

_____14.  The area between the equilibrium price and the demand curve measures producer surplus in a market.

_____15.  A higher price raises consumer surplus.

## B. Multiple-Choice Questions

1. Economic efficiency means maximizing:
   a. total economic well-being.
   b. consumer surplus.
   c. producer surplus.
   d. total equity.
   e. total equity plus total well-being.

2. Producer surplus is the:
   a. total profit.
   b. difference between what the consumer offered and the actual price paid.
   c. difference between price and opportunity cost of production.
   d. inventories that could not be sold at the market price.
   e. the difference between willingness to sell and willingness to buy.

3. Total economic well-being to society is the:
   a. consumer surplus less the producer surplus.
   b. sum of consumer surplus plus producer surplus.
   c. ratio of consumer surplus to producer surplus.
   d. total gains to consumers, producers, and government.
   e. none of the above.

4. Consumer surplus is:
   a. unused products that may be sold at auction.
   b. price less marginal value.
   c. the amount that the consumer would have paid in excess of the actual price.
   d. excess demand for a product.
   e. none of the above.

5. Free markets tend to have which of the following social advantages?  They:
   a. maximize profit.
   b. maximize the number of goods produced.
   c. allocate production to the least-cost producers.
   d. minimize consumer surplus and producer surplus.
   e. maximize equity.

6. Producing less than the market's equilibrium quantity of diet sodas means that:
   a. resources must have had a higher valued alternative use producing something else.
   b. consumer surplus will be higher than otherwise would be the case.
   c. producer surplus will be higher than otherwise would be the case.
   d. an additional unit of diet sodas would add more to society's benefit that to its cost.
   e. all of the above.

7. Scalping of tickets for sports events or rock concerts tends to:
   a. increase social well-being.
   b. benefit both the buyers and the sellers of the scalped tickets.
   c. maximize the sum of consumer and producer surplus.
   d. increase the likelihood that tickets will be used by those who put the highest value on them.
   e. all of the above.

Use the following information to answer questions 8-10. Suppose that you own a classic Fender guitar. You have lost interest, and so it is worth only $50 to you. A friend of yours loves the guitar and would be willing to pay as much as $950 for it.

8. If you sell the guitar to your friend John:
   a. for more than $50, you have gained at his expense.
   b. for less than $950, he has gained at your expense.
   c. for $500, splitting the difference, you both gain; at any other price, somebody loses.
   d. for any positive price, you both gain.
   e. for more than $50 but less than $950, you both gain and social welfare is increased.

9. In the previous question, if you sell the guitar for $100, then social welfare:
   a. decrease by $400.
   b. remains unchanged.
   c. rises by $50.
   d. rises by $850.
   e. rises by $900.

10. It turns out that John is not the only friend who is interested in the guitar. Ben also likes it and would pay $500, Sue would pay $1200, and Bill would actually pay $2000! To maximize this small society's well-being, you should:
    a. sell the guitar to John, because he was the first to offer to buy it, but only if he matches Bill's offer.
    b. sell the guitar to John, even if he doesn't match Bill's offer.
    c. sell the guitar to Bill, but only if he pays $2000.
    d. sell the guitar to Bill, even if he pays no more than the others.
    e. take the guitar off the market until it appreciates some more.

11. Jim is shopping for furniture. He finds a new coffee table that he likes at a big furniture warehouse. The price is only $200. He also has a friend who makes coffee tables in his spare time, charging $500. Disregarding price, Jim is indifferent between the quality of the two tables. He is willing to pay up to $500 for a table of this quality. He could also make one of the same quality himself for $100 in materials, but he feels that his time is worth another $600. If the quality really is the same, then social welfare (ignoring nonmonetary aspects of friendship) is maximized if he buys the coffee table from:
    a. his friend, as long as the price is no more than he is willing to pay.
    b. his friend, as long he will split the difference on the price.
    c. the warehouse, which can produce the table at the lower cost.
    d. neither; he should make it himself for $100.
    e. uncertain without additional information.

12. Your neighbor Alan ran out of coffee, so you gave him a pound. You bought the coffee just before the price shot up because of a freeze in Colombia. You paid $3.00/pound but the coffee would now cost $8.00/pound to replace. He has offered to repay you for the coffee. For him to pay you enough to compensate for your opportunity cost, he would have to pay you:
    a. nothing; the coffee is a sunk cost.
    b. $3.00, which is what you paid for the coffee.
    c. $5.50, which splits the difference between the old and new price.
    d. $8.00, which is your replacement cost.
    e. none of the above.

13. Medical care is vital to our survival. From society's standpoint, we should increase our spending on health as long as:
    a. anyone is sick.
    b. we can afford it.
    c. total benefit increases when we increase spending.
    d. total cost is less than total benefit.
    e. an extra dollar of health care spending generates at least a dollar in added benefits.

14. An auction is socially:
    a. inefficient, because goods go to those with the most money, rather than those who want them the most.
    b. efficient, because it allocates the units of the product to the buyers who value them the most, as evidenced by their willingness to pay.
    c. equitable, because it is only fair for goods to go to those who are willing to pay for them.
    d. inequitable, because not everyone can afford to keep up with the bidding
    e. none of the above.

15. According to Adam Smith's "invisible hand,"
    a. government plays a behind-the-scenes role in making a market economy work efficiently.
    b. individuals who are concerned about the public good will almost invisibly promote increased social welfare.
    c. free markets require only a little intervention to operate smoothly.
    d. many buyers and sellers acting independently out of self-interest can promote general economic well-being without even realizing it.
    e. all of the above.

16. The increase in social welfare associated with the production of a good or service in equilibrium is the:
    a. area between the demand and supply curves.
    b. total difference between the willingness to pay and the willingness to sell.
    c. total benefit from the product minus the opportunity cost of producing it.
    d. sum of the consumer surplus and the producer surplus.
    e. all of the above.

17. If the price of a new car is $20,000, then consumers will continue to buy additional cars until the consumer surplus from the last car purchased is:
    a. zero.
    b. $20,000
    c. maximized.
    d. minimized.
    e. none of the above.

18. In the previous question, auto producers will continue to supply additional cars until the producer surplus from the last car produced is:
    a. zero.
    b. $20,000.
    c. maximized.
    d. minimized.
    e. none of the above.

19. Consumer surplus exists only if:
    a. demand curves are downward sloping.
    b. consumers get products on sale at or below cost.
    c. producer surplus exists.
    d. the market is at equilibrium.
    e. all of the above.

20. Free markets tend to be efficient unless:
    a. market failure occurs.
    b. externalities exist.
    c. government sets prices to make them more fair.
    d. a few firms dominate those markets.
    e. all of the above.

## IV. Advanced Critical Thinking

Some groups argue for legalization of currently illegal drugs, perhaps even cocaine and heroin. They argue that free markets are inherently more efficient than government edicts in allocating resources, and that there is also the issue of freedom involved. Evaluate their arguments. What is the case for legalizing at least some currently illegal controlled substances? What are the arguments against legalization? Do markets operate efficiently in the case of such controlled substances? _____

_____

_____

_____

_____

_____

## V. Solutions

### Terms and Definitions

__5___ Welfare economics
__4___ Willingness to pay
__7___ Consumer Surplus
__1___ Cost
__6___ Producer Surplus
__3___ Efficiency
__9___ Equity
__10__ Market Power
__8___ Externalities
__2___ Market Failure

**Practice Problems**

1. a. Plot the supply and demand diagrams for the used cars in the space below:

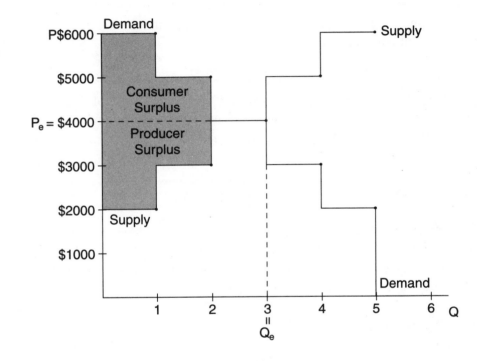

b. Market equilibrium would result in 3 cars sold at a price of $4000 each. It would leave out two buyers with low willingness to pay and two high-cost sellers, but it would maximize efficiency by maximizing total surplus (consumer surplus + producer surplus), as shown on the diagram.

c. The dollar value of consumer surplus is $3000 (Betsy gains $2000 at a price of $4000, and Kathy gains $1000 at that price). The producer surplus is also $3000 (Tim's gains $1000 at a price of $4000, and Buy-a-Bomb gains $2000). The total surplus is therefore $6000.

d. If the highest-cost seller sold to the highest marginal value consumer, and the lowest-cost seller sold to the consumer with the lowest marginal value, and so on, each auto would be sold and each consumer would have a car. However, it would be less efficient: there would be no consumer or producer surplus, because each buyer and seller would have broken even. Compared to the competitive solution, society would lose a $6000 total surplus.

2.  a.  The free market encourages the production of every good that adds more to benefits than it adds to cost. If decisionmakers take into account all of the social benefits and social costs of their actions when they choose, then their decisions will also maximize society's total surplus. This assumes that there is no market failure, due for example to externalities or concentration of market power.

    b.  If production occurs beyond equilibrium, then the additional units will have marginal costs greater than the marginal benefits from their production, resulting in a net loss of social well-being, because total surplus is reduced from its level at equilibrium.

    c.  Stopping short of equilibrium means that society is failing to produce some units of a good or service that have marginal benefits greater than the marginal cost. In this range, willingness to buy is higher than sellers' cost of production, so society would gain from the additional output; that is, total surplus would rise.

## Short-Answer Questions

1.  Efficiency means maximizing the total combined producer and consumer surplus from the market. It does not, however, guarantee any particular distribution of the resulting outcome. Efficiency is objectively measured as what is, but equity requires normative or value judgments about what ought to be.

## True/False Questions

1.  F; welfare economics is the study of how resource allocation affects economic well-being.
2.  F; consumer surplus is the difference between consumers' willingness to pay and the actual market price.
3.  F; producer surplus refers to the difference between market price and sellers' costs of production.
4.  T
5.  F; an efficient allocation of resources is one that maximizes total surplus.
6.  T
7.  F; equity and efficiency often conflict, because there is no reason for the mechanism that maximizes total surplus also to distribute it fairly.
8.  T
9.  F; Adam Smith believed that society's well-being was maximized by individuals operating independently in their own self-interest.
10. F; the major advantage of using supply and demand to allocate resources is the *efficiency* of the outcome, although it may be considered unfair.
11. F; the demand curve measures the quantity of a good or service that a consumer is *willing and able* to buy.
12. F; the equilibrium price is the willingness to pay of the *marginal* buyer.

13. T
14. F; the area between the price and the demand curve measures *consumer* surplus in a market.
15. F; a *lower* price raises consumer surplus.

## Multiple-Choice Questions

| | | |
|---|---|---|
| 1. a | 8. e | 15. d |
| 2. c | 9. e | 16. e |
| 3. b | 10. d | 17. a |
| 4. c | 11. c | 18. a |
| 5. c | 12. d | 19. a |
| 6. d | 13. e | 20. e |
| 7. e | 14. b | |

## Advanced Critical Thinking

It is true that free markets tend to be efficient in maximizing economic efficiency, by ensuring at least under competition that the market will provide every unit of output that adds more to society's benefits than it adds to its costs. One can also make the case that people should have the freedom to decide for themselves what is good for them. However, the counter argument is that there are external costs involved with the production and use of illegal drugs. The buyers and sellers of illegal drugs do not bear all of the costs of their actions. Increased crime rates, declining neighborhoods, health costs, and other social costs are ignored by those in the market. (Of course, some of the external costs are a result of the illegality of the drugs, rather than the drugs themselves.) Such externalities result in market failure, leading to overproduction of those goods that have external costs.

# Chapter 8: Application: The Costs of Taxation

## I. Chapter Overview

### A. Context and Purpose

The previous chapter provided a foundation for welfare economics, looking at the net social gain from production at the competitive equilibrium. We saw in that chapter that maximizing society's total surplus requires production up to but not beyond the point at which the marginal benefit of another unit of output equals its marginal cost. This chapter applies that analysis to policy questions about the efficiency effects of taxation. Specifically, how does taxation distort behavior and cause a deadweight loss to society in excess of the actual taxes paid? This application of welfare analysis will be followed by another applied welfare economics chapter, which will deal with the efficiency implications of international trade.

### B. Learning Objectives

In this chapter you will:

1. Examine how taxes reduce consumer and producer surplus.
2. Learn the meaning and causes of the deadweight loss of a tax.
3. Consider why some taxes have larger deadweight losses than others.
4. Examine how tax revenue and deadweight loss vary with the size of the tax.

After accomplishing these goals, you should be able to:

1. Explain that taxes introduce a wedge between the price paid by consumers and the price received by sellers, preventing the market from reaching the point at which the marginal benefit (willingness to buy) equals the marginal cost (willingness to sell), which in turn, reduces total surplus (consumer plus producer surplus).
2. Show graphically and explain that a tax reduces total surplus (consumer plus producer surplus) by more than it raises tax revenues, and that this gap is known as the deadweight loss of taxation, which results because taxes distort incentives and behavior.
3. Demonstrate that deadweight losses from taxation are greater when supply and/or demand are relatively elastic, because the same tax will cause a greater distortion of behavior when elasticity is high than when elasticity is low.
4. Show graphically and explain that as the size of a tax increases, the deadweight loss rises even faster, for geometric reasons, because the deadweight loss triangle is the square of the size of the tax.

## C. Chapter Review

This chapter applies the tools of welfare economics to the analysis of the social welfare loss from taxation, which is the additional burden of taxation in excess of the actual tax revenues received by government.

### 8-1 The Deadweight Loss of Taxation

Taxes introduce a wedge between the price paid by buyers and the price received by sellers. Depending on whether the tax is levied on consumers or producers, it shifts either the supply or the demand. If demand shifts, then the new demand no longer reflects the value of the marginal unit to the buyer (and society). If supply shifts, then the new supply no longer reflects the opportunity cost to the seller (and society) of providing another unit. Either way, the tax wedge decreases the quantity sold below the socially optimal level that would have resulted under the pretax competitive market. As a result, the tax costs the buyers and sellers more than the actual tax paid; it also costs them a loss of total surplus because of the distortion of behavior that results in underproduction relative to the outcome of the pretax competitive market. As an extreme example, consider the case of a tax so high that it completely eliminates the market for a good. Even though nobody is paying the tax, they are worse off, because they are unable to buy a good that was worth the price to them prior to the tax.

### 8-2 The Determinants of the Deadweight Loss

Remember that deadweight loss results because of the distortion of incentives and behavior caused by a tax. If there were no change in behavior in response to the tax, then there would be no distortion and no deadweight loss. The total cost of taxation to the taxpayer would be the actual tax paid. It makes sense, therefore, that the deadweight loss will be greater, the greater the elasticity of supply and/or demand. As elasticity increases, the responsiveness to the incentive effect of taxation increases. On a supply-and-demand diagram, the triangle of welfare loss is greater when the curves are more elastic.

### 8-3 Deadweight Loss and Tax Revenue as Taxes Vary

Not only does deadweight loss vary with tax rates, it actually increases more than proportionately when tax rates rise. Further, as tax rates rise, tax revenues first rise, then eventually fall as the tax shrinks the quantity sold so much that even higher rates cannot raise additional revenues.

### 8-4 Conclusion

Taxes impose costs on society, in the form of efficiency losses. One major goal of tax policy is to minimize the distortions that reduce the efficiency of the free market.

### D. Helpful Hints

1. *Taxes do more than raise revenue; they also influence people's behavior.* Sometimes that is desirable, for example, when we use cigarette taxes to discourage smoking. Other times, however, the distortion caused by taxation is undesirable and represents the loss of well-being to society.

2. *If taxes did not alter behavior, there would be no net loss of well-being to society.* Even though taxpayers would be worse off by the amount of the taxes paid, the recipients of those revenues would be better off, and the net effect would be zero, because the gains and losses would cancel each other out.

### E. Terms and Definitions

Choose a definition for each key term.

Key terms:

_____Deadweight Loss
_____Laffer Curve

Definitions:

1. A representation of the relationship between tax rates and tax revenues suggesting that when tax rates are above a specified level, further increases in tax rates may actually reduce tax revenues.

2. The reduction in total surplus that results from a tax, because taxes distort incentives.

## II. Problems and Short-Answer Questions

### A. Practice Problems

1. The following graph shows the market for gasoline before and after the imposition of a gasoline tax.

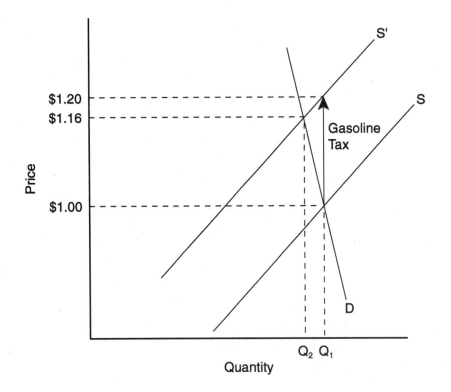

a.  How much is the gasoline tax, and by how much does the price of gasoline rise
    in response to the tax? Explain. By law, is this a tax on the buyer or the seller?
    How can you tell? _____
    _____
    _____
    _____

b.  Label the area of deadweight loss on the diagram and explain. What would
    happen to the total deadweight loss if demand were more elastic? Why?
    _____
    _____
    _____

c.  What would happen to the market for gasoline if the tax were switched to the
    other side of the market, but at the same tax rate? Does it matter whether the
    buyer or the seller is responsible for the tax? Would the equilibrium quantity
    change if the tax is switched? Would there be any change in the deadweight
    loss? Explain. _____
    _____
    _____
    _____
    _____

d.  Who really pays the tax?  The consumer?  The seller?  Both?  How can you tell?  What caused this result? _____

_____

_____

_____

_____

## B.  Short-Answer Questions

1.  Often taxes that promote economic efficiency have negative effects on equity, especially if equity is perceived to require progressive taxes (taxes with a higher average tax rate on those with higher incomes).  Why would this goal conflict with efficiency?_____

_____

_____

_____

_____

_____

2.  In the 19th century, Henry George proposed a tax on land to replace other taxes. Evaluate this proposal on efficiency and equity grounds._____

_____

_____

_____

_____

_____

## III.  Self-Test

### A.  True/False Questions

_____1.       Higher tax rates always lead to higher tax revenues, although the outcome may be inefficient.

_____2.       A tax that raises no tax revenue cannot have a deadweight loss.

_____3.       A tax on salt would be likely to have a lower deadweight loss than a tax on ice cream.

_____4.       The deadweight loss from taxation rises geometrically as tax rates rise.

_____5.       A subsidy tends to cause deadweight loss by encouraging overproduction of a good, beyond the point at which the marginal benefit equals the marginal cost to society.

_____6.       If policymakers desire to minimize deadweight loss from taxation, they should tax goods and services that have relatively close substitutes.

_____7.       A tax on land tends to be passed along to renters.

_____8. Most economists agree that the U.S. would raise more revenue under the individual income tax if tax rates were lowered.

_____9. A lump-sum tax that charges everyone the same amount would have no deadweight loss.

_____10. A tax on producers tends to distort output decisions and result in higher deadweight losses than a tax on buyers.

## B. Multiple-Choice Questions

1. Taxes cause deadweight losses because they:
   a. reduce taxpayers' incomes.
   b. are used to support government programs, which are less valuable than private spending to society.
   c. prevent buyers and sellers from realizing some of the gains from trade.
   d. redistribute income from productive to unproductive members of society.
   e. all of the above.

2. The effect of a tax on behavior will be greater if the tax is levied on the:
   a. buyer.
   b. seller.
   c. buyers and sellers equally.
   d. buyers in the short run, but the sellers in the long run.
   e. none of the above: The tax will have the same effect regardless of where it is levied.

3. The deadweight loss of a tax is equal to:
   a. total taxes paid.
   b. loss of producer and consumer surplus due to the tax.
   c. total taxes paid plus the loss of producer and consumer surplus due to the tax.
   d. loss of producer and consumer surplus minus total taxes paid.
   e. none of the above.

4. Deadweight loss from taxation is likely to be the greatest if:
   a. supply is elastic and demand is inelastic.
   b. both supply and demand are elastic.
   c. supply is inelastic and demand is elastic.
   d. both supply and demand are inelastic.
   e. none of the above: Tax rates matter, but elasticity does not.

5. Which of the following is more likely to increase the deadweight loss of income taxes on labor?
   a. Workers have no control over their hours of work, because the work week is standardized.
   b. Retirement age is mandated by law or custom.
   c. The underground economy becomes more widespread.
   d. Congress shifts the legal burden of the income tax to the employer.
   e. all of the above

6. According to economist Arthur Laffer's predictions regarding the Laffer Curve for the U.S.,
   a. increasing income tax rates will cause tax revenues to fall.
   b. lowering income tax rates will cause tax revenues to fall.
   c. changing income tax rates will not change overall tax revenues.
   d. the demand for and supply of labor are relatively inelastic.
   e. none of the above.

7. Of the following, the tax that would be *least* likely to result in a deadweight loss would be a tax on:
   a. labor.
   b. luxury goods.
   c. housing.
   d. automobiles.
   e. the unimproved value of land.

8. Arthur Laffer's predictions about the effects of changes in tax rates would be most applicable for:
   a. a low-tax country like Singapore.
   b. a high-tax country like Sweden.
   c. the United States.
   d. a very small country.
   e. all of the above.

9. Suppose that beer is taxed at a very low rate. If the government gradually increases the tax rate on beer, tax revenues are likely to:
   a. fall.
   b. rise.
   c. remain unchanged.
   d. rise initially, then eventually fall.
   e. fall initially, then eventually rise.

10. Raising tax rates causes deadweight loss to:
    a. increase more than proportionately.
    b. increase less than proportionately.
    c. decrease less than proportionately.
    d. decrease more than proportionately.
    e. none of the above.

11. To minimize the deadweight loss from real estate taxes, policymakers would have to:
    a. abolish real estate taxes.
    b. lower the tax on the land itself.
    c. lower the tax on buildings and other improvements.
    d. lower the tax on both land and buildings.
    e. tax land only in areas where the demand is inelastic.

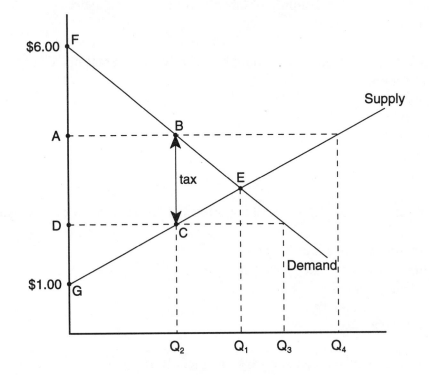

Questions 12-15 refer to the graph above, which shows a market before and after a tax.

12. What effect will the tax have on output? Output will:
    a. increase from $Q_2$ to $Q_1$.
    b. increase from $Q_1$ to $Q_3$.
    c. decrease from $Q_1$ to $Q_2$.
    d. decrease from $Q_3$ to $Q_2$.
    e. none of the above.

13. The deadweight loss from the tax will be area:
    a. FEG.
    b. ABCD.
    c. FBA + DCG.
    d. BEC.
    e. ABECD.

14. If the tax is increased to $5.00, then output will:
    a. drop to zero, as will tax revenues.
    b. decrease, but tax revenues will rise.
    c. decrease (but not to zero), along with tax revenues.
    d. increase, but tax revenues will fall.
    e. none of the above.

15. With the $5.00 tax, the deadweight loss will become:
    a. zero.
    b. area FEG.
    c. area ABCD.
    d. area BEC.
    e. infinite.

## IV. Advanced Critical Thinking

In recent years, proposals to increase the cigarette tax drastically have gained strength. Critics of the proposed tax argue that such an increase would be undesirable, because it would cause tremendous deadweight loss to society. They also argue that it would be unproductive in reducing smoking, because the demand for cigarettes is inelastic. Is this argument consistent? If the demand is inelastic, will the tax have a large impact on total surplus? Is the notion of deadweight loss even appropriate when the goal is to distort behavior away from smoking? Discuss._____

_____

_____

_____

_____

_____

_____

_____

## V. Solutions

### Terms and Definitions

__2__ Deadweight Loss
__1__ Laffer Curve

### Practice Problems

1. The graph below shows the market for gasoline before and after the imposition of a gasoline tax.

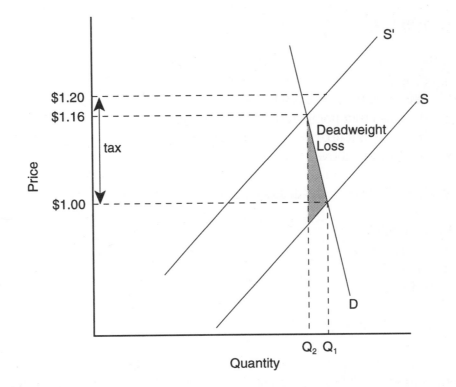

a. The gasoline tax rate is $.20, as shown by the $.20 vertical shift in supply. This shows that willingness to sell has shifted, requiring an additional $.20 for any given quantity to be supplied. The equilibrium price rises by $.16, from $1.00 to $1.16, indicating that the buyer is paying most of the tax. The legal burden is on the seller, as shown by the shift in supply, rather than demand.

b. The deadweight loss is the shaded triangle shown, which is the area between the supply (willingness to sell) and demand (willingness to buy) between the new equilibrium output ($Q_2$) and the old output before the tax ($Q_1$). It represents the lost total surplus due to the loss of output. If demand were more elastic, then the tax would cause a greater loss of output, as quantity demanded falls more dramatically, resulting in a greater deadweight loss (a larger triangle of lost surplus).

c. The effect would be the same if the tax were switched to the buyer instead of the seller. Output would still drop to $Q_2$, and the consumer would still be stuck with $.16 of the $.20 tax. However, the graph would look different, because demand would shift by $.20, rather than supply. The drop in demand would lower the price to $.96, plus the $.20 tax, for a total cost to the consumer of $1.16, which is the same as before. The deadweight loss would be the same.

d. Eighty percent of the tax ($.16 of $.20) is borne by the consumer; the rest of the tax is borne by the seller, as shown by the effect on market price. When demand is less elastic than supply, the consumer is less adaptable and will be stuck with a larger share of the tax. If demand is relatively more elastic, then the seller will bear more of the burden of the tax.

## Short-Answer Questions

1. There is no reason for equity and efficiency to go together. One is objective and the other depends on our values—our sense of what is fair. In fact, taxes that do not alter behavior are most likely to be efficient, yet they are more likely to be lump-sum taxes or taxes on necessities that tend to be more burdensome to the poor.

2. A tax on unimproved land is likely to have no deadweight loss, because it does not influence incentives. Land is fixed in supply, so landowners cannot respond to a tax by producing less. However, if the tax also covers buildings and other improvements, then the landowner can respond by reducing construction or even maintenance on existing buildings. In such a case, the tax would have a deadweight loss, by resulting in reduced output in the construction industry. On equity grounds, the tax may be considered unfair, because taxing land could cause serious cash flow problems for those who own land but do not have much income.

## True/False Questions

1. F; higher tax rates tend to lead to higher tax revenues initially, but after a point, revenue falls.
2. F; a tax that raises no tax revenue can have a large deadweight loss, if it destroys the market for a product.
3. T
4. T
5. T
6. F; if policymakers tax goods and services that have relatively close substitutes, deadweight loss is likely to be greater, because people are more likely to change their behavior in response to the tax.
7. F; a tax on land tends to be paid by the landowners, who cannot change their behavior to avoid the tax unless it covers improvements such as buildings.
8. F; most economists would agree that U.S. tax rates are not so high that they reduce revenue.
9. T
10. F; taxes on producers (supply) have the same effects as taxes on the buyers (demand); the market adjusts price and output to compensate.

## Multiple-Choice Questions

| | | | | | |
|---|---|---|---|---|---|
| 1. | c | 6. | a | 11. | c |
| 2. | e | 7. | e | 12. | c |
| 3. | b | 8. | b | 13. | d |
| 4. | b | 9. | d | 14. | a |
| 5. | c | 10. | a | 15. | b |

## Advanced Critical Thinking

The usual notion of deadweight loss is not appropriate for evaluating the cigarette tax. Normally, distortion of behavior is an undesirable effect of taxation. However, in the case of cigarettes, a major reason for the tax is to discourage consumption, because the free-market equilibrium is not considered to be efficient. There are externalities involved that smokers do not take into account (the health costs of secondhand smoke, for example), and to the extent that cigarettes may be addictive, it is not clear that truly voluntary exchange results from the free market. As a result, the deadweight loss from reducing production and consumption of cigarettes may actually be a social gain. Ironically, the inelastic demand means that even if the distortion of behavior is positive, it is also relatively slight, unless the tax rate is quite high.

# Chapter 9: Application: International Trade

## I. Chapter Overview

### A. Context and Purpose

The previous chapter provided an application of welfare economics to the efficiency effects of taxation. This chapter adds another application of welfare economics, in this case to international trade. The chapter identifies the winners and losers from free trade, as well as the welfare effects of protectionism.

### B. Learning Objectives

In this chapter you will:

1. Consider what determines whether a country imports or exports a good.
2. Examine who wins and who loses from international trade.
3. Learn that the gains to winners from international trade exceed the losses to losers.
4. Analyze the welfare effects of tariffs.
5. Examine the arguments people use to advocate trade restrictions.

After accomplishing these goals, you should be able to:

1. Apply the concept of comparative advantage to show that a country will export goods for which it is the lowest opportunity cost producer and import other goods (for which it is not the lowest opportunity cost producer).
2. Show that exports benefit domestic producers and hurt domestic consumers, and imports benefit domestic consumers and hurt domestic producers who compete with imports.
3. Demonstrate that both imports and exports increase the total surplus, or combined consumer and producer surplus in a country.
4. Identify the deadweight loss caused by tariffs, which distort incentives and move markets away from the competitive equilibrium.
5. List and evaluate five arguments for restricting international trade.

### C. Chapter Review

This chapter applies the tools of welfare economics to the analysis of international trade and the social welfare loss from trade restrictions.

### 9-1 The Determinants of Trade

When the price of a good within a country differs from the world price, then there is an incentive for that country to enter the international market for the good. If the world price is higher than the domestic price, then domestic producers will have an incentive to export the good. If the world price is lower than the domestic price, then domestic consumers will have an incentive to import the good from abroad. Of course, different countries use different currencies, making it difficult to compare prices across countries. An easier approach is to look at *relative price* of one good in terms of another. Relative prices measure opportunity cost, and therefore, comparative advantage. If one country has a lower relative price of corn than another, in terms of wheat, then it has a comparative advantage at corn production.

## 9-2 The Winners and Losers from Trade

Exporting a good causes the domestic price to rise, hurting domestic consumers but helping domestic producers. However, the gains of the sellers are greater than the losses of the buyers, and total surplus rises. Similarly, importing a good causes the domestic price to fall, hurting domestic producers but helping domestic consumers. The gains for the consumers are greater than the losses by the producers, causing total surplus to rise. As a result, both imports and exports cause a net gain in total surplus, and the country's economic well-being rises. In short, the gains of the winners exceed the losses of the losers.

Free international trade hurts some and helps others. When the domestic price deviates from the world price, expansion or contraction of a domestic industry will occur until the domestic price adjusts to the world price. Continuing free trade will keep the domestic price equal to the world price. If tariffs are used to prevent this adjustment to free trade, there will be deadweight losses similar to those of other taxes: tariffs and other taxes prevent buyers and sellers from making all of the mutually advantageous trades that have marginal benefits greater than their marginal costs. Therefore, total surplus is maximized by avoiding tariffs and other trade restrictions.

## 9-3 The Arguments for Restricting Trade

The obvious question is why would countries impose trade restrictions, considering their negative effect on society's well-being? There are several arguments for restricting trade:

- **Jobs**
  Some argue that trade restrictions are necessary to protect jobs. However, free trade both creates and destroys jobs, as countries specialize according to their comparative advantages.

- **National Security**
  Many industries try to defend trade restrictions by claiming that they are essential for national security. Although it can be valid, this argument tends to be overused.

- **Infant Industries**

  New industries often argue for temporary protection; however, these protected infant industries never want to grow up.

- **Unfair Competition**

  Some critics of free trade argue that they want free trade, but it must be "fair" trade. They claim that other countries subsidize their exports, making it hard for domestic firms to compete. However, if another country wants to give its goods away, it benefits the importing country, rather than hurting it.

- **Protection as a Bargaining Chip**

  Others argue that the threat of trade restrictions is simply good politics. Through this threat, we can get other countries to lower their trade barriers. However, the threat may not work, and the result may be a trade war that makes all countries worse off.

## 9-4 Conclusion

Free international trade has the same advantages as voluntary trade within a country: It maximizes total surplus to permit every voluntary exchange. The result will be production of every unit of output that adds more to society's benefit than it adds to society's cost.

## D. Helpful Hints

1. *Countries don't trade, people do.* When someone in the United States buys from someone in Mexico, both parties benefit, just as surely as if both the buyer and seller had been in the U.S.

2. *There are winners and losers from international trade.* It is this fact that accounts for much of the resistance to free trade. The losers tend to be more vocal than the winners, who are more diffused and less visible.

## E. Terms and Definitions

Choose a definition for each key term.

Key terms:

_____World Price
_____Tariff
_____Relative Price

Definitions:

1. The price of one good or service in terms of another
2. The price of a good or service prevailing in global markets
3. A tax on imported goods

## II. Problems and Short-Answer Questions

### A. Practice Problems

1. The graph below shows a country before and after the imposition of a tariff.

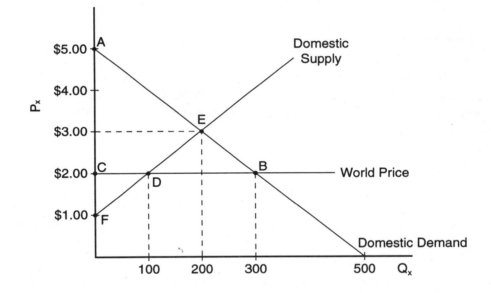

a. Show graphically and calculate the actual change in consumer surplus and producer surplus as a result of the tariff. (Hint: Remember that the area of a triangle is ½ times base times height.) What is the change in the total surplus? How did you calculate the result? _____

_____

_____

_____

_____

b. Why did total surplus change in response to the tariff? _____

_____

_____

_____

_____

2. Economists are generally critical of tariffs and quotas, even though such trade restrictions are often popular with the general public.

   a. Who wins and who loses from tariffs and other trade restrictions? _____

      _____

      _____

      _____

      _____

   b. What effect does a tariff have on economic well-being?  Why? _____

      _____

      _____

      _____

      _____

   c. In light of your answer to part b above, why are trade restrictions so popular?

      _____

      _____

      _____

      _____

   d. List the arguments for trade restrictions and evaluate each briefly.

      1. _____

      _____

      2. _____

      _____

      3. _____

      _____

      4. _____

      _____

      5. _____

      _____

**B. Short-Answer Questions**

1. Alphaland and Utopia can provide widgets and frinzels according to the following production possibilities:

### Daily Output Per Worker

|  | Widgets | Frinzels |
|---|---|---|
| Alphaland | 20 | 20 |
| Utopia | 40 | 80 |

   a. Which country is the lower opportunity cost producer of widgets? of frinzels? Explain. _____
_____
_____
_____
_____

   b. Alphaland seems to be generally less productive than Utopia in terms of both goods. How can they hope to compete in international competition with Utopia? _____
_____
_____
_____
_____

## III. Self-Test

### A. True/False Questions

_____1. The main problem with the argument that tariffs are needed to protect domestic jobs is that such trade restrictions never really save jobs.

_____2. Free international trade raises the economic well-being of all the trading countries.

_____3. International trade creates jobs.

_____4. International trade costs jobs in high-wage countries.

_____5. Free trade benefits everyone in the trading countries.

_____6. A country whose price of steel is less than the world price must be subsidizing its steel industry.

_____7. A country like the U.S., with its large endowment of land, labor and capital, is unlikely to gain from trade with other countries that are less fortunate.

_____8. Voluntary international trade is essentially a zero-sum game; that is, if one side benefits, its gains must come at the expense of the other trading partner.

_____9. As a tax on imports, a tariff causes a deadweight loss similar to that from other taxes.

_____10. When the world price of a good is higher than the domestic price, the result is an increased quantity supplied by domestic suppliers.

## B. Multiple-Choice Questions

1. If the U.S. buys automobiles from Japan, then in the U.S.:
   a. auto producers lose and consumers gain.
   b. auto producers gain and consumers lose.
   c. both auto producers and consumers lose.
   d. both auto producers and consumers gain.
   e. after the market adjusts, neither consumers nor producers are affected.

2. If the U.S. buys automobiles from Japan, then the:
   a. U.S. standard of living will fall, but Japan's will rise.
   b. Japanese standard of living will fall, but that of the U.S. will rise.
   c. standard of living in both countries will fall.
   d. standard of living in both countries will rise.
   e. standard of living may rise or fall, depending on elasticity of demand.

3. If the U.S. sells soybeans to Japan, then:
   a. Japanese soybean farmers are better off.
   b. Japanese soybean consumers are worse off.
   c. U.S. soybean producers are worse off.
   d. U.S. soybean consumers are worse off.
   e. all of the above.

4. A tariff on imported steel in the U.S. would:
   a. raise the total surplus in the U.S. market for steel.
   b. lower the total surplus in the U.S. market for steel.
   c. raise the total surplus of foreign exporters and consumers of steel.
   d. raise the U.S. standard of living at the expense of that of the exporting country.
   e. none of the above.

5. The domestic price of sugar in the U.S. is significantly higher than the world price. This indicates that:
   a. the U.S. market for sugar is experiencing high demand.
   b. the U.S. has a comparative advantage in producing sugar.
   c. other countries are subsidizing their sugar unfairly.
   d. other countries have a comparative advantage in producing sugar.
   e. trade barriers are low in the world market for sugar.

The graph below shows the market for good x in a small country, along with the world price for x. Use the information provided to answer questions 6-9.

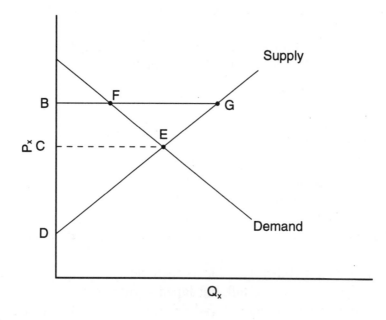

6. The original equilibrium before trade is at:
   a. point G.
   b. point F.
   c. point E.
   d. point D.
   e. none of the above.

7. When this country begins to trade with other countries, it will:
   a. increase exports of good x until the domestic price rises to the world price.
   b. increase exports of good x until the world price falls to the domestic price.
   c. increase imports of good x until the world price falls to the domestic price..
   d. increase imports of good x until the domestic price rises to the world price.
   e. none of the above.

8. The net gain from international trade to this country is area:
   a. AED.
   b. AFB.
   c. FGE.
   d. BGD.
   e. BFED.

9. If this country trades in the world market for good x, then in this country:
   a. everyone will gain.
   b. consumers will gain and producers will lose.
   c. consumers and producers will gain.
   d. consumers and producers will lose.
   e. consumers will lose and producers will gain.

The graph below shows the market for good z in the small country of Alphaland. Use the information to answer questions 10-12.

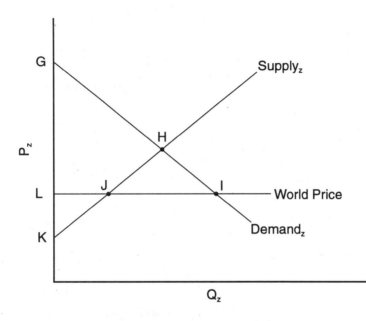

10. To maximize total surplus, Alphaland should:
    a. increase exports of good z until the domestic price falls to the world price.
    b. increase exports of good z until the world price rises to the domestic price.
    c. increase imports of good z until the world price rises to the domestic price.
    d. increase imports of good z until the domestic price falls to the world price.
    e. none of the above.

11. After trade, total surplus will increase by:
    a. GHK.
    b. GIJK.
    c. HIJ.
    d. LJK.
    e. GHJL.

12. In Alphaland, as a result of trade, good z's:
    a. consumers will be better off, but the producers will be worse off.
    b. consumers will be worse off, but the producers will be better off.
    c. consumers and producers will be worse off.
    d. consumers and producers will be better off.
    e. consumers and producers will be no better or worse off.

13. According to the infant industry argument:
    a. new industries should be discouraged, because they cannot compete with established firms.
    b. protecting a new industry from foreign competition may be desirable in the short term, to give it time to become competitive.
    c. new industries may require permanent subsidies from the government in order to be competitive with established foreign firms.
    d. protecting industries that produce products for young children can be a worthwhile investment in the nation's human capital.
    e. none of the above.

14. The national security argument regarding international trade states that:
    a. importing foreign goods may also allow foreign agents free access to our economy and military secrets.
    b. importing key raw materials from other countries, rather than exhausting our own supplies, can strengthen our military preparedness.
    c. key industries that are vital to our national security may require protection from foreign competition.
    d. exporting sensitive products such as computers may compromise our national security and therefore should be strictly regulated.
    e. all of the above are examples of the national security argument regarding trade.

15. If Mexico subsidizes its textiles, making it impossible for U.S. producers to compete, then:
    a. a high tariff on textiles would improve economic well-being in the U.S.
    b. our most appropriate response would be to retaliate with an identical subsidy.
    c. the ideal response would be to threaten retaliation without actually following through on the threat.
    d. we would maximize our economic well-being by purchasing the subsidized textiles from Mexico.
    e. none of the above.

16. In the preceding question, if Mexico subsidizes its textiles, then in Mexico:
    a. textile companies will be worse off.
    b. economic well-being will increase for the society overall.
    c. textile workers will be worse off.
    d. economic well-being will decrease for the society overall.
    e. none of the above.

17. If the U.S. eliminated all tariffs and other trade restrictions, then:
   a. economic well-being would increase for the U.S. but fall for smaller countries.
   b. economic well-being would increase for the U.S. and its trading partners.
   c. consumers would benefit, but the total number of jobs would fall, and wages would fall, in the U.S.
   d. economic well-being would decrease for the U.S. and its trading partners.
   e. economic well-being would increase only if other countries followed suit.

Use the following table to answer question 18:

Hours of labor per unit of goods X and Z produced

|   | U.S. | Japan |
|---|------|-------|
| X | 5 | 4 |
| Z | 10 | 5 |

18. Based on the productivity data above, which of the following is true:
   a. Japan should produce good z and the U.S. should produce good x, and they should trade with each other.
   b. Japan should produce good x and the U.S. should produce good z, and they should trade with each other.
   c. Japan should produce both x and z and export them to the U.S.
   d. the U.S. should enact trade barriers to protect its domestic industries from Japan.
   e. Japan should enact trade barriers, to avoid having its standard of living dragged down by the less productive U.S.

19. In the previous question, Japan had a/an:
   a. absolute advantage in producing good x only.
   b. absolute advantage in producing good z only.
   c. absolute advantage, but not a comparative advantage, in producing both goods.
   d. comparative advantage, but not an absolute advantage, in producing both goods.
   e. both comparative and absolute advantage in producing both goods.

20. Referring back to question 18, Japan's combined consumer and producer surplus will be maximized if Japan:
   a. specializes according to its comparative advantage.
   b. specializes according to its absolute advantage.
   c. uses tariffs to protect its domestic industries.
   d. produces everything for itself, because it is highly productive.
   e. subsidizes good z, which requires 25% more labor than good x to produce.

# IV. Advanced Critical Thinking

Recently, a representative of the United Auto Workers said in support of protection for the U.S. auto industry, "we want free trade, but we want fair trade." He argued that Japanese auto makers are subsidized by their government, and therefore should not be allowed free entry into the U.S. auto market.

a.  Given the large number of auto workers who have lost their jobs in recent decades due to foreign competition, should we act to reduce the number of imported cars if other countries are creating an artificial advantage for their industries? Who would win and who would lose? What would happen to society's overall economic well-being? Explain. What if another country subsidized every industry? Could they put us out of business? _____

    _____

    _____

    _____

    _____

    _____

    _____

b.  Using the supply/demand diagram below, fill in the world price, and label the equilibrium quantity and price with free international trade, as well as after import restrictions eliminate all imported cars.

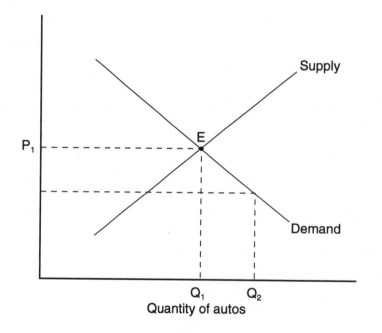

# V. Solutions

## Terms and Definitions

__2___World Price
__3___Tariff
__1___Relative Price

## Practice Problems

1.

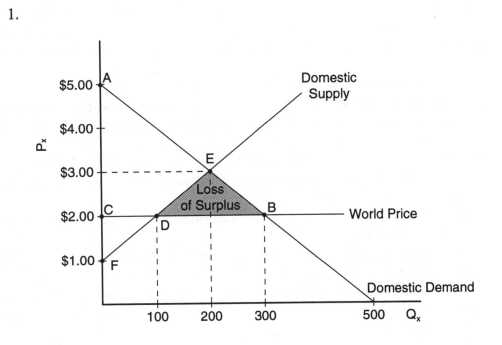

1 a. Total surplus falls from $500 to $400. With trade, the equilibrium is at point B, with a price of $2.00 and consumption (including imports) of 300. Of this quantity of 300, 100 are produced by domestic firms and 200 are imported. The original surplus, with trade, is the area ABC, representing consumer surplus, plus area CDF, which is producer surplus. Numerically, this surplus is ½($5.00-$2.00)(300) + ½($2.00-$1.00)(100) = $500. After eliminating trade, the equilibrium shifts to point E, at a price of $3.00 and a total domestic output of 200. The total surplus is triangle AEF, or ½($5.00-$1.00)(200) = $400. Thus, the total surplus falls by $100, which is also the area of triangle DEB = ½ ($3.00-$2.00)(300-100).

b. Total surplus falls because buyers and sellers are prevented from making all of the exchanges that are in their best interest. Cutting consumption of good x back from 300 to 200 units means that consumers will not be able to buy 100 units that had a marginal value (or benefit) to society that exceeds the marginal cost of producing it.

2 a. Winners include domestic producers, who face less competition, and foreign consumers, who have more of their products left to consume at home. Losers include domestic consumers, who face a restricted supply, and foreign producers, whose foreign markets are restricted by tariffs.

b. A tariff lowers overall economic well-being by reducing the sum of producer and consumer surplus, just as any other tax would do—by distorting behavior and reducing output below the competitive market equilibrium.

c. The winners from trade restrictions are highly visible and tend to be quite vocal in their opposition to free trade. The losers—the general public—are more diffused and harder to identify. If consumers in general pay slightly higher prices, it may not be obvious that trade restrictions are the cause, even though the total loss is great.

d. 1. Trade restrictions can protect some jobs in industries that compete with imports, but at the expense of others that are in export-related industries. Our imports from other countries provide the dollars that our trading partners use to buy our exports.
   2. They can also provide temporary protection for new or "infant" industries until they get established, but the problem is that infant industries never want to grow up.
   3. National security is another possibly valid argument, but every industry tries to claim that it is vital.
   4. Retaliation against unfair competition is another argument, but retaliation ends up hurting the economic welfare of the retaliating country.
   5. The threat of protectionism can be used to encourage trading partners to reduce their trade barriers, but it can also backfire and lead to trade wars that make both trading partners worse off.

**Short-Answer Questions**

1. Alphaland and Utopia can provide widgets and frinzels according to the following production possibilities:

### Daily Output Per Worker

|  | Widgets | Frinzels |
|---|---|---|
| Alphaland | 20 | 20 |
| Utopia | 40 | 80 |

a. Alphaland is the lower opportunity cost producer of widgets, even though its workers are only half as productive as Utopia's (20/day vs. 40/day). This is because Alphaland's opportunity cost of producing widgets is the frinzels that it could have produced instead. At a ratio of 20:20, the opportunity cost of a widget is one frinzel. In Utopia, the ratio is 40:80, for an opportunity cost of 2 frinzels per widget. Utopia, however, is the lower opportunity cost producer of frinzels (80 frinzels to 40 widgets, or 2 frinzels to 1 widget) vs. 20 frinzels to 20 widgets or 1 frinzel for 1 widget in Alphaland. As a result, even though Utopia has an absolute advantage in either good, it has a comparative advantage only in producing frinzels. Alphaland has the comparative advantage in widgets. Both countries gain if they specialize according to their comparative advantages.

b. Even though Utopia has an absolute advantage in producing both goods, it nevertheless gives up more to produce widgets than if it produces frinzels and trades them for Alphaland widgets at any relative price less than 2:1. Similarly, Alphaland would gain at any relative price greater than 1:1. At any relative price between 1 and 2 frinzels per widget, both countries gain.

## True/False Questions

1. F; tariffs save some domestic jobs (those in competition with imports) at the expense of other domestic jobs (those in export industries).
2. T
3. F; international trade redistribute jobs from less productive to more productive uses.
4. F; international trade redistributes jobs in both high- and low-wage countries.
5. F; there are both winners and losers from free trade, although net social welfare rises, because the winners' gains in surplus exceed the losers' reduction in surplus.
6. F; if a country has a price of steel that is less than the world price, this indicates that the country has a comparative advantage in steel.
7. F; no matter how affluent a country is, it gains from trade as long as its opportunity cost, or relative price, is different from other countries.
8. F; voluntary international trade is a positive-sum game; both trading partners benefit or they would not trade.
9. T
10. T

## Multiple-Choice Questions

| | | | | | |
|---|---|---|---|---|---|
| 1. | a | 8. | c | 15. | d |
| 2. | d | 9. | e | 16. | d |
| 3. | d. | 10. | d | 17. | b |
| 4. | b | 11. | c | 18. | a |
| 5. | d | 12. | a | 19. | c |
| 6. | c | 13. | b | 20. | a |
| 7. | a | 14. | c | | |

**Advanced Critical Thinking**

a. Although it would be politically popular to protect auto workers, it would actually reduce our total surplus from automobiles. It would help auto workers and auto companies in the U.S., but it would hurt U.S. auto buyers and foreign auto producers. It would also help foreign consumers of automobiles, who would find that more of their supply would stay at home, holding down the price they pay. Most industries seem to make the claim that imports are subsidized, but it is not possible for another country to subsidize everything and drive all industries out of business. When a country subsidizes one industry and makes it more competitive internationally, it makes it harder for its other industries to compete. Jobs are not created, but merely redistributed from less subsidized to more subsidized industries.

b. Using the supply/demand diagram below, fill in the world price, and show the equilibrium with free international trade, as well as after import restrictions eliminate all imported cars.

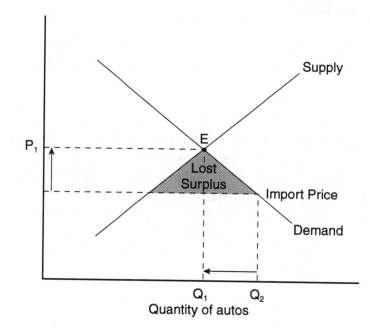

# Chapter 10: Externalities

## I. Chapter Overview

### A. Context and Purpose

Earlier chapters developed the rationale for the market as a means to maximize society's well-being. Markets are generally an efficient way to decide how to use society's scarce resources. We have seen that voluntary exchange is generally a win-win situation, one in which both parties (and society as a whole) are made better off.

This chapter considers the situation in which the market does not perform efficiently—when decisionmakers do not bear all of the costs or realize all of the benefits of their actions. The chapter also looks at the role of government in correcting such market imperfections.

### B. Learning Objectives

In this chapter you will:

1. Learn what an externality is.
2. See why externalities can make market outcomes inefficient.
3. Examine how people sometimes can solve the problem of externalities on their own.
4. Consider why private solutions to externalities sometimes do not work.
5. Examine various government policies aimed at solving the problem of externalities.

After accomplishing these goals, you should be able to:

1. Define and give examples of both positive and negative externalities.
2. Show graphically and explain how either positive or negative externalities can prevent the market from achieving the socially optimal level of output, which maximizes the sum of consumer and producer surplus.
3. Use the Coase theorem to demonstrate that when transactions costs are low, those affected by an externality may be able to negotiate a solution through the market.
4. Explain why externalities sometimes require government intervention.
5. Compare the effects of pollution taxes or subsidies with the effects of traditional government regulation as ways to internalize the social costs of pollution.

## C. Chapter Review

### 10-1 Externalities and Market Inefficiency

Previous chapters illustrated that the market maximizes the sum of producer and consumer surplus as individual decisionmakers make choices based on the marginal costs and benefits of their actions. This assumed that all costs of production are borne by the producer, and all benefits of consumption are captured by the buyer. If a third party is affected by an activity, either by bearing some of the costs or by receiving some of the benefits, the market equilibrium quantity will not be efficient. The impact of these activities on third parties is called externalities.

When externalities exist, decisionmakers make choices without taking into account all of the marginal effects of their actions, namely, the effects on others. When the externalities are negative, as in the case of pollution, production will be excessive because the external portion of the marginal cost of production is ignored. The supply curve represents the private cost to the decisionmaker without taking into account the external social cost of pollution. For the outcome to be socially optimal, the supply curve must include all of the social costs of production, even those that are external to the producer. These additional costs would reduce the supply (shift the supply curve to the left), reducing equilibrium quantity and raising price. In short, negative externalities result in too much production being sold at too low a price for efficiency.

When positive externalities exist, the market underproduces. In the case of consumption externalities, the private value from the product is less than the social value, including benefits to third parties. The result is a private demand curve that understates the benefits of the product to society. An example is education: Much of the benefit from education goes to society at large. Consequently, without a public subsidy, the individual would look only at his or her personal benefits and underconsume education relative to society's optimal level.

In the case of production externalities, the private cost overstates the social cost because of the spillover benefits to society. As a result, the private supply curve lies to the left of society's true cost, and underproduction occurs. For example, businesses look only at internal costs and benefits in deciding on the level of research even though there may be significant benefits to society. Therefore, the market tends to underallocate resources to research.

### 10-2 Private Solutions to Externalities

It is a logical extension of the earlier discussion of markets to apply the concept of voluntary exchange to the internalization of external costs or benefits. Remember that the inefficiency from externalities results because the marginal costs and marginal benefits to the individual fail to include effects on a third party. If a change in behavior would benefit a third party, then it is reasonable to think that the third party could negotiate with the decisionmakers to change their behavior. If the change in behavior is worth more to the third party than it would cost the decisionmakers, then they should be able to make a deal that would benefit everyone concerned. This is the basic premise of the *Coase theorem*: When the interested parties can get together to negotiate, they can work out a voluntary deal that makes everyone better off and increases society's well-being. For example, those who are hurt by pollution from a paper mill can negotiate a solution with the company. They can either pay the mill to cut back on pollution or negotiate compensation for the damage that they incur from the mill's pollution. Either way, the mill will take into account the social cost of pollution in its future production decisions, and the externality disappears.

Unfortunately, such private solutions do not always work. Negotiating is not costless, especially when it requires coordinating the actions of large numbers of people throughout a large geographic area. Private solutions work best when there are small numbers of third-party victims who are easily identified and can be organized to work together in negotiating a solution.

## 10-3 Public Policies toward Externalities

Traditional control of externalities such as pollution has been in the form of direct regulation. With regulation, the government simply mandates the level of cleanup that must occur. This works reasonably well in cases in which the external costs to society are so high that fine-tuning the level of cleanup is not as important as simply stopping pollution quickly. For example, after the publication in 1969 of Rachel Carson's book, *Silent Spring*, which described the long-term environmental damage done by certain pesticides, the government banned the use of the pesticide DDT. In most cases, however, the proper level of cleanup is difficult to determine. Direct regulation puts the entire burden for measuring social costs and benefits on the government, and it provides no incentive for polluters to develop better cleanup technology. On the contrary, if producers develop new technology, the government might respond simply by tightening the environmental standards.

As an alternative, society can use market-based policies that provide incentives for individual decision-makers to take into account all of the relevant costs of production. These incentives can take the form of pollution taxes, subsidies, or tradable pollution permits. Each of the policies has the same effect: It would internalize the external cost of pollution by raising the opportunity cost of polluting. Instead of mandating the level of reduction of sulfur dioxide by a paper mill, for example, the EPA could impose a $5 tax on each unit of pollutant emitted. Clearly, this would raise the private opportunity cost of polluting by $5/unit. However, as suggested by the Coase theorem, a $5/unit subsidy to not pollute would have the same effect as a $5 tax on each unit of pollution. If polluting means giving up a $5 subsidy, then the opportunity cost of polluting is still $5 under the subsidy, just as it would have been under the tax. Similarly, if the EPA distributes pollution permits that are tradable, then the opportunity cost of using a permit to release sulfur into the atmosphere is the forgone income from selling the permit. If the permit has a market value of $5, then the opportunity cost of polluting is still $5. In each case, the market-based policy internalizes the cost of pollution. Unlike the case of direct regulation, such market-based policies also provide an incentive for the polluter to develop better technology in order to reduce the internal cost of pollution. In the previous example, every one-unit reduction in pollution saves the firm $5, unlike direct regulation, which provides no financial incentive to reduce the quantity of pollution below the mandated maximum level.

## D. Helpful Hints

1. *You really can have too much of a good thing.* We live life at the margin, so even if we put a high value on a clean environment, at some point we are likely to decide that a little more cleanup costs more than it is worth (at the margin). Suppose that we choose to clean up 99% of the air pollution from producing paper. Even though we put a high value on a clean environment, we may choose to leave the remaining 1% if we discover that eliminating the last 1% of air pollution will cost as much to clean up as the first 99% did. That is, the marginal cost exceeds the marginal benefit for the final 1%.

2. *It is difficult to identify the most efficient level of environmental cleanup because many of the benefits are hard to measure.* For example, how much value do we put on a life saved through pollution control? The typical reaction is that each life has an infinite value, but people do not behave that way. Rational people take risks with their lives every day as they drive cars, eat, work, and play. The economic value of a human life is difficult to measure, but it is nevertheless a real factor to consider in evaluating environmental cleanup or other government programs.

## E. Terms and Definitions

Choose a definition for each key term.

Key terms:

\_\_\_\_\_Externality
\_\_\_\_\_Internalizing externalities
\_\_\_\_\_Technology spillover
\_\_\_\_\_Technology policy
\_\_\_\_\_Coase theorem
\_\_\_\_\_Transactions costs
\_\_\_\_\_Pigovian taxes

Definitions:

1. Taxes set equal to the external cost of pollution in order to internalize the negative externality.
2. A positive externality that results when a firm's investment in new technology has external benefits for society as a whole.
3. A positive or negative effect on a third party as a result of a transaction between a buyer and seller.
4. For any initial distribution of property rights, if transactions costs are relatively small, the affected parties can negotiate to internalize the externality and reach a bargain that will make everyone better off.
5. The costs of negotiating and implementing an agreement between buyers and sellers.
6. Giving buyers and sellers an incentive (through a tax or other market-based scheme) to take into account the external effects of their actions.
7. Government policy designed to subsidize industries that produce technology spillovers throughout the economy.

## II. Problems and Short-Answer Questions

### A. Practice Problems

You are economics consultant for Brewster, New York. The city is faced with a massive cleanup bill for trichlorethylene, which has been found in the town drinking water. A local manufacturing business dumped solvents into a pit on its property for a number of years because it cost the firm less than proper disposal. The firm has gone out of business, leaving contamination with an estimated cost of $6.5 million. The State Board of Health has presented the following options: (a) Do nothing: Live with the problem or move out; (b) Boil water for drinking and avoid long showers (which release the chemical into the air); (c) Drill new water wells and cap the old contaminated wells; or (d) Find the source of contamination and clean it up completely.

1. The following table shows estimated costs and benefits of each cleanup option. The cost is the cost of cleanup, not the cost of pollution itself. The benefit is the reduction in the damage due to the contamination. Note that the maximum potential benefit is $6.5 million, which represents total elimination of the damage from trichlorethylene. Fill in the missing blanks.

## EPA Cleanup Options for Brewster, New York

| Option | Total Cost | Total Benefit | MC | MB | Net Benefit |
|---|---|---|---|---|---|
| a. Do nothing | 0 | 0 | ___ | ___ | ___ |
| b. Boil water | $1 mil | $4 mil | ___ | ___ | ___ |
| c. New wells | $2 mil | $5.5 mil | ___ | ___ | ___ |
| d. Total cleanup | $5 mil | $6.5 mil | ___ | ___ | ___ |

Note: All benefits and costs are social rather than private. Specifically: MC = the marginal cost to society of one additional level of cleanup; MB = the marginal benefit to society (social value) of one additional level of cleanup; and Net Benefit = Total Benefit less Total Cost (to society). Total benefit is the reduction in pollution damage, up to the point of complete elimination of the $6.5 million in damage from trichlorethylene contamination.

1. Based on these numbers, what level of cleanup would you recommend and why?
   _____
   _____
   _____

2. How would you interpret the Total Benefit column? That is, what kinds of benefits would you include here? What kinds of problems would you anticipate in measuring the benefits of such an environmental cleanup project?
   _____
   _____
   _____
   _____

3. What would be the dollar value of the deadweight loss from total cleanup (option d)? Why would total cleanup result in a deadweight loss to society even though we would like to have a clean environment? _____
   _____
   _____
   _____
   _____

4. If total cleanup (option d) were the only alternative to doing nothing (option a), would you recommend it? Explain why or why not. _____
   _____
   _____

5. You have just discovered that the polluter could have disposed of the solvent properly for $1 million, avoiding all contamination of the water supply.

a. Why didn't the market take care of the problem before the contamination occurred? Wouldn't that have been more efficient? _____

_____

_____

_____

_____

b. What conditions would have been required to achieve a market solution so that the victims and the polluters could have avoided this problem?

_____

_____

_____

_____

c. Would the contamination have occurred if the polluter also had owned the Brewster Water Company? Why or why not? _____

_____

_____

_____

_____

## B. Short-Answer Questions

1. According to the Coase theorem, the market can often solve problems of negative externalities on its own.

a. What conditions must hold for the market solution to work?

_____

_____

_____

b. When the private parties involved can negotiate a solution to a negative externality, does it matter for economic efficiency who pays whom? For example, if the problem is water pollution, does it matter whether the polluter is penalized for polluting or the victim subsidizes the polluter for not polluting? Or if government is involved, will a pollution tax have a different effect from a subsidy to polluters to not pollute? Your answer should include an explanation of how such different assignments of property rights to the environment affect the opportunity cost to the polluter of continuing to pollute.

_____

_____

_____
_____
_____
_____

2.  Critics argue that tradable pollution permits look like a good idea at first glance, but there are several reasons why they are not likely to work: (1) It would be very difficult to decide who should get them, since some firms with older factories may not be able to clean up as much as newer firms; (2) Permits would give firms a license to pollute, putting a dollar value on a priceless resource; and (3) Some firms might make money by selling their permits rather than using them themselves. How would you respond?   Are these criticisms valid reasons why such a system would not be efficient for society? _____

_____
_____
_____
_____
_____

## III.  Self-Test

### A.  True/False Questions

_____ 1.   A subsidy is less likely than a tax to reduce the amount of pollution.

_____ 2.   Tradable pollution permits have the same effect on output and the level of pollution as a Pigovian tax on polluters.

_____ 3.   The most efficient way to clean up pollution is direct regulation.

_____ 4.   Internalizing the cost of pollution eventually will result in totally clean air and water.

_____ 5.   For pollution permits to be efficient for society, they need to be tradable.

_____ 6.   A Pigovian tax reduces economic efficiency by distorting taxpayers' behavior.

_____ 7.   A disadvantage of market-based policies to clean up the environment is that they treat the environment as if it were a commodity rather than a priceless resource.

_____ 8.   Unlike direct regulation, a market-based policy provides an incentive for polluters to develop new technology to clean up pollution.

_____ 9.   If studded snow tires do an estimated $10 damage to the highways per vehicle each year, then the most efficient outcome for society would be to ban their use.

_____10. Economic efficiency suggests that once we determine the optimal level of pollution cleanup, all firms should share equally in that cleanup.

_____11. Tradable pollution permits will internalize negative externalities efficiently only if the government auctions off the permits.

_____12. According to the Coase theorem, negative externalities require government action because the market fails to take into account external social costs.

_____13. A negative externality in consumption results in a demand curve that overstates the social value of a product.

_____14. A positive production externality results in a supply curve that overstates the social cost of a product.

_____15. It would be more efficient for government to stay out of the business of environmental cleanup because government policies will inevitably distort the market.

## B. Multiple-Choice Questions

1. Private solutions to negative externalities are *least* likely to be effective when:
   a. the costs of pollution are high.
   b. the costs of pollution cleanup are high.
   c. property rights are clearly assigned to one party.
   d. transactions costs are high.
   e. there are only a few people involved.

2. Which of the following statements is true? The most *efficient* solution for a negative externality would be:
   a. an outright ban.
   b. direct regulation to control the amount of the externality.
   c. either a pollution tax or subsidy equal to the amount of the negative externality.
   d. a tax on the good or service associated with the pollutant.
   e. a subsidy to not produce the good or service associated with the pollutant.

3. The most efficient goal for society with regard to the environment is to clean up pollution until:
   a. all pollution is eliminated.
   b. we have eliminated all pollution that it is technically feasible to stop.
   c. the total benefit of pollution cleanup is maximized.
   d. we have eliminated all pollution that does not cost us any jobs.
   e. the marginal benefit to society from the last dollar spent on pollution cleanup is exactly one dollar.

4. According to the Coase theorem,
   a. the market can internalize external costs and benefits and achieve efficiency if private parties can negotiate solutions to the externalities.
   b. government can improve upon the operation of the market by environmental controls.
   c. the market can internalize externalities if all parties involved have roughly equal bargaining power.
   d. correcting externalities through the market can work, but only if the innocent third parties have clearly established and enforceable property rights.
   e. none of the above.

5. Which of the following is a market-based pollution control policy?
   a. specific limits on allowable pollution in each market.
   b. total deregulation, allowing the market to eliminate pollution without government action.
   c. the issuance of tradable pollution permits by the Environmental Protection Agency.
   d. government expenditures on research and development to clean up the environment.
   e. all of the above.

6. The inefficiency that results from cleaning up the environment beyond the socially optimal level is the:
   a. loss of the jobs in the economy.
   b. higher taxes on polluters.
   c. deadweight loss from providing units of pollution cleanup that have a social value less than their social cost.
   d. transfer of resources from the private to the public sector.
   e. all of the above.

7. Relative to market-based pollution control policies, direct regulation:
   a. requires less detailed information to set the pollution limits.
   b. provides more of an incentive to develop better technology to clean up beyond the minimum.
   c. allows polluters to pollute at no charge up to the limits set by the government.
   d. makes it easier to fine-tune regulations for different situations.
   e. all of the above.

8. The existence of a positive production externality suggests that society's well-being would be increased by:
   a. lowering price and increasing output.
   b. raising price and increasing output.
   c. lowering price and decreasing output.
   d. raising price and decreasing output.
   e. taxing the externality and letting the market determine price and output.

9. A negative externality in production leads to:
   a. overproduction relative to the socially optimal level.
   b. underproduction relative to the socially optimal level.
   c. an imbalance between quantity supplied and quantity demanded.
   d. a demand curve that is not at the socially optimal level.
   e. a supply curve that fails to include all of the benefits to society.

10. Which of the following statements is true?
    a. Social cost = private cost - the external cost of pollution.
    b. Social cost = private cost + the external cost of pollution.
    c. Social cost = cost of pollution.
    d. Social cost + cost of pollution = private cost.
    e. Social cost + private cost = supply.

11. A deadweight loss from pollution cleanup occurs whenever:
    a. pollution cleanup imposes costs on society.
    b. society puts a price tag on pollution, providing a "license to pollute."
    c. government gets involved.
    d. jobs are lost.
    e. some units of pollution cleanup cost more than their marginal benefit to society.

12. If the last unit of output produced at a paper mill has a value to society of $10 and a social cost of $15, but the private cost to the company is $10, and the current price is $10, then the:
    a. market is in equilibrium, but a lower output would make society better off.
    b. market is in equilibrium, but a higher output would make society better off.
    c. output and price are too low for equilibrium.
    d. output is too low, and price is too high, for equilibrium.
    e. output is too high, and price is too low, for equilibrium.

13. In the presence of technology spillovers, the market tends to_____ the product relative to society's best interest.
    a. overproduce and underprice
    b. overproduce and overprice
    c. underproduce and underprice
    d. underproduce and overprice
    e. efficiently produce

14. A major criticism of technology policy is that
    a. technology is a mixed blessing: It involves costs as well as benefits.
    b. subsidies for technology may be awarded more on political than economic grounds.
    c. such subsidies are inherently inefficient.
    d. if new technology is socially desirable, the market will automatically provide it.
    e. it will distort the economy in favor of technology-enhancing industries.

15. The most efficient pollution control system would ensure that each polluter:
    a. cleans up to the point where total social benefits are maximized.
    b. cleans up just to the point where that polluter's last unit of cleanup has a social value exactly equal to its social cost
    c. must meet exactly the same pollution standards as everyone else.
    d. meets all standards that do not result in layoffs or financial losses.
    e. cleans up to the maximum level that is technically feasible.

## IV. Advanced Critical Thinking

The Optimal Level of Crime Prevention: How Many Robberies Are Too Many?

A public official recently argued that our goal as a society should be to eliminate crime, that we should not stop until there is not a single robbery or murder. His assertion is that even one robbery is one too many. Even if society has enough resources to make it feasible to eliminate crime, would it make sense? Or is this bad economics? Can you make an analogy with pollution control? Write a short essay explaining what's wrong with this way of thinking._____

_____
_____
_____
_____
_____
_____
_____

In order to answer these and other questions, consider the hypothetical case study of the small town of Knock-em-Stiff, Ohio. The number of robberies has increased over the past decade, and the town council is under pressure from the voting public to clean up crime. They have hired a consultant to estimate the economic effects of forming a professional police department instead of relying on a volunteer who works part time when he is not working at his regular job as clerk at the local hardware store. The council has just received the consultant's report and must decide how many police officers to hire.

According to the consultant, the projected social cost of crime without any police protection at all is $200,000 per year. This includes explicit costs such as for property loss, medical costs, and lost earnings due to injuries, as well as intangible costs such as loss of peace of mind or reduced quality of life due to the higher crime rate. The benefit from each additional police officer hired is the estimated reduction in the total social cost of crime in the village; therefore, the maximum possible benefit from crime prevention is $200,000, which represents the total elimination of crime (and its social costs) in the village. The consultant has found that the village can hire police officers at an annual cost of $30,000 each, including salary and fringe benefits.

The consultant's estimates of costs and benefits follow. Fill in the missing numbers and answer the questions that follow. The first line is done for you. At the end of the table is a list of terms and their definitions, in case you need to review before filling in the blanks.

## Consultant's Report: Annual Costs and Benefits of Various Levels of Police Protection for Knock-em-Stiff, Ohio

| # of Police Officers | Total Social Cost | Marginal Social Cost | Total Social Benefit | Marginal Social Benefit | Net Social Benefit |
|---|---|---|---|---|---|
| 0 | 0 | — | 0 | — | 0 |
| 1 | 30,000 | | 30,000 | | |
| 2 | 60,000 | | 70,000 | | |
| 3 | 90,000 | | 105,000 | | |
| 4 | 120,000 | | 134,000 | | |
| 5 | 150,000 | | 160,000 | | |
| 6 | 180,000 | | 180,000 | | |
| 7 | 210,000 | | 190,000 | | |
| 8 | 240,000 | | 196,000 | | |
| 9 | 270,000 | | 200,000 | | |
| 10 | 300,000 | | 200,000 | | |

1. Some people argue that the town should hire enough police officers to eliminate crime. Based on the consultant's report, how would you respond? How many police officers should they hire and why?

2. Plot Marginal Social Cost (MSC) and Marginal Social Benefit (MSB) on the graph at the top of the next page, and label the socially optimal amount of crime prevention. Plot the Total Cost (TC) and Total Benefit (TB) on the lower graph, and identify the point that maximizes Net Benefit (TB-TC). (This point should coincide with your answer to Question 1.)

Marginal Social Cost (msc) and Marginal Social Benefit (msb) of Crime Prevention

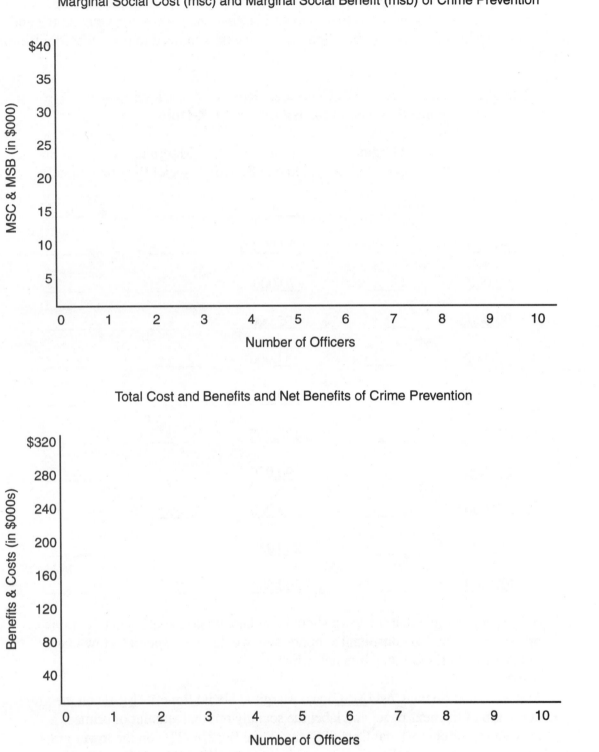

Total Cost and Benefits and Net Benefits of Crime Prevention

# V. Solutions

## Terms and Definitions

__3___Externality
__6___Internalizing externalities
__2___Technology spillover
__7___Technology policy
__4___Coase theorem
__5___Transactions costs
__1___Pigovian taxes

## Practice Problems

### EPA Cleanup Options for Brewster, New York

| Option | Total Cost | Total Benefit | MC | MB | Net Benefit |
|---|---|---|---|---|---|
| a. Do nothing | 0 | 0 | — | — | 0 |
| b. Boil water | $1 mil | $4 mil | $1 mil | $4 mil | $3 mil |
| c. New wells | $2 mil | $5.5 mil | $1 mil | $1.5 mil | $3.5mil |
| d. Total cleanup | $5 mil | $6.5 mil | $3 mil | $1.0 mil | $1.5 mil |

Note: All benefits and costs are social rather than private. Specifically:  MC = marginal cost to society; MB = marginal benefit to society (social value); and Net Benefit = Total Benefit less Total Cost (to society)

1.  The most efficient level of cleanup is option c: drill new wells. To maximize social well-being, we should take every action that has a marginal benefit greater than the marginal cost. This means that option c is the best choice: its MB is $1.5 million, while its MC is only $1.0 million. Society gains another $0.5 million (MB-MC) by moving from option b to c. Even though we would like to have total cleanup (option d), it is not worth the cost to society. Option d has a marginal cost of $3.0 million, which exceeds its marginal benefit of $1.0 million to society.

2.  The Total Benefit from pollution cleanup is actually the reduction in the cost of pollution to society. In this example, the total benefit from eliminating the source of pollution is $6.5 million, which represents the benefit from avoiding the damage from the pollutant. These benefits would include such factors as reduced risk to property or human health, including lost hours of work and medical bills, as well as pain and suffering. Measurement of the factors is difficult because the health effects are uncertain and likely to be long term. Even if the health effects are

known, it is difficult to estimate the full dollar value of pain and suffering and other intangible health costs.

3.  Total cleanup would reduce Net Benefits from $3.5 million to $1.5 million, making society $2.0 million worse off. Another way to see this is to look at the Marginal Benefit and Marginal Cost of option d: At that point, the <u>MC</u> of $3.0 million exceeds the <u>MB</u> of $1.0 million by $2.0 million. This $2.0 million shortfall reduces the Net Benefit of the cleanup program by $2.0 million relative to the previous option.

4.  If the choice were all or nothing, then total cleanup would make sense because the Net Benefit is positive. A $1.5 million Net Benefit is better than nothing.

5a. To the polluter, dumping the solvent was costless even though it imposed a $6.5 million cost on society. Clearly, it would have been more efficient to spend $1 million to avoid a $6.5 million cost rather than spending much more later without even cleaning up completely. The problem is that the $6.5 million is an external cost, leading to excessive pollution. If the polluter had been paying the full social cost of pollution, it would have paid the $1 million to avoid contamination rather than $6.5 million in environmental damage.

b.  If property rights to the environment had been defined clearly, and if the victims had been identified, then the victims could have negotiated with polluters not to pollute. The cost of pollution would have been internalized, and the polluters would have paid the $1 million to avoid contamination rather than bearing the full $6.5 million in environmental damage.

c.  If the same company owned both the polluter and the water supply, then the company would have had an incentive to pay the $1 million in disposal costs for the trichlorethylene rather than do $6.5 million in damage to a resource that it owned. This would have internalized the cost, similar to the answer to 5(b) above.

**Short-Answer Questions**

1.  a.  The affected parties must be able to negotiate a settlement. For this to happen, the transactions costs must be low enough to make it worthwhile. As a result, the market is more likely to work efficiently when the affected population is small. With a large population, it is difficult to identify everyone and work out a settlement.

    b.  According to the Coase theorem, if the affected parties can negotiate a solution to an externality, the result will be the same improvement in economic efficiency regardless of who pays whom. If the victims of pollution own the property rights to the environment, they can charge the polluter for using their scarce resource. If the polluter owns the rights, the victims can subsidize the polluter to cut back on pollution. Either way, the polluter will internalize the pollution cost. Losing a subsidy has the same opportunity cost as paying an equivalent pollution charge.

2. These arguments are invalid. First, if newer factories can clean up more easily than older factories, then it is more efficient for the newer factories to clean up relatively more. We should clean up wherever it can be done at the lowest cost. Second, permits put a price on a scarce resource that had been underpriced (free to the user) in the past, which encouraged overconsumption. We put a price on other scarce resources, so why exclude this one? Third, if some firms sell their permits, it means that other firms put a higher value on them. As long as the total number of permits issued equals the amount of pollution that society will accept, why not let the firms decide who can clean up at the lowest cost?

## True/False Questions

1. F; both will have the same effect on pollution and economic efficiency.
2. T
3. F; market-based policies are more flexible and provide incentives for polluters to solve the problem themselves.
4. F; internalizing the cost will mean that pollution will be reduced only to the point that the marginal benefit of the last unit of pollution cleanup will just equal its cost.
5. T
6. F; it improves efficiency by eliminating a distortion of behavior caused by not pricing a scarce resource.
7. F; an advantage of market-based policies is that they put a price on a scarce resource that had previously been treated as a free good.
8. T
9. F; even if they do $10 in damage to the highways, it is efficient to use them if their benefit exceeds their cost, including the $10 in external cost to society. A $10 tax would let the market determine whether or not they were worth their full cost to society.
10. F; to get the most cleanup with the fewest resources, polluters that can clean up at the lowest cost should do more of the cleaning up.
11. F; the government could give the permits away, and the result would still be efficient (although not necessarily equitable) as long as the recipients could sell their permits.
12. F; according to the Coase theorem, the market may be able to internalize externalities when negotiating costs are not excessive.
13. T
14. T
15. F; government action may be necessary for efficiency when the market is unable to internalize the costs of pollution.

## Multiple-Choice Questions

| | | | | | |
|---|---|---|---|---|---|
| 1. | d | 6. | c | 11. | e |
| 2. | c | 7. | c | 12. | a |
| 3. | e | 8. | a | 13. | d |
| 4. | a | 9. | a | 14. | b |
| 5. | c | 10. | b | 15. | b |

## Advanced Critical Thinking

This is bad economics. Because we cannot have everything we want, we have to make choices. Marginalist thinking tells us that no matter how much we value something, we should still stop at the point at which the next unit provides an additional benefit that is less than its cost. We would like to stop crime, but we should never use more resources to prevent an additional crime than that prevention is worth to us. The cure should never cost more than the problem that we are solving. Pollution is similar to crime: In both cases, we would like less of the activity, but we don't want to spend $100,000, for example, to save $10,000 in social costs.

### Consultant's Report: Annual Costs and Benefits of Various Levels of Police Protection for Knock-em-Stiff, Ohio

| # of Police Officers | Total Social Cost | Marginal Social Cost | Total Social Benefit | Marginal Social Benefit | Net Social Benefit |
|---|---|---|---|---|---|
| 0 | 0 | — | 0 | — | 0 |
| 1 | 30,000 | 30,000 | 30,000 | 30,000 | 0 |
| 2 | 60,000 | 30,000 | 70,000 | 40,000 | 10,000 |
| 3 | 90,000 | 30,000 | 105,000 | 35,000 | 15,000 |
| 4 | 120,000 | 30,000 | 134,000 | 29,000 | 14,000 |
| 5 | 150,000 | 30,000 | 160,000 | 26,000 | 10,000 |
| 6 | 180,000 | 30,000 | 180,000 | 20,000 | 0 |
| 7 | 210,000 | 30,000 | 190,000 | 10,000 | (20,000) |
| 8 | 240,000 | 30,000 | 196,000 | 6000 | (44,000) |
| 9 | 270,000 | 30,000 | 200,000 | 4000 | (70,000) |
| 10 | 300,000 | 30,000 | 200,000 | 0 | (100,000) |

1. The town should hire police officers as long as the last officer hired costs no more than the estimated value of that officer to the town. That is, keep hiring as long as $\underline{MB} > \underline{MC}$; stop hiring when $\underline{MB} = \underline{MC}$. This means hiring three officers because the first three officers have marginal benefits greater than the $30,000 marginal cost, but even one additional officer would have a marginal benefit to the town of less than the $30,000 marginal cost. Note that hiring three officers also maximizes the Net Benefit to society.

2.

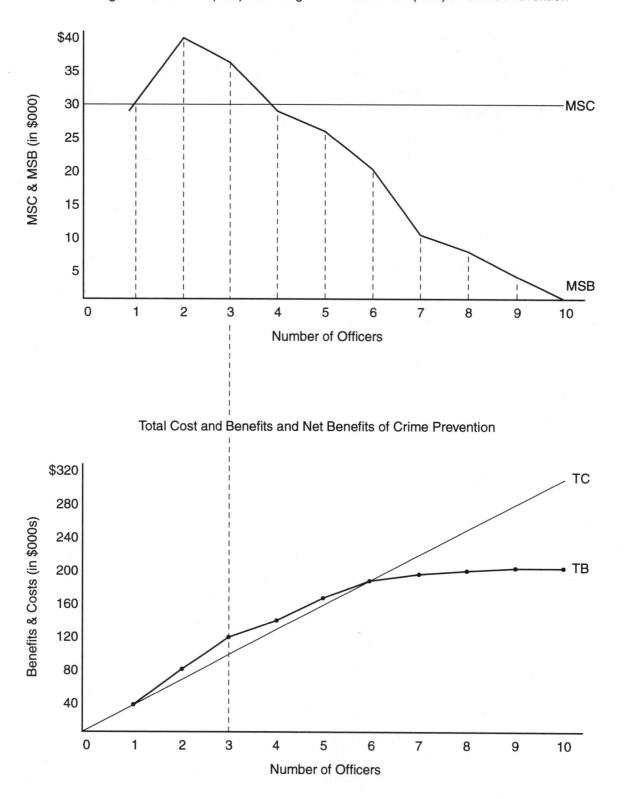

Marginal Social Cost (msc) and Marginal Social Benefit (msb) of Crime Prevention

Total Cost and Benefits and Net Benefits of Crime Prevention

# Chapter 11:  Public Goods and Common Resources

## I. Chapter Overview

### A.  Context and Purpose

The market works well at allocating resources when everyone bears the costs and benefits of his actions.  Unfortunately, this restriction does not always hold, which leads to imperfections in the market.  Chapters 10-12 analyze the role of government in correcting for such market imperfections.

The previous chapter investigated the role of government in correcting the problems that externalities cause for the market.  The next chapter covers the tax system.  This chapter extends the analysis of the role of government to cover public goods, which are those goods that are consumed simultaneously by multiple users, even those who do not pay for the goods.

### B.  Learning Objectives

In this chapter you will:

1.  Learn the defining characteristics of public goods and common resources.
2.  Examine why private markets may fail to provide public goods.
3.  See why the cost-benefit analysis of public goods is both necessary and difficult.
4.  Examine why people tend to use common resources too much.
5.  Consider some of the important common resources in our economy.

After accomplishing these goals, you should be able to:

1.  Interpret what is meant by *rival consumption* and *excludable goods* and why public goods are neither excludable nor rival.
2.  Distinguish public from private goods and identify the effect of the free-rider problem on the ability of private markets to provide public goods.
3.  Evaluate the role and limitations of cost-benefit analysis in evaluating government programs.
4.  Explain  the significance of poorly defined or nonexistent property rights in causing overconsumption of common resources.
5.  Apply the concept of common resources to such diverse examples as underground petroleum reserves, public highways, and even whales.

## C. Chapter Review

### 11-1  The Different Kinds of Goods

For the market to allocate goods efficiently, the goods must be both *excludable* and *rival*. An excludable good is one that others can be prevented from using. A rival good is a good for which one person's consumption takes away from another's enjoyment. Goods can be categorized according to those criteria. Consider the following cases:

- *Private goods*: Goods that are both excludable and rival, such as hamburgers.
- *Public goods*: Goods that are neither excludable nor rival, such as national defense.
- *Common resources*: Goods that are rival but not easily excludable, such as whales in the ocean.
- *Natural monopoly*: The market for a good that is excludable but not rival, such as cable-television signals.

### 11-2  Public Goods

Public goods are neither excludable nor rival in consumption. It is not feasible to exclude those who do not pay for a public good, and additional users can consume the good without detracting from the satisfaction received by others. National defense is a public good. For example, the security provided by a nuclear submarine is non-excludable in the sense that it protects the entire country, not just those who paid for it. It is also nonrival in that it can protect a growing population without reducing the benefits received by the original consumers. Because it is not feasible to exclude those who do not pay for national defense, there is a free-rider problem—some users will not pay their share—when the production of national defense is left to the private market.

### 11-3  Common Resources

Common resources share the characteristic of nonexcludability with public goods. Unlike public goods, however, common resources are rival: One person's consumption of a common resource detracts from others' consumption. Common resources differ from private goods in that they lack clearly defined and enforced property rights. This makes exclusion difficult or impossible. An example of a common resource is underground petroleum reserves. They are clearly rival because if one company pumps the oil out of the ground, then that oil is no longer available for others. However, it is difficult to define and protect the property rights to underground oil. Not only can it extend under several owners' property, but drillers can drill diagonally to reach oil under someone else's land. Iraq made this claim about Kuwait's petroleum exploration just before invading Kuwait. If property rights to underground petroleum were clear-cut, then petroleum reserves would be a simple case of a private good that the market could allocate efficiently. Because oil reserves are a common resource, the market tends to overproduce under the "use it or lose it" mentality.

## D. Helpful Hints

1. *Not all public goods are provided by government, and not all private goods are provided by markets.* However, in those cases where markets provide public goods, finding an efficient way to pay for the good can be tricky. Consider commercial television as an example. Exclusion is not feasible with present technology, and consumption is nonrival. In short, a commercial television signal is a public good. Because of the difficulty in excluding free riders, the broadcast companies have turned to another way to generate revenues: They sell advertising.

2. *It is possible to satisfy the demand for public goods without providing a separate good for each consumer.* Suppose that 250 million Americans would like to have one nuclear submarine for protection. Only one submarine is required to satisfy the entire demand. Conversely, if 250 million Americans each demand a private good such as one hamburger, then 250 million hamburgers are required to satisfy the market demand. Because of the nonrival nature of consumption, we can "pass the hat" or ask everyone to contribute toward the purchase of a public good for the group. Because of the free-rider problem, that "contribution" may have to be mandatory, in the form of taxes.

3. *Some essentially private goods share characteristics with public goods.* The same logic about "passing the hat" to pay for a public good applies to some goods that are neither purely public nor purely private. Suppose that you and a few friends would like to rent a new video. As long as everyone wants to see the same movie, you need only one copy to meet everyone's demand. Up to the point that the room gets crowded, the video rental behaves in part like a public good in that it has nonrival consumption. One more user watching the film doesn't take away from others' enjoyment.

4. *Public goods differ from private goods not because of who provides them, but because of innate characteristics of the goods themselves.* Government may provide goods that are essentially private (excludable and rival), such as a congested state campground. Similarly, markets may provide goods that are essentially public (nonexcludable and nonrival). Commercial television signals, for example, are essentially public goods, with infeasible exclusion (without using different broadcast technology) and nonrival consumption (additional viewers do not detract from others' enjoyment). To avoid the free-rider problem, broadcasters use commercial advertising to pay for the good.

5. *Common resources tend to be overproduced and overconsumed.* If it seems unlikely that common pools of petroleum would lead to overproduction and consumption of oil, consider two children who must share a box of popcorn or a soft drink at the movies. Granted, drilling for oil is a bit more difficult than sipping soda through a straw, but the basic analysis is the same. In each case, property rights are not assigned clearly, causing the parties involved to use the resource at a

faster than desirable rate. With the popcorn, each kid might prefer to eat slowly, making the popcorn last for the entire movie. However, if he waits, the other child may finish off the popcorn. Both eat faster to make sure that they get their share. Similarly with oil, companies that choose to leave oil in the ground for later use will be left out as others drill the wells dry.

## E. Terms and Definitions

Choose a definition for each key term.

Key terms:

_____Excludability
_____Rivalness
_____Private goods
_____Public goods
_____Common resource
_____Natural monopoly
_____Free-rider problem
_____Cost-benefit analysis
_____Tragedy of the Commons

Definitions:

1. Those goods that are both excludable and rival in consumption; an example is an automobile.
2. A good that is rival but not excludable, such as underground petroleum reserves without established mineral rights.
3. A good that it is possible to prevent others from using.
4. What is owned by everyone is valued by nobody; that is, when people act individually, they tend to overuse common resources because they do not take into account the costs that they impose on others; if they acted together, they would have the incentive to use less of the resource.
5. A good for which one person's consumption detracts from that of others.
6. Those goods that are nonrival yet excludable, such as an uncongested public swimming pool.
7. Those goods that are neither rival nor excludable; an example is basic research or general knowledge.
8. The incentive for people to use a nonexcludable good such as a public good or common resource without paying for it.
9. The study of the benefits and costs of public projects to society in order to plan for the efficient provision of government programs.

## II. Problems and Short-Answer Questions

### A. Practice Problems

1. Consider the following goods and services. Identify their characteristics in terms of rivalry and excludability, then categorize each as either private, public, natural monopoly, or common resource. Explain your answers.

   a. Commercial television signals: _____
   _____
   _____
   _____
   _____

   b. Congested city streets: _____
   _____
   _____
   _____
   _____

   c. A poem: _____
   _____
   _____
   _____
   _____

   d. General medical research on the relationship between lifestyle and heart disease:
   _____
   _____
   _____

   e. A congested public swimming pool: _____
   _____
   _____
   _____
   _____

   f. An uncongested private swimming pool: _____
   _____
   _____
   _____
   _____

2.  The following table shows four possible categories of goods according to degree of rivalness and excludability.

**Categories of Goods**

RIVAL?

|  | YES | NO |
|---|---|---|
| **EXCLUDABLE?** | | |
| **YES** | TYPE:_____ EXAMPLE:_____ EXPLAIN:_____ _____ _____ _____ _____ _____ _____ _____ _____ _____ _____ | TYPE:_____ EXAMPLE:_____ EXPLAIN:_____ _____ _____ _____ _____ _____ _____ _____ _____ _____ _____ |
| **NO** | TYPE:_____ EXAMPLE:_____ EXPLAIN:_____ _____ _____ _____ _____ _____ _____ _____ _____ _____ _____ | TYPE:_____ EXAMPLE:_____ EXPLAIN:_____ _____ _____ _____ _____ _____ _____ _____ _____ _____ _____ |

a.  Label the four types as either public goods, private goods, common resources, or natural monopolies.

b.  Give an example not already used in the text of a good in each category.

c. Explain briefly under each example why it belongs in the category that you chose.

## B. Short-Answer Questions

1. Why do we need regulations to protect game against excessive hunting and fishing? Wouldn't it be rational for people to cut back voluntarily on the quantity of game that they take, when it is obvious that everyone benefits if we all agree to some restraint in order to avoid exhaustion of the resource? _____

   _____

   _____

   _____

   _____

2. A lighthouse is often given as an example of a public good. Why? (How does it satisfy the criteria for a public good?) Can you think of any reasons why a lighthouse might fail to meet the test for a public good? Explain. _____

   _____

   _____

   _____

   _____

3. Food is more of a basic necessity than highways, yet government builds roads for the general public and normally does not provide food for everyone. Why?

   _____

   _____

   _____

   _____

## III. Self-Test

### A. True/False Questions

_____1. A public good is one that is provided by government.

_____2. A private good is characterized by nonrival consumption.

_____3. An uncongested road is a common resource.

_____4. A fireworks display at a private amusement park is a public good.

_____5. The free-rider problem results when exclusion is not feasible.

_____6. The main weakness of national defense as an example of a public good is that defense is actually provided privately in a market economy through aerospace companies and other defense contractors.

_____7. Human life is priceless.

_____8. The socially optimal price for admission to our national parks is zero.

_____9. A private good is one that is always provided by the market.

_____10. A public good is one that doesn't cost anything to produce.

## B. Multiple-Choice Questions

1. Fire protection is an example of a:
   a. public good.
   b. private good.
   c. natural monopoly.
   d. common resource.
   e. public or private good depending on who provides it.

2. The whaling industry has driven some species of whales nearly to extinction. Cattle, however, continue to thrive on farms throughout the world. The major reason for this difference between cattle and whales is that:
   a. whales are a common resource and cattle are private property.
   b. whales are more valuable than cattle, and whalers are simply responding to economic incentives.
   c. the technology for harvesting whales has improved faster than is the case for cattle.
   d. whaling is an international industry but cattle are raised locally.
   e. whales have a longer gestation period than cattle.

3. There is more litter along highways than there is along private driveways because:
   a. driveways are shorter than highways.
   b. there is more traffic on highways.
   c. nobody cares about litter along highways.
   d. highways are a common resource.
   e. tax dollars are scarce.

4. National parks are:
   a. public goods.
   b. private goods.
   c. natural monopolies.
   d. common resources.
   e. none of the above.

5. Which of the following is the best example of the "Tragedy of the Commons"?
   a. an AIDS epidemic.
   b. overconsumption when McDonald's misjudges and underprices its basic hamburger.
   c. tomatoes in a community garden are picked before they are fully ripe.
   d. the failure of communism and the downfall of the Soviet Union.
   e. all of the above.

6. The main reason that public housing projects become run down is that:
   a. poor people are irresponsible.
   b. government is inefficient.
   c. taxpayers fail to vote for adequate funds for maintenance.
   d. they are common property, and nobody takes responsibility for them.
   e. none of the above.

7. Assigning exclusive whaling rights in the ocean would:
   a. encourage even more overharvesting of whales.
   b. discourage the overharvesting of whales.
   c. discourage overharvesting in the short run, but lead to even more intensive whaling in the long run.
   d  encourage overharvesting in the short run, but lead to more controlled whaling in the long run.
   e. have no effect on the level of whaling.

8. Public goods:
   a. cost nothing to produce.
   b. can be consumed by additional people without additional cost once they are produced.
   c. tend to be overconsumed from the standpoint of society.
   d. are overproduced by the market.
   e. all of the above.

9. Private firms are not likely to fund the socially optimal amount of basic research because basic research:
   a. has no payoff.
   b. yields benefits that cannot be measured in dollars.
   c. provides long-term but not short-term benefits.
   d. produces benefits to society as a whole, including those who do not pay for it.
   e. None of the above: When free, the market will provide the optimal amount of research.

10. Unlike the case with public goods, when someone consumes a common resource, he or she:
   a. engages in rival consumption.
   b. diminishes the benefits received by other consumers.
   c. tends to overconsume it from the standpoint of society.
   d. imposes a negative externality on others.
   e. all of the above.

11. What makes cable television a natural monopoly?
    a. Even though it is excludable, additional users do not diminish its enjoyment by others.
    b. By law each cable company has an exclusive franchise.
    c. There are no close substitutes for cable television.
    d. No one else is willing to compete with a successful cable company.
    e. None of the above.

12. A public good is
    a. subject to rival consumption.
    b. overproduced by the market.
    c. consumable by additional users without reducing the consumption by other users.
    d. excludable.
    e. all of the above.

13. A common resource has which of the following in common with a private good?
    a. rival consumption.
    b. excludability.
    c. efficient provision by the market.
    d. nonrival consumption.
    e. none of the above.

14. Both private goods and natural monopolies are:
    a. excludable.
    b. nonrival.
    c. produced efficiently by the market.
    d. consumable by additional users without making existing users worse off.
    e. all of the above.

15. The relationship between public goods and externalities is that:
    a. both always result in underproduction by the market.
    b. a public good is essentially a good with benefits that are mostly external.
    c. a public good imposes negative externalities on others.
    d. public goods do not involve externalities.
    e. none of the above.

## IV. Advanced Critical Thinking

1. According to the late Jacques Cousteau, "our goal for the environment should be total cleanup: We should not stop until all effluent should be drinkable and all smokestack gases should be breathable."

a.  Do you agree? If we had achieved 99.9% cleanup, would you agree that our goal should be to eliminate the final 0.1% pollution? Would it change your opinion if there were clear evidence that cleaning up the final 0.1% residual pollution would save 10 lives per year? What if the cost to society for the final 0.1% cleanup were $1 trillion? Write a critique of Cousteau's statement, explaining clearly why you agree or disagree. _____

_____

_____

_____

_____

_____

_____

b.  In what sense is the environment a common resource? Does this help to explain why achieving the optimal level of environmental cleanup tends to require government action? _____

_____

_____

_____

_____

_____

_____

2.  Irving Kristol, in a *Wall Street Journal* article entitled "The Hidden Cost of Regulation," wrote that environmental cleanup is an "economically unproductive expenditure" because it does not contribute to profit. Kristol argued that "cleaner water is a free 'social asset' to the population in the neighborhood." He also argued that environmental regulations "render . . . economic costs invisible." Write a critique of Kristol's statement, in the form of a Letter to the Editor, explaining clearly the ways in which you agree or disagree. Include a discussion of whether or not environmental cleanup is a "productive expenditure." Could it be productive for society overall but not for the individual firm? What is Kristol assuming about the property rights to the environment? In what sense is he right that regulation renders costs invisible? In what sense does environmental regulation have the opposite effect, making explicit some existing costs that had been invisible to polluters?

_____

_____

_____

_____

_____

_____

## V. Solutions

### Terms and Definitions

__3__ Excludability
__5__ Rivalness
__1__ Private goods
__7__ Public goods
__2__ Common resource
__6__ Natural monopoly
__8__ Free-rider problem
__9__ Cost-benefit analysis
__4__ Tragedy of the Commons

### Practice Problems

1. a. Commercial television signals: Nonrival because an additional viewer does not reduce the strength of the signal received by other viewers. Nonexcludable (with current equipment) because anyone with a tuner can receive the signal without paying. This makes it a public good even though it is provided privately.

   b. Congested city streets: Rival consumption because additional users impose costs on other drivers by increasing the congestion. Nonexcludable because it would be very difficult to charge tolls on city streets with virtually unlimited access. This is a common resource that tends to be overconsumed.

   c. A poem: Nonrival consumption because many people can enjoy the same poem at the same time. Nonexcludable because users can read the poem or even memorize it and enjoy it without paying for it. As such, it is a classic case of a public good.

   d. General medical research on the relationship between lifestyle and heart disease: Consumption is nonrival because the same research can benefit one or one billion people simultaneously. It is also nonexcludable because once knowledge is gained, it is virtually impossible to keep it away from people who do not pay for it. Basic research is a public good.

   e. A congested public swimming pool: This good is rival because of the crowding. More users clearly will detract from the benefits received by existing users. It is also excludable because it is very easy to admit only those who buy an admission ticket. It meets both criteria for a private good even though it is publicly provided.

f. An uncongested private swimming pool: This good is nonrival because it is not crowded. As long as it is not crowded, additional swimmers do not impose costs on other users. It is also excludable, not because it is privately owned, but because it is easy to require purchasing a ticket for admission. Therefore, it meets the requirements for a natural monopoly. The fact that it is privately owned is irrelevant.

2.

**Categories of Goods**

**RIVAL?**

| | YES | NO |
|---|---|---|
| **EXCLUDABLE?** | | |
| **YES** | TYPE: Private <br><br> EXAMPLE: sirloin steak <br><br> EXPLAIN: My consumption of a steak prevents you from consuming it, and those who do not pay can be excluded. (any similar example would work here.) | TYPE: Natural Monopoly <br><br> EXAMPLE: a nearly empty theater <br><br> EXPLAIN: Because it is not crowded, consumption is nonrival, yet exclusion is still possible (those who do not buy tickets are not admitted). |
| **NO** | TYPE: Common Resource <br><br> EXAMPLE: wild mushrooms <br><br> EXPLAIN: People who pick wild mushrooms tend to pick all that they can find, because they know that if they leave any to reseed, someone else will come along and pick them anyway. They would be more likely to do a controlled harvest if they could keep the mushroom patch | TYPE: Public Good <br><br> EXAMPLE: a song <br><br> EXPLAIN: A song can be enjoyed by additional people without taking away any enjoyment by others. It is also very difficult to exlude nonpayers from enjoying it, although copyright owners try to collect royalties from public use (an action that is not always successful). |

## Short-Answer Questions

1. Because wild game is a common resource, there is a tendency toward overhunting and overfishing. Even if everyone individually would like to cut back in order to maintain the population of game over time, this will not happen without collective action such as regulation. If individuals try to cut back voluntarily, someone else will kill the game. Without enforceable property rights, there is no incentive for rational people to conserve.

2. Traditionally, a lighthouse has been used as an example of a public good. Consumption is nonrival in the sense that the light is available for everyone simultaneously; additional users do not diminish the value received by others. Supposedly it is also very difficult to exclude those who refuse to pay. However, the claim of nonexclusion may be overstated: It is certainly possible for a lighthouse owner to contract with ship owners to turn on the light only when their ships are passing, while leaving the light off at other times to avoid free riders.

3. Food is a private good subject to rival consumption and easy exclusion of nonpayers. As such, food lends itself easily to efficient provision by the market. Highways, however, are nonrival, at least during uncongested periods, and exclusion is difficult for other than limited-access highways. Although there are some strong arguments for pricing roads to ration their usage during congested periods, it is still more challenging to price roads than to price food.

## True/False Questions

1. F; some public goods, like commercial television signals, are provided privately; the characteristics that make a good public or private are innate and not determined by outside institutional factors.
2. F; private goods are rival in consumption because one person's consumption takes away from another's.
3. F; an uncongested road is not a common resource because the consumption is not rival; rather, if exclusion is not practical, it is a public good (until it becomes crowded).
4. T
5. T
6. F; this is irrelevant: nonrivalness and nonexclusion make national defense a public good, which would be true even if an aerospace firm ran the military as a private company.
7. F; at least in an economic sense, we do not put an infinite value on life; we take risks with human life every day in a variety of ways.
8. F; at a zero price, our national parks would be hopelessly overcrowded, indicating that the price is too low for equilibrium. Price serves to ration scarce resources efficiently, including space in our national parks.

9. F; private goods sometimes are provided by government (surplus food, for example); some goods are private because of their innate characteristics of rivalness and excludability.
10. F; public goods are not free; producing them means giving up something else.

## Multiple-Choice Questions

| | | |
|---|---|---|
| 1. c | 6. d | 11. a |
| 2. a | 7. b | 12. c |
| 3. d | 8. b | 13. a |
| 4. d | 9. d | 14. a |
| 5. c | 10. e | 15. b |

## Advanced Critical Thinking

1.  a.  Although the goal is noble, it is impractical and would actually make society worse off. Even without factories, cars, furnaces, or even campfires, human beings themselves cannot even meet the standard of zero effluent. Zero tolerance on the environment would mean cleaning up every vestige of pollution, even if the residual pollution were trivial, yet would cost billions of dollars to correct. Even if we had the technology, we would make our society worse off by cleaning up pollution beyond the point at which the last dollar spent provided a dollar's worth of benefit to society. Even when lives are involved, we need to weigh costs and benefits. Suppose that society could eliminate the residual pollution and save 10 lives/year at a social cost of $1 trillion per year. We could save more lives each year by reallocating that $1 trillion to other lifesaving activities, such as making our highways safer or in medical research. The $1 trillion has to come from somewhere; nothing is free. If the alternative is other lifesaving activities, then spending the $1 trillion on the environment may actually cost lives!

    b.  Unless property rights to the environment are established, clean air and water are owned by nobody, and, therefore, they tend to be treated as free goods. If the marginal cost of using the environment is zero to the individual, then in the absence of restrictions, he or she will use it as long as an additional unit has any positive marginal benefit. Although rational for the individual, it is overconsumption from the standpoint of society.

2.  Kristol makes a valid point that environmental cleanup is not free; it takes resources away from other uses. To call it unproductive, however, suggests that it has no value. He glosses over the distinction between private and public benefits. Certainly, a clean environment has benefits to society, even if cleanup does not add to profit. The fact that pollution is a negative externality is, of course, the rationale for government intervention: The individual polluter does not consider the social good in making a decision about environmental cleanup. Kristol argues that

regulation hides some costs to society in the sense that, unless forced to do so by law, regulators will not measure the costs of their regulations to business and society as a whole. However, the purpose of environmental policy is to make explicit some costs that polluters traditionally ignored because they were able to shift those costs to others. When regulators internalize negative externalities, they actually make visible to the polluter some costs that had been invisible. Kristol apparently treats the property rights to the environment as "first come first serve." Otherwise, it makes no sense to state that when a polluter cleans up after itself, it is providing a "free social asset" to the community. Only if you accept the argument that the polluter owns the environment does it follow that restoring it to its original state is somehow a gift to the victims of pollution.

# Chapter 12: The Design of the Tax System

## I. Chapter Overview

### A. Context and Purpose

In the last two chapters, we looked at the role of government in correcting the problems caused by externalities and public goods in a market economy. The emphasis was on government expenditures, with little consideration of how the government generates the revenues to pay for those spending programs.

This chapter concludes the three-chapter sequence on the role of government by analyzing the characteristics and economic impact of the U.S. tax system. The chapter explores the efficiency cost or deadweight loss from taxes, the incidence of taxes (who actually bears the burden), and the equity effects of taxation.

### B. Learning Objectives

In this chapter you will:

1. Get an overview of how the U.S. government raises and spends money.
2. Examine the efficiency costs of taxes.
3. Learn alternative ways to judge the equity of the tax system.
4. Learn why studying tax incidence is crucial for evaluating tax equity.
5. Consider the tradeoff between efficiency and equity in the design of a tax system.

After accomplishing these goals, you should be able to:

1. Identify the major sources of revenue for governments at the federal, state, and local levels in the U.S.
2. List and explain the various costs of taxes, including the deadweight loss that results when taxes distort behavior.
3. Define and give examples of the benefits and ability-to-pay principles of tax equity.
4. Explain and give examples of the ways in which the market may shift taxes away from statutory or legal taxpayers, resulting in a final burden or tax incidence that may differ greatly from that intended by law.
5. Explain the equity-efficiency tradeoff as it applies to tax policy: It is very difficult to design taxes that promote either economic efficiency or equity without having a negative impact on the other goal.

## C. Chapter Review

### 12-1 A Financial Overview of the U.S. Government

The U.S. has a system of fiscal federalism in which federal, state, and local governments collectively comprise "the government". Roughly two-thirds of the taxes collected, along with the programs that they fund, are by the federal government.

The federal government relies primarily on the individual income tax, followed closely by payroll taxes. A distant third as a source of federal revenue is the corporation income tax. These revenues are used to fund, in order of greatest expenditure, Social Security, national defense, welfare, interest on the national debt, Medicare, health, and other expenditures.

State and local governments together rely primarily on sales taxes, followed closely by property taxes, and then federal funding as revenue sources. Individual income taxes rank fourth, with corporate income taxes a distant fifth.

### 12-2 Taxes and Efficiency

Government uses taxes to free resources for public use. Inevitably, they reduce private purchasing power. However, taxes also impose efficiency costs on the economy in the form of deadweight losses when they (1) alter people's behavior and (2) impose administrative and compliance costs.

Taxes alter behavior. If a tax discourages someone from buying a good or service, then, for that taxpayer, there is no revenue generated. Even so, there is a cost because that person was prevented from selecting his or her first choice because of the existence of a tax. The deadweight loss results because there is a loss for one person without a corresponding gain for anyone else.

Taxes also impose administrative and compliance burdens. They are not costless to administer. Like the deadweight loss, the administrative cost is an efficiency loss because there is a cost to one person without an offsetting gain to someone else. The time that you spend filling out your tax forms benefits nobody.

Although we can imagine hypothetical taxes that cause no deadweight loss to society, all real-world taxes impose efficiency losses on the economy. Taxes that reduce inefficiency often violate society's standards of equity. A lump-sum tax would avoid the distortion of individuals' behavior because it would be unavoidable, but it would be unacceptable on equity grounds. It would require the billionaire and the homeless person to pay the same number of dollars in taxes. On equity grounds, the individual income tax is more acceptable to most people, even though there may be a deadweight loss when a high marginal tax rate (the rate on the last dollar earned) discourages work effort. This efficiency loss is especially pronounced under the progressive tax rates that many people support on ability-to-pay grounds.

## 12-3 Taxes and Equity

If efficiency were the only consideration, tax policy would be much easier to implement. However, tax equity is also a major criterion for evaluating tax proposals. Unfortunately, equity is difficult to assess because fairness is very subjective. One way to determine the fairness of a tax is through the *benefits principle*: Taxes should be assessed according to the benefits that people receive from the government programs that these taxes finance. Unfortunately, most taxes go into general revenue funds and cannot be easily linked to the benefits received. An alternative is the *ability-to-pay principle*: Taxes should be assessed according to taxpayers' financial capability. The goal is both vertical and horizontal equity. *Vertical equity* means that taxpayers with more ability to pay should pay more taxes. *Horizontal equity* means that taxpayers with the same ability to pay should pay the same taxes. Taxes can be either *proportional* (all taxpayers pay the same percent of income), *progressive* (the rich pay a higher percent), or *regressive* (the rich pay a lower percent).

To determine tax equity, it is necessary first to determine the actual tax incidence—who actually pays the taxes. For example, many people argue for increasing the tax rate on rich corporations without analyzing who actually pays corporate taxes. People ultimately pay corporate taxes: either consumers, through higher prices, or employees, through lower wages, or stockholders, through lower profits (and therefore dividends).

## 12-4 Conclusion: The Tradeoff between Equity and Efficiency

The tradeoff between equity and efficiency is one of the biggest issues in economics, so it should not be surprising to find that this tradeoff is a major obstacle to reaching consensus on proper tax policy. Alan Blinder, formerly of the President's Council of Economic Advisers, wrote a book entitled *Hard Heads, Soft Hearts, Tough-Minded Economics for a Just Society*, with a major theme that we need government policies that promote both efficiency (hard-headedness) and equity (soft-heartedness). We cannot eliminate the conflict between efficiency and equity, but we can consider both criteria in our planning. Nowhere is that more true than in tax policymaking.

## D. Helpful Hints

1. *Taxes are designed to transfer real resources—land, labor, and capital—from the private to the public sectors.* If you are skeptical, keep in mind that government has printing presses and could always print more money to pay for its spending. The problem is that printing money would not make scarcity go away. Printing money is essentially another way to tax people to pay for government expenditures. Everything has an opportunity cost. If we want more public roads or schools or bombers, we must be willing to give up something else to get them. Taxes are simply a way to reduce private spending when public spending goes up.

2. *If you want more of something, subsidize it. If you want less of something, tax it.* Taxes distort behavior by increasing the opportunity cost of doing whatever is taxed. Sometimes this is desirable, for example, when we raise cigarette taxes to discourage smoking. Other times, taxes discourage behavior that is desirable. For example, payroll taxes like Social Security are essentially taxes on employment. As such, they introduce a wedge between the wage paid and the wage received (after taxes), resulting in fewer people working.

3. *People pay taxes.* This may seem obvious, but often we hear arguments for taxing rich corporations. Corporations are neither rich nor poor, rather, they are merely conduits through which money flows from people to other people. Corporate taxes are paid by people—owners, customers, and/or employees. The actual mix, or tax incidence, is determined by the elasticities of supply and demand in the relevant markets for the corporation's products, labor, and capital.

## E. Terms and Definitions

Choose a definition for each key term.

Key terms:

_____Average tax rate
_____Marginal tax rate
_____Budget deficit
_____Budget surplus
_____Lump-sum tax
_____Benefits principle
_____Ability-to-pay principle
_____Vertical equity
_____Horizontal equity
_____Proportional tax
_____Regressive tax
_____Progressive tax

Definitions:

1. The principle of tax equity stating that a fair tax is one that taxes people according to their income or other measure of financial capability to handle the burden of taxation.
2. An extension of the ability-to-pay principle stating that those with the same financial capabilities should pay the same in taxes—equal treatment of equals.
3. Additional tax paid as a percent of additional income.
4. Total tax paid as a percent of income.
5. The principle of tax equity stating that a fair tax is one that taxes people according to the benefits that they receive from the resulting government programs.

6. A tax under which higher-income taxpayers pay a higher fraction of their incomes in taxes; the tax rate rises as income rises.

7. A shortfall that results whenever government spending exceeds government revenues.

8. An excess of revenues over expenditures when government spends less than it takes in.

9. A tax under which taxpayers in lower-income brackets pay a higher fraction of income in taxes; the tax rate falls as income rises.

10. A tax under which taxpayers in all income brackets pay the same fraction of income in taxes; the tax rate stays the same as income rises.

11. A tax that is the same absolute amount for everyone, regardless of income, and therefore does not distort behavior.

12. An extension of the ability-to-pay principle stating that those with a greater financial capability should pay more in taxes than those with lesser financial capabilities—unequal treatment of unequals.

## II. Problems and Short-Answer Questions

### A. Practice Problems

1. The table below presents a case study of taxable consumption by income bracket for taxpayers in a hypothetical state with a 5% sales tax.

   a. Fill in the blanks in the table below.

### Tax Paid and Effective Tax Rate under a 5% State Sales Tax

| Income | Taxable Consumption | Tax Paid | Average Tax Rate (% of income) |
|--------|---------------------|----------|-------------------------------|
| $10,000 | $10,000 | $_____ | _____ |
| $20,000 | $18,000 | $_____ | _____ |
| $30,000 | $26,000 | $_____ | _____ |
| $40,000 | $34,000 | $_____ | _____ |
| $50,000 | $42,000 | $_____ | _____ |

b. Is the tax regressive, progressive, or proportional? Why? Is your answer consistent with its nature as a flat-rate tax at 5%? Explain.

_____

_____

_____

_____

_____

_____

_____

c. Do you think that the numbers and your answer to part (b) would change if the state exempted certain basic necessities like food and clothing? Explain.

_____

_____

_____

d. Is a consumption tax, such as the sales tax, likely to be more or less efficient than an income tax with a comparable yield? Would exempting food and clothing make the sales tax more or less efficient? Explain.

_____

_____

_____

_____

_____

_____

## B. Short-Answer Questions

1. Lump-sum taxes are sometimes promoted as superior to other forms of taxation, yet they are rarely included in real-world tax structures.

   a. What are lump-sum taxes and what are their advantages over traditional taxes? Explain. _____

   _____

   _____

   _____

   _____

   b. What characteristics of lump-sum taxes keep them from becoming more commonly used? _____

   _____

   _____

   _____

_____
_____
_____

2. The benefits principle seems much more objective as a measure of equity than the ability-to-pay principle. In spite of this, the benefits principle is not used very often to justify a tax proposal. Why isn't it used more often? (Why is it easier to justify most taxes on ability-to-pay grounds?) _____

_____
_____
_____

3. Congress has built many incentives into the tax code to encourage certain types of behavior, such as deductions for charitable giving and home mortgage interest. Even if these expenditures are socially desirable on efficiency grounds (as either public goods or positive externalities), can you think of any ways that they might interfere with the achievement of equity? _____

_____
_____
_____
_____
_____
_____

## III. Self-Test

### A. True/False Questions

_____1.  The average tax rate is the most important factor in how much a particular tax will distort behavior.

_____2.  A lump-sum tax would be more efficient than our current tax system.

_____3.  The biggest source of revenue at the state and local level is the individual income tax.

_____4.  Horizontal equity means that everyone should pay the same dollar amount of taxes regardless of income.

_____5.  A tax that collects more dollars from a rich person than a poor person is known as a progressive tax.

_____6.  A marginal tax rate is the actual taxes paid divided by income.

_____7.  Deadweight losses are tax revenues used to fund government programs that are not worth the cost to society.

_____8.  Overall, the U.S. federal tax system is progressive.

_____9.  Replacing the income tax with a consumption tax would encourage saving.

_____10. A regressive tax takes a smaller fraction of income from a rich person than from a poor person.

_____11. The marginal tax rate is more important than the average tax rate in causing deadweight losses from taxation.

_____12. The Social Security tax is proportional.

_____13. If the federal government enacts a 20% increase in income tax rates, the most likely result will be a 20% increase in income tax revenues.

_____14. If consumption rises more slowly than income, a 5% sales tax is likely to be proportional.

_____15. A federal budget deficit means that federal spending exceeds federal tax revenues.

## B. Multiple-Choice Questions

1. A progressive tax collects:
   a. more dollars from a rich person than a poor person.
   b. a higher percentage of income from a rich person than a poor person.
   c. revenues according to benefits received from government programs.
   d. revenues used only for politically correct programs.
   e. none of the above.

2. Deadweight losses result because of the:
   a. distortion of behavior caused by taxes.
   b. inevitable inefficiency caused by all government programs.
   c. inherent reduction in standard of living caused by the payment of taxes.
   d. inequities caused by taxes.
   e. all of the above.

3. The best example of a tax justified under the benefits principle is:
   a. a gasoline tax used to pay for highways.
   b. a sales tax used to build a sports arena.
   c. a state lottery tax used for higher education.
   d. an income tax used for defense spending.
   e. all of the above.

4. The biggest share of total federal taxes paid in the U.S. is by the _____ quintile in terms of personal income.
   a. lowest
   b. second
   c. third
   d. fourth
   e. highest

5. The marriage tax refers to the fact that:
   a. most states charge for marriage licenses.
   b. some couples find that their combined income tax burden rises after they marry.
   c. as inflation drives up incomes and prices, married couples = taxes also rise.
   d. there are costs associated with marriage.
   e. all of the above.

6. Replacing the income tax with a flat-rate consumption tax would:
   a. encourage more saving.
   b. make the tax system less progressive.
   c. mean that two families with the same income would not necessarily have the same tax bill.
   d. increase the after-tax interest rate received on bank accounts.
   e. all of the above.

7. Simplifying the individual income tax code would:
   a. reduce the administrative and compliance costs of the tax.
   b. lower the tax revenues generated.
   c. make it more progressive.
   d. increase equity according to the benefits principle.
   e. increase the vertical equity of the tax system.

Use the following information to answer Questions 8-10. The state legislature is considering a new tax that will collect $100 from families with incomes of $10,000, $150 from families with incomes of $50,000, and $200 from families with incomes of $100,000.

8. The tax rate on families earning $10,000 is:
   a. $100
   b. 0.1%
   c. 1.0%
   d. 10%
   e. none of the above.

9. The tax rate on families earning $100,000 is:
   a. $200
   b. 0.2%
   c. 2.0%
   d. 20%
   e. none of the above.

10. The new tax would be:
    a. proportional.
    b. regressive.
    c. progressive.
    d. horizontally inequitable.
    e. none of the above.

11. The entire burden or the incidence of the corporate income tax is certainly on:
    a. consumers.
    b. owners.
    c. workers.
    d. the company itself.
    e. people.

12. Of the following, the most basic tradeoff in economics is between:
    a. efficiency and equity.
    b. vertical and horizontal equity.
    c. business taxes and individual taxes.
    d. the benefits and ability-to-pay principles.
    e. the needs of the many vs. the desires of the few.

13. The biggest source of revenue for the federal government is
    a. social insurance taxes.
    b. corporate income taxes.
    c. excise taxes.
    d. individual income taxes.
    e. other taxes.

14. The biggest category of spending by the federal government is:
    a. Social Security.
    b. national defense.
    c. welfare.
    d. net interest on the national debt.
    e. health.

15. The biggest single source of revenue for state and local governments is:
    a. property taxes.
    b. individual income taxes.
    c. corporate income taxes.
    d. federal government aid.
    e. sales taxes.

16. The largest budget item for state and local governments is:
   a. highways.
   b. public welfare.
   c. education.
   d. criminal justice.
   e. health care.

17. The most efficient tax is the:
   a. lump-sum tax.
   b. individual income tax.
   c. corporate income tax.
   d. consumption tax.
   e. property tax.

18. The best example of a tax usually justified on ability-to-pay grounds is the:
   a. sales tax.
   b. property tax.
   c. payroll tax.
   d. corporate income tax.
   e. progressive income tax.

19. Which of the following features of the tax code cause changes in individuals = behavior?
   a. The federal government taxes alcoholic beverages.
   b. Charitable contributions are deductible under the federal income tax.
   c. Interest paid on home mortgages is deductible, but interest paid on car loans is not.
   d Individual income tax rates are higher for some married couples than for unmarried couples with the same incomes.
   e. all of the above.

20. An efficient tax is one that:
   a. raises large amounts of money quickly.
   b. generates revenues at the least cost to the taxpayers.
   c. satisfies both vertical and horizontal equity.
   d. is easy to administer.
   e. imposes no costs on the taxpayer.

## IV. Advanced Critical Thinking

Before World War II, the corporate income tax was the second largest revenue source for the federal government, behind only the individual income tax. In recent decades it has fallen in importance to a distant third behind federal payroll taxes. In spite of the movement away from this tax, the general public continues to support the corporate income tax under the belief that rich corporations should pay their share of the tax burden. On the other hand, some critics argue that the corporate income tax could be integrated into the individual income tax by eliminating the corporate tax and raising individual income tax rates to make up for the lost tax revenue. They argue that equity and efficiency could be improved and the tax system streamlined by combining both income taxes into a single individual income tax.

What do you think? Would corporations get away without paying their fair share of taxes if the two income taxes were combined? Who really pays business taxes? The corporations themselves? Write a critique of the corporate income tax, addressing the issues raised by both the critics and the supporters. Be sure to include the following issues: vertical and/or horizontal equity, administrative costs, and deadweight losses. Conclude with a summary evaluation of the prospects for integrating the corporate and individual income taxes. _____

_____

_____

## V. Solutions

### Terms and Definitions

__4____Average tax rate
__3____Marginal tax rate
__7____Budget deficit
__8____Budget surplus
__11___Lump-sum tax
__5____Benefits principle
__1____Ability-to-pay principle
__2 ___Vertical equity
__12___Horizontal equity
__10___Proportional tax
__9____Regressive tax
__6____Progressive tax

## Practice Problems

1. a. Tax Paid and Effective Tax Rate under a 5% State Sales Tax

| Income | Taxable consumption | Tax paid | Average tax rate (% of income) |
|--------|--------------------|-----------| -------------------------------|
| $10,000 | $10,000 | $ 500 | 5.0% |
| $20,000 | $18,000 | $ 900 | 4.5% |
| $30,000 | $26,000 | $1300 | 4.33% |
| $40,000 | $34,000 | $1700 | 4.25% |
| $50,000 | $42,000 | $2100 | 4.2% |

   b. The tax is regressive: The average tax rate falls from 5% to 4.2% as income rises from $10,000 to $50,000. This occurs because consumption rises at a slower rate than income. Taxpayers earning only $10,000 spend their entire incomes and therefore pay the 5% sales tax on their whole incomes. Taxpayers earning $50,000 spend only 84% of it, so the 5% tax is on only a part of their incomes, making the effective rate on income less than 5%. Note that 84% of 5% is 4.2%, which is the average sales tax for those earning $50,000.

   c. Exempting necessities would reduce taxes for all taxpayers, but the biggest percentage reduction would be for lower-income taxpayers, who spend proportionately more on such goods. This would make the tax less regressive, although it would be unlikely to eliminate regressivity completely.

   d. Consumption taxes tend to be more efficient than income taxes in the sense that they do not discourage saving by taxing interest received. The income tax introduces a tax wedge between suppliers and demanders of saving. A consumption tax avoids this source of inefficiency, and resulting deadweight loss when the interest received by savers is less than the interest paid by banks because of taxes on interest. However, exempting food and clothing to improve equity introduces a new source of inefficiency by distorting consumer behavior away from taxable and toward nontaxable consumption.

## Short-Answer Questions

1. a. A lump-sum tax is one that requires everyone to pay the same number of dollars in taxes regardless of their economic status or behavior. By their nature, lump-sum taxes do not distort behavior because there is no behavior change that can alter them; therefore, they are a model of efficiency. The cost to the taxpayer is the tax itself, without any deadweight loss.

b.  In spite of their efficiency advantages, lump-sum taxes have a major drawback in terms of equity. Because everyone pays exactly the same amount, the tax is highly regressive. The millionaire pays exactly the same number of dollars in taxes as the homeless person. Few people would accept this on vertical equity grounds. In fact, it is not even possible for a person at the subsistence level to pay taxes without starving.

2.  In general, it is difficult to link most taxes to the benefits of the government programs that they fund. In most cases, tax revenues go directly into general revenues to fund programs in general. The income tax, for example, can be defended based on ability-to-pay but would be hard to link to specific programs and their beneficiaries. Only in a few cases, such as the gasoline tax used to build and maintain highways, can beneficiaries be identified closely enough to use the benefits principle.

3.  Such tax breaks can interfere with both vertical and horizontal equity. Because higher-income taxpayers are more likely to give to charity and to own homes, this tax break will tend to reduce the tax burden more for them, reducing the progressivity of the income tax. It also means that two taxpayers with identical incomes (ability-to-pay) may have different tax bills if one gives more to charity or owns a home with a mortgage when the other is paying rent. This violates the criterion of horizontal equity.

**True/False Questions**

1.  F; the marginal tax rate has the primary effect on behavior because people make decisions at the margin.
2.  T
3.  F; it is the sales tax.
4.  F; it means that people with equal incomes should pay the same taxes.
5.  F; only if the rich person pays a higher tax *rate* (not just more dollars) is it progressive.
6.  F; marginal tax rate is *additional* dollars as a percent of *additional* income.
7.  F; deadweight losses are costs of taxation in addition to the actual taxes paid; they are caused by changes in taxpayer behavior.
8.  T
9.  T
10. T
11. T
12. F; the rate drops abruptly above a certain income level, which varies annually to keep up with inflation.
13. F; the only way that tax revenues would go up by the same amount as tax rates would be if there were no change in behavior as a result of the tax hike; for example, if the supply of labor were perfectly inelastic and work effort were unchanged.

14. F; when consumption rises more slowly than income, a flat-rate tax on consumption is regressive relative to income.
15. T

## Multiple-Choice Questions

| | | |
|---|---|---|
| 1. b | 8. c | 15. e |
| 2. a | 9. b | 16. c |
| 3. a | 10. b | 17. a |
| 4. e | 11. e | 18. e |
| 5. b | 12. a | 19. e |
| 6. e | 13. d | 20. b |
| 7. a | 14. a | |

## Advanced Critical Thinking

The corporate income tax is an inefficient way to raise revenue for the federal government. As the revenues decline, the administrative costs for the government and the taxpayers continue. In some cases, the administrative cost to the taxpayers is actually greater than the tax payment itself. This is not efficient. Integrating the corporate tax into the individual income tax with the same revenue yield would eliminate an entire layer of bureaucracy and administrative cost. Generating the same revenue from the individual income tax would reduce the distortion caused by taxing some businesses (corporations), but not others. This additional taxation of corporations distorts their behavior. Eliminating the corporate tax would end a distortion of behavior caused by treating incorporated and unincorporated businesses differently. On equity grounds, the corporate income tax is ambiguous, mainly because we cannot agree entirely on who pays it. We do know, however, that it is not rich corporations that pay the tax. Corporations are neither rich nor poor. Only people pay taxes. When a corporation is taxed, the tax may be shifted to consumers in the form of higher prices, or workers in the form of lower wages, or owners (stockholders) in the form of lower profits leading to lower dividends and lower value of their shares of stock. Under the individual income tax, the degree of progressivity is controlled by society in setting tax rates. Under the corporate tax, the market controls tax incidence, which makes it harder for policymakers to achieve vertical and horizontal equity goals.

# Chapter 13: The Costs of Production

## I. Chapter Overview

### A. Context and Purpose

Earlier chapters introduced the workings of the market system (Chapters 1-7), then explored the role of government in improving efficiency when the market is less than perfect. We now return to the analysis of the market system, examining business structure and operation in the next five chapters (13-17).

This chapter looks at the firm's cost of production, revenue and profit, and distinguishes economic cost and profit from traditional accounting cost and profit. We will see that cost and profit take on very specific meanings in economics that differ from the everyday use of the terms. The analysis in this chapter will provide the tools necessary to understand how all firms, from the largest to the smallest, behave under different types of market conditions.

### B. Learning Objectives

In this chapter you will:

1. Examine what items are included in a firm's cost of production
2. Analyze the link between a firm's production process and its total cost.
3. Learn the meaning of average total cost and marginal cost and how they are related.
4. Consider the shape of a typical firm's cost curves.
5. Examine the relationship between short-run and long-run costs.

After accomplishing these goals, you should be able to:

1. Calculate economic cost by adding implicit opportunity costs to the explicit costs that make up accounting cost and compare and contrast economic and accounting profit.
2. Explain why the marginal product of an additional worker declines as more workers are hired and relate this diminishing marginal product to the increasingly steep total-cost curve.
3. Use total cost to derive both marginal and average cost, then differentiate between the two and explain how marginal cost affects average cost.
4. Identify the relationships between marginal cost, average total cost, average variable cost, and average fixed cost.
5. Explain why fixed cost disappears in the long run, identify the effect on the long-run costs curves of all costs being variable, and distinguish diminishing marginal product (short run) from decreasing returns to scale (long run).

## C. Chapter Review

### 13-1 What Are Costs?

The firm's goal is to maximize profit. This is simply the total revenue that it receives from selling its product minus the total cost of producing that product:

$$\text{Profit} = \text{Total Revenue minus Total Cost}$$

where

$$\text{Total Revenue} = \text{Price x Quantity sold}$$

As you can see, total revenue is pretty straightforward, but total cost can be a bit tricky. To an economist, cost means opportunity cost. It includes the explicit costs or money outlays that comprise accounting costs, of course, but it also includes implicit costs whenever resources that could have been used elsewhere are used by the firm. A small business that shows an accounting profit actually may be losing money in an economic sense, if we deduct all of the implicit costs of resources that the owner ties up in the firm rather than using elsewhere. The owner's labor, for example, is a real cost of operating the business even if there is no actual salary paid. The cost is the lost earnings from giving up the opportunity to work for someone else rather than the owner's actual salary from his or her own business. Similarly, the lost interest income on money the owner invests in the business is a real cost of doing business even though it is not an accounting cost. Specifically, consider the following relationships:

$$\text{Economic Cost} = \text{Accounting Cost} + \text{Implicit Cost} = \text{Total Opportunity Cost}$$
$$\text{Accounting Cost} = \text{Explicit Cost}$$
$$\text{Economic Profit} = \text{Total Revenue minus Total Economic Cost}$$
$$\text{Accounting Profit} = \text{Total Revenue minus Total Accounting Cost}$$

### 13-2 Production and Costs

The production function shows the relationship between inputs and outputs. In the short run, this means looking at the relationship between the amount of labor used and the amount of output because we define the short run as a time period too short to allow increases in other inputs.

Adding additional labor increases output, although at some point additional workers are subject to *diminishing marginal product*, which means that the last unit of labor hired adds less to total output than did the previous one. Diminishing marginal product occurs when workers are added without additional capital and land. In the long run, expansion need not result in diminishing marginal product because land, labor, and capital can be increased simultaneously.

As marginal product diminishes, the firm's total cost begins to rise at a more rapid rate because additional units of output cost more to produce (the same wage per worker results in less additional output, so the cost per additional unit produced rises).

## 13-3  The Various Measures of Cost

If total cost is known for the various levels of output, it is possible to calculate all other measures of cost.  The relationships between the cost measures are as follows:

$$\text{Total Cost (TC)} = \text{Fixed Cost (FC)} + \text{Variable Cost (VC)}$$

$$\text{Average Fixed Cost (AFC)} = FC/Q$$

$$\text{Average Variable Cost (AVC)} = VC/Q$$

$$\text{Average Total Cost (ATC)} = \text{Total Cost (TC)/Quantity of Output (Q)};$$

also,

$$ATC = AFC + AVC$$

$$\text{Marginal Cost (MC)} = \Delta TC/\Delta Q = \Delta VC/\Delta Q$$

where $\Delta$ = "change in."

Marginal cost (MC)  rises with output as soon as the point of diminishing marginal product is reached.  However, the Average = total = cost (ATC) curve is U-shaped. It declines initially because of the dominance of average fixed cost (AFC), which always declines as the fixed cost is spread over more units of output.  Eventually, however, the rising MC curve  intersects the ATC curve at minimum ATC and ATC begins to rise.

## 13-4  Costs in the Short Run and in the Long Run

Because we define the long run as the time period long enough to vary capital and all other  inputs, all costs become variable in the long run.  As a result, diminishing marginal product is no longer a problem.  There are no fixed inputs.  Given enough time, firms can vary their scale of operation by acquiring more land and building additional factories in addition to hiring more labor  (or they can cut back on their use of all inputs). This eliminates a major reason for the U-shaped ATC curve: the existence of fixed inputs. As a result, the long-run ATC curve is likely to be flatter than the short-run curve.  To the extent that it is still U-shaped, the decreasing part of the curve is an area of *economies of scale*, in which increasing all inputs actually lowers ATC.  The increasing part of the curve exhibits *diseconomies of scale*, a range in which increasing all inputs raises the average total cost.  If there is a horizontal range, this is the area of *constant returns to scale*, in which increasing all inputs causes a proportionate increase in output, keeping ATC constant.

## D. Helpful Hints

1.  *The distinction between short run and long run in economics is somewhat arbitrary.*
    We define short run as a period in which some inputs (typically capital and land) are
    fixed while at least one (typically labor) is variable, and the long run as a period
    long enough to vary all inputs or even enter or exit the industry. Although arbitrary,
    it makes a lot of sense: A firm desiring to increase output quickly could expand
    labor immediately, but it would take a while to build a new factory.

2.  *Diminishing marginal product is the rule, not the exception.* As long as only labor
    can vary, it shouldn't be surprising that output will not rise in proportion with labor
    input. Imagine growing strawberries in your backyard in a plot that is only 20x10
    feet. You might be able to pick 3 pints of strawberries in 15 minutes. However,
    additional workers in the same small plot could not be expected to maintain that
    level of output per worker. Eventually, the marginal product of an additional
    worker will fall because land and capital are fixed. With enough workers, the
    marginal product actually becomes negative when the patch is so crowded that
    people are getting in each others' way and trampling the berries.

3.  *Diminishing marginal product is not the same thing as negative marginal product.*
    In everyday language people often confuse the two concepts. In the strawberry
    patch, diminishing marginal product is not bad—even if all workers are identical,
    we shouldn't expect each worker to add the same amount to output—but negative
    marginal product means that another picker actually reduces total product and
    should not be hired (or even allowed to help for free!).

4.  *Marginal cost always intersects average total cost and average variable costs at
    their lowest points.* The marginal value contributes to the average, so if marginal is
    less than average, it pulls the average down, and if marginal is greater than average,
    it pulls the average up. Think about what happens to the overall GPA (grade point
    average) of the class when another student adds the course. The marginal GPA of
    the additional student either raises or lowers the average. Overall GPA for the class
    falls as long as the marginal GPAs are below the average, and rises when the
    marginal GPAs exceed the average.

## E. Terms and Definitions

Choose a definition for each key term.

Key terms:

_____Total revenue
_____Total cost
_____Profit

_____Production function
_____Marginal product
_____Diminishing marginal product
_____Fixed cost
_____Variable cost
_____Average total cost
_____Average fixed cost
_____Average variable cost
_____Marginal cost
_____Efficient scale
_____Economies of scale
_____Diseconomies of scale
_____Constant returns to scale

Definitions:

1. Amount that the firm pays to buy its inputs.
2. Amount the firm receives for the sale of its product.
3. Variable cost divided by quantity of output.
4. Range in which long-run average total cost does not vary with output.
5. Total revenue minus total cost.
6. Relationship between quantity of inputs and quantity of output.
7. *Change* in total cost for a given *change* in output.
8. Range of increasing long-run average total cost as output rises.
9. Costs that do not vary with the level of output.
10. Additional output that results from an additional unit of an input.
11. A decline in the *addition* to total output that results from an additional unit of a variable input.
12. The level of output that minimizes short-run average total cost.
13. Costs that vary with the level of output.
14. Range of declining long-run average total cost as output rises.
15. Total cost divided by quantity of output.
16. Fixed cost divided by quantity of output.

## II. Problems and Short-Answer Questions

### A. Practice Problems

1. Wendell's Widget Works (WWW) faces the following cost schedule :

| Quantity (Q) | Fixed Cost (FC) | Variable Cost (VC) | Total Cost (TC) | Marginal Cost (MC) | Average Variable Cost (AVC) | Average Fixed Cost (AFC) | Average Total Cost (ATC) |
|---|---|---|---|---|---|---|---|
| 0 | $46 | $ 0 | | | | | |
| 1 | | 30 | | | | | |
| 2 | | 50 | | | | | |
| 3 | | 58 | | | | | |
| 4 | | 64 | | | | | |
| 5 | | 84 | | | | | |
| 6 | | 114 | | | | | |
| 7 | | 150 | | | | | |
| 8 | | 190 | | | | | |
| 9 | | 240 | | | | | |

## Wendell's Widgets

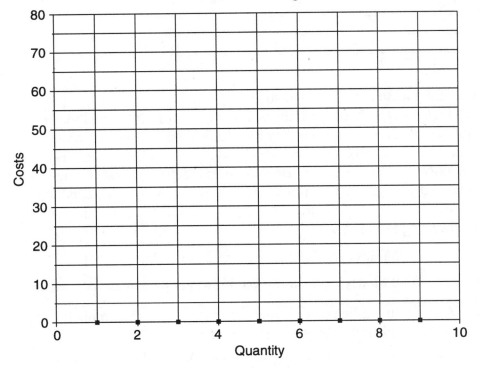

a. Fill in the table and graph the results.

b. From these cost curves, can you tell where diminishing marginal product sets in? Explain._____
_____
_____
_____

c. What is the relationship between <u>TC</u>, <u>VC</u>, and <u>FC</u>? Explain.
_____
_____

d. What is the relationship between <u>ATC</u>, <u>AVC</u>, and AFC? Explain.
_____
_____
_____

e. What is the relationship between <u>ATC</u> and <u>MC</u>? Between AVC and <u>MC</u>? Explain. _____
_____
_____

f.  What is Wendell's efficient scale? Explain. _____

_____

_____

_____

2.  Bob's Burger Box has been operating continuously since 1962. The original
investment was $100,000, but the business is worth a lot more today. In fact, Bob's
chief competitor would like to buy him out and has made a standing offer of $1
million any time that Bob wants to sell. He is also willing to hire Bob for
$50,000/year if Bob sells out. Bob has been tempted because he figures that he
could earn 10% on the $1 million if he invests it wisely. You need to help him
decide. Currently, Bob figures that he is earning a profit of $100,000/year based on
the following information:

Total Revenue: $200,000 (from 100,000 hamburgers @$2.00)

Total Money Outlays: $100,000 (wages paid, materials, utilities)

a.  What are his explicit (accounting) costs? What are his implicit costs? What is
his total economic (opportunity) cost? Explain. _____

_____

_____

b.  If his goal is to maximize profit, should he stay in business or sell out? Is he
earning any money? Would an accountant and an economist give the same
answer to the question about how much he is earning? Explain.

_____

_____

_____

_____

c.  Would it affect your answer to (b) above if he inherited the business from his
uncle, and therefore had no money of his own invested in the business?

_____

_____

d.  Suppose that instead of owning the business free and clear, Bob owed $1
million to the bank on a 10% loan, or $100,000/year, in interest. What effect
would this have on your answer to (a)? Specifically, would it affect his explicit
(accounting) cost? His implicit cost? His total economic (opportunity) cost?
How would this affect his economic and accounting profit? Explain.

_____

_____

_____

_____

## B. Short-Answer Questions

1. Consider the following production function for a pet supply manufacturer, Linda's Lemming Runs:

| Number of workers hired: | 0 | 1 | 2 | 3 | 4 | 5 | 6 | 7 | 8 | 9 | 10 |
|---|---|---|---|---|---|---|---|---|---|---|---|
| Output: | 0 | 10 | 25 | 40 | 50 | 59 | 61 | 62 | 62 | 62 | 60 |
| Marginal product: | __ | __ | __ | __ | __ | __ | __ | __ | __ | __ | __ |

   a. Fill in the missing values for marginal product.

   b. With which worker does *diminishing* marginal product set in? When does marginal product actually become *negative*? Compare the two cases in terms of the effect on total output. _____
   _____
   _____
   _____
   _____

2. What is the relationship between diminishing marginal product and marginal cost? Explain why this occurs. _____
   _____
   _____
   _____

3. Explain in your own words the difference between accounting profit and economic profit. Include discussion of the distinction between explicit and implicit costs and how they relate to economic cost and opportunity cost. _____
   _____
   _____
   _____
   _____
   _____

## III. Self-Test

### A. True/False Questions

_____1. Economic profit is typically higher than accounting profit.
_____2. Economic cost is accounting cost plus implicit costs.
_____3. Implicit costs are opportunity costs for which there is no actual money outlay.
_____4. Average total cost + average variable cost = average fixed cost.
_____5. Average fixed cost equals zero in the long run.
_____6. All costs are variable in the short run.

_____7. Accounting profit does not take implicit cost into account.
_____8. When output equals zero, total cost = fixed cost.
_____9. Variable cost = total cost minus fixed cost.
_____10. In the long run, all costs are fixed.
_____11. The average-total-cost curve has the most pronounced U-shape in the short run.
_____12. Average total cost reaches a minimum where it intersects average variable cost.
_____13. The average-fixed-cost curve is U-shaped.
_____14. Profit = price x quantity.
_____15. Marginal cost rises because of diminishing marginal product.

## B. Multiple-Choice Questions

1. Which of the following costs is variable in the *short run*?
   a. wages paid to labor.
   b. payments to suppliers to buy new capital equipment.
   c. rent on land.
   d. interest on business loans to buy capital equipment.
   e. all of the above.

2. Which of the following costs is variable in the *long run*?
   a. wages paid to labor.
   b. payments to suppliers to buy new capital equipment.
   c. rent on land.
   d. interest on business loans to buy capital equipment.
   e. all of the above.

3. Diseconomies of scale result when:
   a. diminishing marginal product occurs.
   b. falling average total cost occurs.
   c. output increases more than proportionately to changes in inputs.
   d. increasing all inputs proportionately results in increasing ATC.
   e. modern production techniques require larger numbers of workers, in order to take advantage of specialization.

4. Which of the following is an example of an implicit cost?
   a. wages paid to part-time workers.
   b. wages that the owner could have earned by going to work for someone else.
   c. interest paid on a business loan.
   d. costs of raw materials purchased now for use later.
   e. all of the above.

5. Marginal cost always equals average total cost at:
   a. minimum average total cost.
   b. minimum marginal cost.
   c. maximum average total cost.
   d. average variable cost.
   e. none of the above.

Use the data for Bob's Bootery to answer Questions 6-10 below:

| Q | Total Cost |
|---|---|
| 0 | $100 |
| 1 | $110 |
| 2 | $125 |
| 3 | $150 |
| 4 | $220 |

6. The variable cost when Q = 3 is:
   a. $0.
   b. $25.
   c. $50.
   d. $150.
   e. none of the above

7. Fixed cost is:
   a. $0.
   b. $10.
   c. $15.
   d. $25.
   e. $100.

8. The marginal cost of the second unit of output is:
   a. $0.
   b. $10.
   c. $15.
   d. $25.
   e. $100.

9. The average total cost when Q = 3 is:
   a. $8.33.
   b. $25.00.
   c. $50.00.
   d. $150.00.
   e. none of the above

10. The average variable cost when $Q = 2$ is:
    a. $10.
    b. $12.50.
    c. $25.00.
    d. $62.50.
    e. $125.00.

11. The average fixed cost when $Q = 3$ is:
    a. $25.00.
    b. $33.33.
    c. $50.00.
    d. $150.00.
    e. none of the above

12. The efficient scale of operation for Bob's Bootery is:
    a. 0.
    b. 1.
    c. 2.
    d. 3.
    e. 4.

13. Diminishing marginal product occurs whenever:
    a. business is operating inefficiently, resulting in high per-unit costs.
    b. the quality of the available labor pool deteriorates and production costs rise.
    c. business becomes so large that it is unwieldy to manage and productivity declines.
    d. diseconomies of scale occur.
    e. additional workers add less to output than did the workers who came before.

To answer Questions 14-17, use the following information for Fred's Fabulous Franks, a hot dog stand that has been a downtown institution for 50 years:

| | |
|---|---|
| Cost of supplies and other materials: | $10,000 |
| Rent: | $20,000 |
| Wages paid: | $25,000 |
| Interest on a $10,000 bank loan: | $ 1,000 |
| Fred's salary offer from a competitor: | $20,000 |

14. What is the total explicit (accounting) cost of running Fred's Franks?
    a. $11,000
    b. $36,000
    c. $56,000
    d. $76,000
    e. none of the above

15. What is the total opportunity (economic) cost of running Fred's Franks?
    a. $11,000
    b. $36,000
    c. $56,000
    d. $75,000
    e. $76,000

16. If Fred pays off the bank loan and invests $10,000 of his own money in the business, giving up the chance to earn $1,000 in interest elsewhere, his:
    a. accounting and economic costs will both rise by $1,000.
    b. accounting and economic costs will both fall by $1,000.
    c. accounting cost will fall by $1,000, but economic cost will not change.
    d. accounting cost will not change, but economic cost will fall by $1,000.
    e. accounting and economic costs will remain unchanged.

17. If Fred has a new job offer of $100,000/year to sell out and go into sales, his:
    a. implicit cost of staying in business will rise.
    b. explicit cost of staying in business will rise.
    c. implicit cost of staying in business will fall.
    d. explicit cost of staying in business will fall.
    e. implicit and explicit costs will be unchanged as long as he doesn't accept.

18. A firm's profit is most closely related to:
    a. producer surplus.
    b. consumer surplus.
    c. total revenue.
    d. total cost.
    e. total revenue + total cost.

Use the data below for Acme Manufacturing to answer question 18.

| Quantity (in thousands) | 1 | 2 | 3 | 4 | 5 | 6 |
|---|---|---|---|---|---|---|
| Long-term ATC | $100 | $90 | $100 | $120 | $150 | $160 |

19. Acme is experiencing:
    a. economies of scale at output of two or less and diseconomies at higher quantities.
    b. diseconomies of scale at output of two or less and economies at higher quantities.
    c. diseconomies of scale at all levels of output.
    d. economies of scale at all levels of output.
    e. diminishing marginal product.

20. Constant returns to scale occur when:
    a. increasing all inputs proportionately increases output by the same proportion, keeping long-run average total cost the same.
    b. doubling output causes average total cost to double.
    c. firms are able to increase labor input in the short run without a change in average total cost.
    d. increasing all inputs proportionately results in constant output because of zero marginal product.
    e. all of the above.

21. Which of the following statements is true?
    a. Diseconomies of scale is a short-run concept.
    b. Diminishing marginal product is a short-run concept.
    c. Diminishing marginal product results when the firm doubles in size without doubling output.
    d. Diseconomies of scale result when only one input increases and output fails to keep up.
    e. all of the above.

## IV. Advanced Critical Thinking

Your uncle, who farms 1,000 acres in central Illinois, has always claimed that he is losing money in farming. However, according to his tax returns, he earns a decent profit. Is someone not telling the truth, or does he simply need a better tax accountant? Why do you suppose he stays in agriculture if he is incurring losses as he claims?

_____
_____
_____
_____
_____
_____
_____
_____
_____
_____

## V. Solutions

### Terms and Definitions

___2___ Total revenue
___1___ Total cost
___5___ Profit
___6___ Production function

___10__ Marginal product
___1___ Diminishing marginal product
___9___ Fixed cost
___13__ Variable cost
___15__ Average total cost
___16__ Average fixed cost
___3___ Average variable cost
___7___ Marginal cost
___12__ Efficient scale
___14__ Economies of scale
___8___ Diseconomies of scale
___4___ Constant returns to scale

**Practice Problems**

1. a. Wendell's Widget Works (WWW) faces the following cost schedule :

| Quantity | Fixed Cost | Variable Cost | Total Cost | Marginal Cost | Average Variable Cost | Average Fixed Cost | Average Total Cost |
|---|---|---|---|---|---|---|---|
| Q | FC | VC | TC | MC | AVC | AFC | ATC |
| 0 | $46 | $ 0 | $ 46 | $ — | $ — | $ — | $ — |
| 1 | 46 | 30 | 76 | 30 | 30 | 46 | 76 |
| 2 | 46 | 50 | 96 | 20 | 25 | 23 | 48 |
| 3 | 46 | 58 | 104 | 8 | 19.3 | 15.3 | 34.7 |
| 4 | 46 | 64 | 110 | 6 | 16 | 11.5 | 27.5 |
| 5 | 46 | 84 | 130 | 20 | 16.8 | 9.2 | 26 |
| 6 | 46 | 114 | 160 | 30 | 19 | 7.7 | 26.7 |
| 7 | 46 | 150 | 196 | 36 | 21.4 | 6.6 | 28 |
| 8 | 46 | 190 | 236 | 40 | 23.8 | 5.8 | 29.5 |
| 9 | 46 | 240 | 286 | 50 | 26.7 | 5.1 | 31.8 |

   b. Yes, diminishing marginal product sets in at the output level at which marginal cost begins to rise, with the fifth unit of output. It is diminishing marginal product that causes marginal cost to rise by increasing the labor cost of each additional unit of output.

   c. Costs are either variable or fixed. Therefore, Total Cost = Variable Cost + Fixed Cost.

   d. If $\underline{TC} = \underline{VC} + \underline{FC}$, then dividing both sides by $\underline{Q}$ maintains the equality and gives us the following identity: $\underline{ATC} = \underline{AVC} + \underline{AFC}$.

   e. $\underline{MC}$ always intersects $\underline{ATC}$ and $\underline{AVC}$ at their minimum points. In each case, the average either is influenced by the marginal value: If $\underline{MC} > \underline{ATC}$ or $\underline{AVC}$, then the average rises, and if $\underline{MC} < \underline{ATC}$ or $\underline{AVC}$, then the average is pulled down by the low marginal cost.

f. Wendell's efficient scale is an output of 5. At this quantity, average total cost reaches a minimum at 26.

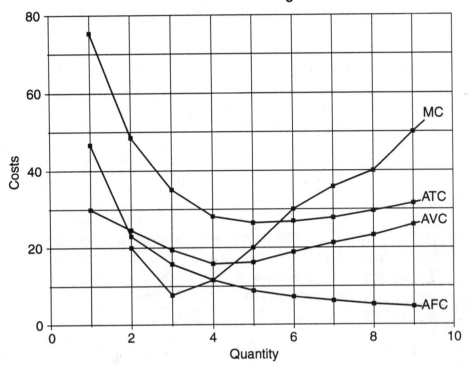

**Wendell's Widgets**

2. a. Bob's accounting cost = $100,000. These are the explicit costs or money outlays required to stay in business. His implicit costs include forgone earnings of $50,000 by not accepting the job offer + $100,000 in lost interest by not selling out and investing the $1 million at 10% interest. His total economic cost is the total opportunity cost of staying in business, including both explicit and implicit costs. This opportunity cost equals $250,000 ($100,000 in explicit costs + $50,000 in forgone wages + $100,000 in forgone interest).

b. To maximize his profit, he should sell out. When he takes into account all of the costs of staying in business, he is losing money. His economic profit is negative: $200,000 in total revenue minus $250,000 in total (opportunity) cost equals a profit (loss) of ($50,000). To an accountant (and the IRS), however, he is earning $100,000 ($200,000 in revenues minus $100,000 in explicit cost).

c. The answer would be unchanged. The opportunity cost of staying in business would still include the interest on the $1 million because, regardless of its source, it is available for him to invest if he sells out.

d.  If Bob owes $1 million to the bank, the $100,000 in interest becomes an explicit cost that would be deducted from accounting profit. However, his economic cost already included the $100,000 in interest as an implicit cost, so his economic profit (in this case a loss) would be unchanged at ($50,000). His accounting profit would be 0 ($200,000 in revenues minus $200,000 in explicit cost).

## Short-Answer Questions

1.  a.  Consider the following production function for a pet supply manufacturer, Linda's Lemming Runs:

| Number of workers hired: | 0 | 1 | 2 | 3 | 4 | 5 | 6 | 7 | 8 | 9 | 10 |
|---|---|---|---|---|---|---|---|---|---|---|---|
| Output: | 0 | 10 | 25 | 40 | 50 | 59 | 61 | 62 | 62 | 62 | 60 |
| Marginal product: | — | 10 | 15 | 15 | 10 | 9 | 2 | 1 | 0 | 0 | -2 |

b.  Diminishing returns sets in with the 4th worker hired because this is the first drop in marginal product (from 15 to 10). When marginal product begins to decline, total output continues to rise, although at a slower rate. With the 10th worker hired, the marginal product actually becomes negative, which means that *total* product begins to fall.

2.  When diminishing marginal product sets in, the drop in output per additional worker makes it more expensive to produce additional output (because output per additional dollar spent on labor declines). Therefore, at the hiring and output level at which diminishing marginal product occurs, marginal cost begins to rise.

3.  Accounting profit is based on money flows; it equals the firm's total revenues minus all of the explicit money outlays required to generate those revenues. Economic profit takes into account all opportunity costs, even those that did not result in money outlays. Economic profit equals the firm's total revenues minus the full opportunity cost of earning those revenues, including both money outlays and any implicit opportunity costs of production.

## True/False Questions

1.  F; economic profit is accounting profit minus implicit cost.
2.  T
3.  T
4.  F; average total cost = average variable cost + average fixed cost.
5.  T
6.  F; all costs are variable in the *long run*.
7.  T
8.  T
9.  T

10. F; in the long run, all costs are *variable*.
11. T
12. F; average total cost reaches a minimum where it intersects *marginal* cost.
13. F; average fixed cost declines as output rises.
14. F; *total revenue* = price x quantity.
15. T

## Multiple-Choice Questions

1. a
2. e
3. d
4. b
5. a
6. c
7. e
8. c
9. c
10. b
11. b
12. d
13. e
14. c
15. e
16. c
17. a
18. a
19. a
20. a
21. b

## Advanced Critical Thinking

This is not inconsistent. His tax returns show his accounting profit equal to total revenue minus total explicit cost. Accounting profit fails to consider any implicit cost of production, such as the value of his time or the interest on his investment in the business. The farmland alone could be worth millions of dollars. If he were not in farming, this money could be invested elsewhere earning hundreds of thousands of dollars per year. His economic profit reflects these implicit costs. If the implicit costs are substantial enough to offset the positive accounting profit, then economic loss will result. If he stays in business in spite of incurring an economic loss, this could mean that he gets enough utility out of working (and owning) the land to make him willing to incur the loss. Another possibility is that he is willing to hold the land as an investment. Every year that the land appreciates in value, it earns a return equal to its rate of appreciation.

# Chapter 14:  Firms in Competitive Markets

## I.  Chapter Overview

### A.  Context and Purpose

The previous chapter provided an overview of costs of production.  This chapter extends that analysis to cover profit maximization by competitive firms in the short and long run.  The next three chapters adapt this model to cover other types of firms.

### B.  Learning Objectives

In this chapter you will:

1.  Learn what characteristics make a market competitive
2.  Examine how competitive firms decide how much output to produce.
3.  Examine how competitive firms decide when to shut down production temporarily.
4.  Examine how competitive firms decide whether to exit or enter a market.
5.  See how firm behavior determines a market's short-run and long-run supply curves.

After accomplishing these goals, you should be able to:

1.  Explain why a competitive market requires a large number of buyers and sellers, a standardized product, and easy entry and exit.
2.  Interpret the profit-maximization rule for competitive firms (produce additional output until price-marginal cost) and explain how this is a special case of the general profit-maximization rule, which results in production until marginal revenue = marginal cost.
3.  Demonstrate that  a profit-maximizing competitive firm will shut down temporarily if its total revenue is less than its variable costs.
4.  Explain the role of positive economic profit as a signal for competitive firms to enter an industry, and negative economic profit (economic loss) as a signal for firms to leave an industry.
5.  Show that the market supply curve is the summation of all of the individual firms' marginal-cost curves above average variable cost; in the long run, new firms will enter until economic profit is exactly zero so that long-run industry supply will be more elastic than short-run supply.

## C. Chapter Review

### 14-1 What Is a Competitive Market?

In a perfectly competitive market, there are so many buyers and sellers of a standardized good that no individual buyer or seller can influence price. That is, buyers and sellers are all price takers. In addition, competitive markets have no barriers to entry, so firms can enter or exit the industry easily in response to changing market conditions.

### 14-2 Profit Maximization and the Competitive Firm's Supply Curve

Just like other firms, competitive firms desire to maximize profit. Remember that rational people make decisions at the margin. Everyone, from individuals to firms to societies, maximizes well-being by following a general decisionmaking rule:

> *Do anything as long as marginal benefit is greater than or equal to marginal cost.*

The corollary to this rule is:

> *Stop when the marginal benefit equals the marginal cost.*

For a business trying to maximize profit, this rule becomes:

> *Produce as long as the marginal (additional) revenue is equal to or greater than the marginal (additional) cost, and stop when marginal revenue equals marginal cost.*

Note that fixed costs are irrelevant for making future decisions. Economists refer to fixed costs as sunk costs because, once they are incurred, they cannot be recovered. A firm determines how much output to produce by equating marginal revenue and marginal cost, neither of which is affected by fixed cost.

The profit-maximizing firm needs to consider the following revenue measures:

$$\text{Average Revenue} = \text{Total Revenue/Quantity}$$
$$\text{Marginal Revenue} = \Delta\text{Total Revenue/}\Delta\text{Quantity}$$

For the competitive firm, all sales occur at the market price, which does not change as the firm increases output. As a result, in perfect competition:

$$\text{Average Revenue} = \text{Marginal Revenue} = \text{Price}$$

To maximize profit using marginal analysis, the perfectly competitive firm produces until:

$$\text{Marginal Revenue} = \text{Price} = \text{Marginal Cost}$$

So for any price, the firm will choose the quantity supplied by looking at the marginal-cost curve, which makes that curve the firm's supply curve. The only qualification is that firms will not sell at a price below the average variable cost. If price is below average variable cost, the firm is losing more money than if it were to shut down. Therefore, the competitive firm's supply curve in the short run is the portion of the marginal-cost curve above the average variable cost.

The analysis is similar in the long run, except that all costs are variable. Remember that in the long run all inputs and costs are variable. Consequently, the profit-maximizing firm in the long run will not produce below average total cost (ATC). With P < ATC, the firm is incurring losses and will go out of business. On the other hand, if P > ATC, the firm will earn an economic profit, encouraging it to stay in business and encouraging other firms to enter the industry. Keep in mind the difference between economic and accounting profit. Economic profit includes all opportunity costs of time and capital. When a firm has zero economic profit it is enjoying a normal accounting profit. It is for this reason that firms are willing to continue to produce at a point of zero economic profit. In addition, any positive economic profit provides an incentive for firms to enter the industry.

### 14-3 The Supply Curve in a Competitive Market

Market supply is the summation of all of the individual supply curves. Long-run market supply includes potential as well as current competitors. If economic profits exist, new firms will enter the market in the long run, increasing supply and driving down price until the economic profits disappear. If economic losses exist, firms will exit the industry in the long run, decreasing supply and resulting in rising prices until economic losses disappear. The situation stabilizes in the long run only when economic profit = zero, which means that price = average total cost. This long-run equilibrium occurs at minimum average total cost, with each firm operating at its efficient scale.

### D. Helpful Hints

1. *Sunk costs are sunk.* That is, fixed costs cannot be recovered and therefore are irrelevant for future decisions. In the short run, a business cannot avoid its fixed costs even by shutting down. This is why it is rational for a business to continue to produce at a loss in the short run as long as its revenues cover the variable costs. Any revenues in excess of the variable cost will offset part of the fixed cost and reduce losses. However, if the firm shuts down, it will incur losses equal to the full fixed cost.

2. *Sunk costs are really sunk.* This is worth a second hint. Thinking at the margin is what distinguishes economists from noneconomists. Even if you now accept this axiom, its implications still may not be obvious. A business that is maximizing profit ignores fixed costs. This means that in the short run (when there are some fixed costs), a business that just replaced an expensive piece of equipment or made an expensive repair will not find it profitable to raise price even by a slight amount. This is probably counterintuitive, but remember that the firm is already charging whatever the market will bear, up to the point at which $\underline{MC} = \underline{MR}$. Just ask yourself this question: If it is profitable for the firm to raise price now to recoup the cost, why wasn't it profitable to raise price before the big investment just to make more profit? The answer is that if the firm can raise price to make more profit, it would have already done so! If it is rational, however, it won't make the decision based on sunk costs. Similarly, if you go to a concert that turns out to be a waste of time, you shouldn't stay until the end just because you paid $50 for a ticket. The $50 is gone; don't make yourself even more miserable by sitting through a worthless concert.

## E. Terms and Definitions

Choose a definition for each key term.

Key terms:

_____Competitive market
_____Average revenue
_____Marginal revenue
_____Shutdown point
_____Breakeven point

Definitions:

1. The minimum price that a business will accept rather than go out of business in the long run, equal to the minimum average total cost.
2. The minimum price that a business will accept rather than shut down in the short run, equal to the minimum average variable cost.
3. A market with many buyers and sellers trading identical products so that each buyer and seller is a price taker.
4. The change in total revenue from an additional unit sold.
5. Total revenue divided by the quantity sold; identical to price.

## II. Problems and Short-Answer Questions

### A. Practice Problems

1. The graph below shows a competitive firm maximizing profits. However, the curves are not labeled. Assume that the firm is initially in equilibrium earning a positive economic profit.

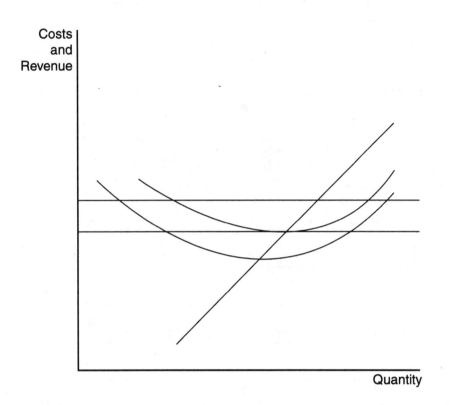

a. Label the following: <u>P</u>, <u>AR</u>, <u>MR</u>, <u>MC</u>, <u>ATC</u>, and <u>AVC</u>. Show the equilibrium quantity and price as $Q_e$ and $P_e$. Label the short-run shutdown point as point A and the breakeven point as point B.

b. Why is it rational for the firm to produce at $Q_e$? Should it continue to produce temporarily if the price falls below point B but stays above point A? Why or why not? Would your answer be different in the longrun? Explain.

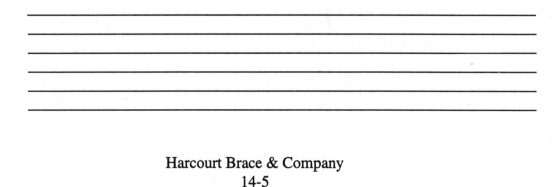

c. Is the firm in short-run equilibrium? Long-run equilibrium? How can you tell?

_____

_____

_____

d. What is likely to happen to the price in the long run? Why? Show the new price line on the graph and explain what happened in the market to cause this shift. _____

_____

_____

_____

2. In Chapter 13 you calculated production costs for Wendell's Widget Works (WWW). The cost schedule is as follows:

| Quantity (Q) | Variable Cost (VC) | Total Cost (TC) | Marginal Cost (MC) | Average Variable Cost (AVC) | Average Total Cost (ATC) | Marginal Revenue (MR) | Profit (TR-TC) |
|---|---|---|---|---|---|---|---|
| 0 | $ 0 | $ 46 | $ — | $ — | $ — | ____ | ____ |
| 1 | 30 | 76 | 30 | 30 | 76 | ____ | ____ |
| 2 | 50 | 96 | 20 | 25 | 48 | ____ | ____ |
| 3 | 58 | 104 | 8 | 19.3 | 34.7 | ____ | ____ |
| 4 | 64 | 110 | 6 | 16 | 27.5 | ____ | ____ |
| 5 | 84 | 130 | 20 | 16.8 | 26 | ____ | ____ |
| 6 | 114 | 160 | 30 | 19 | 26.7 | ____ | ____ |
| 7 | 150 | 196 | 36 | 21.4 | 28 | ____ | ____ |
| 8 | 190 | 236 | 40 | 23.8 | 29.5 | ____ | ____ |
| 9 | 240 | 286 | 50 | 26.7 | 31.8 | ____ | ____ |

a. Wendell is selling in a competitive market at a price of $40. Fill in the missing blanks for marginal revenue and profit.

b.  What is the profit-maximizing output for Wendell?  What is his profit or loss?
Should he continue to produce in the long run? _____

_____

_____

c.  If the price falls to $20, what is Wendell's profit-maximizing output in the short
run?  What is his profit or loss?  What should he do in the long run?

_____

_____

_____

d.  If Wendell's price falls to $15, what would be his profit or loss if he continued
to produce at a price of $15?  What would be his profit or loss if he temporarily
shut down in the short run?  Which action should he take in the short run?
Explain. _____

_____

_____

_____

_____

3.  The following graph shows the effects of a tax hike on a competitive industry that
shifts the short-run supply curve from $S_1$ to $S_2$.

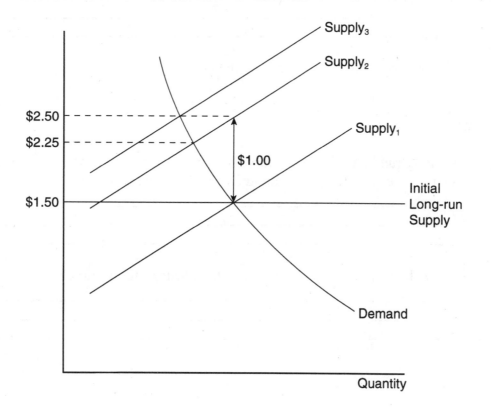

a. How much is the tax? How much will price rise in the short run? (Who pays the tax in the short run?) _____

_____

_____

_____

_____

b. What happens to quantity in the short run? Identify the initial equilibrium quantity and the new short-run equilibrium quantity after the tax.

_____

_____

_____

c. If the industry was initially in long-run equilibrium at a price of $1.50, what will happen to profit (or loss) in the short run? Explain. _____

_____

_____

_____

d. How will firms respond in the long run? What are the implications for long-run industry supply and the resulting price? Who pays the tax in the long run? Explain. _____

_____

_____

_____

e. Show the new long-run supply curve on the graph.

## B. Short-Answer Questions

1. How can the long-run industry supply curve be horizontal even though the short-run supply has a positive slope for both individual firms and the industry?

_____

_____

_____

2. What would explain a positively sloped long-run industry supply curve?

_____

_____

_____

3. What constitutes the competitive firm's supply curve? Explain.

_____

_____

_____

4. What is the significance of a firm's efficient scale for competitive equilibrium?

_____

_____

_____

5. How would a rational, profit-maximizing, competitive firm respond in the short run to an increase in fixed costs? Will there be any change in equilibrium price or quantity in the short run? Why or why not? _____

_____

_____

6. Your father-in-law runs a small plumbing and heating business in rural Indiana. He charges $35 for a basic service call, which he estimates just covers his costs including his overhead. One of his customers, who is a real miser, has lived with a malfunctioning water softener for the past year rather than pay $35 to have it adjusted. The miser has said that he is not willing to pay more than $10 for the adjustment, but he is willing to wait until the plumber has some down time with nothing else to do. What do you recommend? Should your father-in-law accept the $10 if he is in the neighborhood anyway and has no more jobs that day? Or is your father-in-law right in saying that he would lose the difference between his average total cost of $35 and the extra revenue of $10 if he accepts? Does he make $10 or lose $25? Explain. _____

_____

_____

_____

_____

_____

_____

## III. Self-Test

### A. True/False Questions

_____1.  A firm earning zero economic profit will exit the industry in the long run.

_____2.  Positive accounting profits will attract more firms into an industry in the long run.

_____3.  A firm facing a price that is less than average total cost will shut down temporarily until the situation improves.

_____4.     Sunk costs are not part of opportunity cost.

_____5.     A profit-maximizing competitive firm will produce until $\underline{P} = \underline{MC}$.

_____6.     A firm producing where $\underline{MC} > \underline{MR}$ is producing more than the profit-maximizing quantity.

_____7.     Long-run supply is always horizontal for competitive industries.

_____8.     For a competitive firm, $\underline{P} = \underline{MR}$ only at equilibrium.

_____9.     In perfect competition, the sellers are price takers, and the buyers are price setters.

_____10.    The market demand curve for a competitive industry is downward sloping.

_____11.    A competitive industry includes many buyers and sellers of a standardized product.

_____12.    A firm that is not covering its variable cost should shut down unless it is at least covering fixed cost.

_____13.    The industry supply curve is the summation of all of the individual firms' supply curves.

_____14.    The best signal that investing in an industry would be desirable is high accounting profit.

_____15.    If $\underline{MC} = \underline{MR}$, but $\underline{P} < \underline{ATC}$, then the firm is in short-run but not long-run equilibrium.

## B. Multiple-Choice Questions

1. A firm earning zero economic profit
   a. is not covering its full opportunity cost of doing business.
   b. is earning a zero or negative accounting cost.
   c. will shut down in the short run.
   d. will go out of business in the long run.
   e. none of the above.

2. In the long run, a competitive firm will operate at:
   a. its efficient scale.
   b. minimum marginal cost.
   c. $\underline{TR} > \underline{TC}$.
   d. maximum $\underline{MR}$.
   e. all of the above.

3. A profit-maximizing competitive firm will produce up to the point at which:
   a. total revenue is maximized.
   b. marginal revenue is maximized.
   c. total cost is minimized.
   d. price minus total cost is maximized.
   e. marginal revenue = marginal cost.

4. Dolly's Doughnuts is a competitive firm producing where $\underline{MR}$ = $4.00 and $\underline{MC}$ = $2.00. To maximize profit, the firm should:
   a. expand output.
   b. cut back on output.
   c. keep doing what it is doing.
   d. raise price to increase total revenue.
   e. cut price to increase total revenue.

5. Long-run supply is more elastic than short-run supply for the industry because in the long run:
   a. costs are higher.
   b. costs are lower.
   c. firms can enter or exit the industry.
   d. firms can expand or contract the number of workers they hire.
   e. none of the above.

6. The long-run market supply curve is likely to slope upward if:
   a. additional firms are attracted into the industry in the long run.
   b. not all firms have the same costs of production.
   c. diminishing marginal product sets in.
   d. there are no barriers to entry into the industry.
   e. economies of scale exist.

7. Suppose that the government imposes a $1/unit tax on the output of a competitive industry in long-run equilibrium with a horizontal long-run supply curve. The short-run supply and demand curves have comparable elasticities. The most likely result of the tax will be:
   a. an immediate and permanent price hike of $1, leaving profit unchanged as the tax is passed along entirely to the consumer.
   b. a $1 price hike in the short run, dropping back to the original price in the long run.
   c. an immediate and permanent price hike of less than $1, leaving profit permanently reduced.
   d. a price hike of less than $1 in the short run, resulting in losses until the price eventually rises by the full $1 tax, leaving economic profit at zero.
   e. a $1 price hike in the short run, dropping back part way between the new and old prices in the long run, resulting in slightly reduced long-run profit.

8. A firm should shut down in the short run if it is not covering its:
   a. variable costs.
   b. fixed costs.
   c. total costs.
   d. reasonable return on investment.
   e. money outlays or explicit costs.

9. A firm should shut down in the long run if it is not covering its:
   a. fixed costs.
   b. accounting costs.
   c. money outlays.
   d. economic costs.
   e. average fixed cost.

10. An increase in demand in a competitive industry leads to:
    a. higher prices and profit in the short run only.
    b. higher prices and profit in the long run only.
    c. higher prices and profit as long as demand remains high.
    d. no change in either price or profit.
    e. none of the above.

11. A rational entrepreneur should enter a competitive industry only if:
    a. price exceeds average variable cost.
    b. price exceeds average total cost.
    c. price exceeds marginal cost.
    d. price exceeds average fixed cost.
    e. profit is significantly greater than zero.

12. Suppose that demand increases for the output of a competitive industry, driving up price. Each of the 1,000 current firms is willing to increase quantity supplied by 2 units in response to the higher price. Assuming free entry and exit, the total quantity supplied by the industry eventually will increase by:
    a. less than 2,000.
    b. exactly 2,000.
    c. more than 2,000.
    d. 2,000 initially, then fall back to the original level in the long run.
    e. none of the above.

13. According to your father-in-law, business is terrible and he would sell out and retire, except that he just spent $100,000 to upgrade his equipment and needs to stay in business at least long enough to recover his investment. His logic is:
    a. sensible, as long as he can afford the negative cash flow.
    b. sensible, unless he can recoup his investment by adding the value of the upgraded equipment to the selling price of his business.
    c. flawed, because nobody should continue to produce at a loss.
    d. flawed, because the equipment upgrade is a sunk cost.
    e. none of the above.

Use the information below to answer Questions 14-16.

| Quantity | Total Revenue | Total Cost |
|----------|---------------|------------|
| 0 | $ 0 | $ 5 |
| 1 | $ 5 | $ 7 |
| 2 | $10 | $10 |
| 3 | $15 | $16 |
| 4 | $20 | $25 |

14. The marginal cost of the third unit of output is:
   a. $1.
   b. $6.
   c. $10.
   d. $16.
   e. none of the above.

15. The firm should produce output of:
   a. 0.
   b. 1.
   c. 2.
   d. 3.
   e. 4.

16. If the firm's fixed cost were $5 higher, then the firm in the short run should produce:
   a. 0.
   b. 1.
   c. 2.
   d. 3.
   e. 4.

17. A competitive firm in long-run equilibrium will satisfy the following:
   a. $P = MC$.
   b. $MR = MC$.
   c. $P = ATC$.
   d. $P = MR$.
   e. all of the above.

Use the following graph for a competitive firm to answer Questions 18-20.

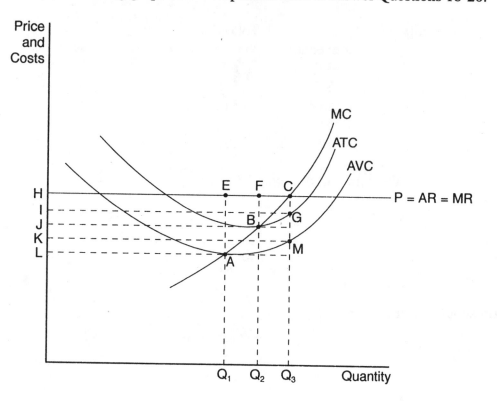

18. The firm shown in the diagram will produce at output level:
    a. 0.
    b. $Q_1$.
    c. $Q_2$.
    d. $Q_3$.
    e. $Q_4$.

19. The firm is realizing a:
    a. zero profit.
    b. profit equal to area HCGI.
    c. profit equal to area HCMK.
    d. profit equal to area HFBJ.
    e. loss equal to area ECMA.

20. What will happen to this firm in the long run?
    a. More firms will enter the industry, driving down price until profit equals zero.
    b. More firms will enter the industry, lowering cost and raising profit because of economies of scale.
    c. More firms will enter the industry, increasing average total cost but leaving price unchanged until profit equals 0.
    d. Firms will leave the industry, increasing price until profit equals zero.
    e. Nothing; the firm is in long-run equilibrium.

## IV. Advanced Critical Thinking

Your campus newspaper has run an editorial attacking the fast-food restaurants in the food court for anticompetitive behavior when they raised prices simultaneously last week. Demanding equal time, the restaurants responded that the higher prices were necessitated by a rent hike by the university for all restaurants in the food court. They argued further that they were behaving perfectly competitively by raising price because, under competition, all costs are passed along to the consumer. Evaluate both sides of this argument. Are the restaurants behaving like perfect competitors? Should a profit-maximizing business consider the rent in setting the price of its product? Would your answer vary depending on the length of time involved? Explain. _____

_____

_____

_____

_____

_____

_____

_____

## V. Solutions

### Terms and Definitions

__3___Competitive market
__5___Average revenue
__4___Marginal revenue
__2___Shutdown point
__1___Breakeven point

## Practice Problems

1. a.

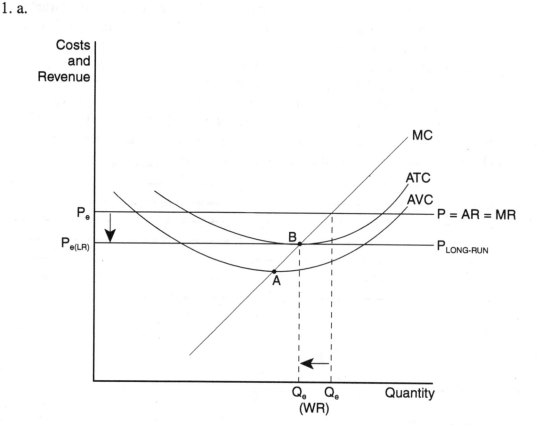

b. Output level $Q_e$ maximizes profit because it means producing every unit of output that adds more to revenue than it adds to cost. If price falls below point B, the firm will have negative profit (incur a loss). However, in the short run the firm should continue to produce as long as it is above point A, the <u>AVC</u> curve. Any price in excess of <u>AVC</u> contributes to fixed cost, reducing the losses that result below point B. In the long run, the firm can avoid all costs (nothing is fixed); therefore, it should not produce at a loss (below point B). It can go out of business and avoid all losses.

c. The firm is in short-run equilibrium only. It is earning an economic profit. In long-run equilibrium, entry of new firms will continue until all firms are earning zero economic profits.

d. In the long run, the profit will encourage new firms to enter the industry. The additional industry supply will drive down price until the profit is eliminated. Each firm then will produce at minimum average total cost (its efficient scale) in order to survive. The new price line will be tangent to <u>ATC</u> (at point B).

2. a. Costs and revenues for Wendell's Widget Works (WWW) at price = $40.

| Quantity (Q) | Variable Cost (VC) | Total Cost (TC) | Marginal Cost (MC) | Average Variable Cost (AVC) | Average Total Cost (ATC) | Marginal Revenue (MR) | Profit (TR-TC) |
|---|---|---|---|---|---|---|---|
| 0 | $ 0 | $ 46 | $ — | $ — | $ — | = | ($46) |
| 1 | 30 | 76 | 30 | 30 | 76 | $40 | (36) |
| 2 | 50 | 96 | 20 | 25 | 48 | 40 | (16) |
| 3 | 58 | 104 | 8 | 19.3 | 34.7 | 40 | 16 |
| 4 | 64 | 110 | 6 | 16 | 27.5 | 40 | 50 |
| 5 | 84 | 130 | 20 | 16.8 | 26 | 40 | 70 |
| 6 | 114 | 160 | 30 | 19 | 26.7 | 40 | 80 |
| 7 | 150 | 196 | 36 | 21.4 | 28 | 40 | 84 |
| 8 | 190 | 236 | 40 | 23.8 | 29.5 | 40 | 84 |
| 9 | 240 | 286 | 50 | 26.7 | 31.8 | 40 | 74 |

b.  Wendell maximizes profit by producing up to the point at which MC = MR, or Q = 8.  Because the eighth unit adds $40 each to cost and revenue (MC = MR = $40), Wendell is indifferent between stopping with Q = 7 and continuing to Q = 8. Either way, his profit is $84.  Because it is greater than zero, he should continue to produce in the long run.

c.  At a price (and marginal revenue) of $20, MR = MC at an output of 5.  He should produce up to 5 units for a loss of $30 (TR - TC = $100 - $130 = -$30). Because it exceeds his AVC of $16.80, he is better off producing in the short run to avoid losing his entire fixed cost of $46.  A $30 loss is $16 better than a $46 loss.  Note that his $20 price exceeds his AVC by $3.20, leaving $3.20 times 5 units, or $16, to contribute to fixed cost.  In the long run, however, all costs are variable, and Wendell would be better off leaving the widget industry rather than continuing to lose money.

d.  At a price of $15, if Wendell continued to produce, his output would be 4 (this is the most he could produce without MC > MR).  However, this doesn't even cover his variable cost.  His loss would be $50 (TR - TC = $60 - $110), which is worse than the $46 that he would lose if he shut down. Therefore, he should shut down and lose only his fixed cost.

3.  a.  The tax is $1.00. It will raise the price to $2.25 in the short run, which means that the consumer pays $0.75 ($2.25-$1.50), and the seller pays the remaining $0.25.

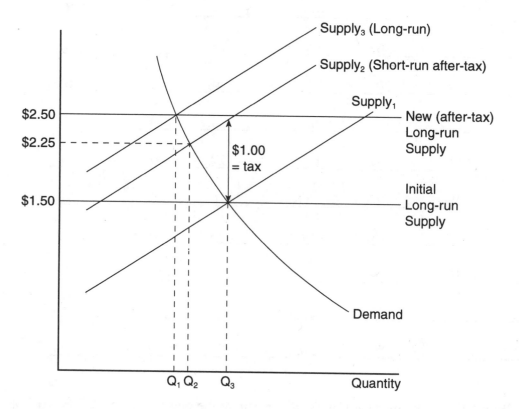

b.  Equilibrium quantity falls from $Q_1$ to $Q_2$ as a result of the tax.

c.  If the industry was in long-run equilibrium, profit was zero. The $0.25 portion of the tax absorbed by the sellers will result in losses in the short run.

d.  In the long run, firms will respond to losses by leaving the industry until price rises by the full $1.00 tax. The long-run industry supply curve will shift upward by $1.00, which is the price hike required to restore long-run equilibrium at zero profit. Therefore, the consumer pays the full tax in the long run.

e.  Show the new long-run supply curve on the graph.

## Short-Answer Questions

1. Long-run supply is horizontal if all firms have identical cost curves and there are constant returns to scale. The positive slope of the short-run supply curve results from diminishing returns when some inputs are fixed. In the long run, all inputs are variable.

2. The long-run supply curve can have a positive slope if not all firms have the same cost curves. The more efficient firms would be in the industry at a lower price, but as price rises, higher-cost firms could enter the industry and survive. In addition, some resources may be unavailable in sufficient quantities for firms to expand without driving up the price of those resources. Either factor would result in higher costs (and therefore higher price) as the industry expands.

3. The competitive firm's supply curve is the marginal-cost curve above the average variable cost. The firm will produce as long as it is worth it at the margin. The competitive firm's marginal revenue is the price, so it will expand as long as $P > \underline{MC}$ and it is covering its variable cost ($P > \underline{AVC}$). If it does not cover variable cost, then it should shut down.

4. In the long run, competitive firms produce at a zero profit, that is, where $\underline{ATC}$ is just tangent to the price line. Because the price line is horizontal for a price taker, price can be tangent to average total cost only at the minimum average total cost, which is the efficient scale. Therefore, perfect competition ensures production at the efficient scale in the long run.

5. A rational firm would ignore fixed cost in setting its output. Firms maximize profit where $\underline{MC} = \underline{MR}$. Fixed cost affects neither because sunk costs are irrelevant. They do not affect the cost of producing an additional unit of output. Neither price nor quantity will change in the short run.

6. If the adjustment does not take any materials, then the $35 overhead cost is a sunk cost. Whether he makes the call or not, he must pay his overhead. If a customer will pay even $10 toward that overhead, it is better than losing the whole $35 during a slow period with no other customers. He makes $10 on the call. (Of course, he doesn't want word to get around, or everyone will want the lower price.)

## True/False Questions

1. F; zero profit covers all costs of doing business, including a normal return on investment; therefore, there is no reason to enter or exit the industry.
2. F; positive *economic* profits will attract more firms into an industry in the long run.
3. F; a firm facing a price that is less than average *variable* cost will shut down temporarily.
4. T

5. T
6. T
7. F; a competitive market can have an upward-sloping long-run supply curve.
8. F; for the competitive firm price always equals marginal revenue.
9. F; in perfect competition, both buyers and sellers are price takers.
10. T
11. T
12. F; a firm that is not covering its variable cost should shut down regardless of fixed cost.
13. T
14. F; the best signal that investing in an industry would be desirable is high *economic* profit.
15. T

## Multiple-Choice Questions

| | | | |
|---|---|---|---|
| 1. e | 6. b | 11. b | 16. c |
| 2. a | 7. d | 12. c | 17. e |
| 3. e | 8. a | 13. d | 18. d |
| 4. a | 9. d | 14. b | 19. b |
| 5. c | 10. a | 15. c | 20. a |

## Advanced Critical Thinking

The fast-food restaurants are not behaving perfectly competitively. Under competition, the consumer ultimately pays all costs of production, but this occurs in the long run through free entry and exit. If competitive firms are losing money, they cannot raise price to recoup the losses. Some firms eventually go out of business, and price rises because of the reduction in supply in the long run. Profit-maximizing firms do not consider rent and other fixed costs in setting price in the short run because fixed costs are sunk and do not affect marginal cost or marginal revenue.

# Chapter 15: Monopoly

## I. Chapter Overview

### A. Context and Purpose

The previous chapter introduced market structure by investigating the characteristics of perfect competition. This chapter extends the analysis to monopoly, the case in which barriers to entry protect a single seller from competition. These barriers to entry allow monopolists to earn economic profit in the long run.

### B. Learning Objectives

In this chapter you will:

1. Learn why some markets have only one seller.
2. Analyze how a monopoly determines the quantity to produce and the price to charge.
3. See how the monopoly's decisions affect economic well-being.
4. Consider the various public policies aimed at solving the problem of scarcity.
5. See why monopolies try to charge different prices to different customers.

After accomplishing these goals, you should be able to:

1. Identify the three barriers to entry and explain their role in making monopoly possible.
2. Compare and contrast the general profit-maximization rule, $MC = MR$, for perfect competitors, where $P = MR$, and with monopolists, for whom $P > MR$.
3. Show the deadweight loss from underproduction in the monopoly case.
4. Compare four public policy responses to the inefficiency of monopoly: (1) procompetitive policies, (2) regulation, (3) government-run monopolies, and (4) doing nothing.
5. Demonstrate that monopolists can use price discrimination to capture consumer surplus.

### C. Chapter Review

### 15-1 Why Monopolies Arise

A monopolist is the sole seller of a product without close substitutes. Monopolists can continue to earn economic profit in the long run due to *barriers to entry* that prevent new competitors from entering the industry and driving down price and profit. Such barriers to entry usually arise for one of three reasons:

- Control over a key resource, for example, water rights in the Old West.

- Exclusive rights grants by government, such as patent protection.

- Falling average total cost that makes a single producer more efficient than many smaller firms, as in the case of a power company, which experiences economies of scale.

## 15-2 How Monopolies Behave

In general, firms maximize profit by producing up to, but not beyond, the point at which $\underline{MC} = \underline{MR}$ (marginal revenue = marginal cost). For competitive firms, every extra unit of output adds the exact amount of its price to total revenue, so $\underline{P} = \underline{MR}$, and the profit-maximization rule becomes $\underline{P} = \underline{MC}$. The primary difference between monopoly and competition is control over price. Monopolists are price setters who can alter price within the constraints of the demand curve, but competitors are price takers who have no control over price.

A monopolist's marginal revenue is always less than the price, because partially offsetting the *output effect* that raises total revenue when output rises is a *price effect* that lowers total revenue because of the cut in price required to sell the extra output. This occurs because, in order to sell more units, the monopolist must cut price on all its sales, not just the additional units. For example, suppose that Ben is a monopolist who sells widgets for $5.00 each (never mind what a widget is, we just know that Ben sells them for $5.00). At $5.00, he can sell 20 widgets per day. If he wants to sell more, he has to cut the price. To sell one more widget, he must cut the price to $4.80. The problem is that his marginal revenue from a 21st widget is much less than the price. His 21st widget sold brings in $4.80, but he loses $0.20 each in revenue on each of the first 20 widgets (or $4.00 in total) by cutting the price from $5.00 to $4.80. The net effect on his revenue is an increase of $4.80 minus a decrease of $4.00, for a net increase, or marginal revenue, of $0.80. Another way to see this is to look at total revenue for 20 units ($5.00 x 20 = $100), then compare that with the total revenue from 21 ($4.80 x 21 = $100.80). The $0.80 difference is the marginal revenue of the 21st unit.

Note that the monopolist does not have a supply curve. A supply curve shows the quantity that the seller will supply at each price, independent of demand. However, monopolists set price and quantity by looking at marginal cost and marginal revenue. A supply curve should be the same for any demand curve; the monopolist's "supply" is different for each demand and marginal-revenue curve. Therefore, a distinct supply curve does not exist for a monopolist.

## 15-3 The Welfare Cost of Monopoly

Monopoly imposes efficiency costs on society in the form of *deadweight losses* from underproduction of the good. Society maximizes well-being whenever output expands up to the point at which the extra value, or marginal benefit, is just equal to the

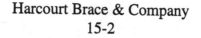

marginal cost. This maximizes the sum of the consumer and producer surplus, or the value of the good to the consumer minus the cost of making the good. By producing the output at which $MC = P$, the competitive firm produces the efficient level of output. By producing where $MC = MR < P$, the monopolist produces less than the efficient output. The outcome is a reduction in the total surplus that would result from producing at the efficient output level. The deadweight loss is the lost surplus on the withheld output. That is, the monopolist fails to produce some output that society values more than it costs to produce. This is the same logic that applies to a tax wedge between the consumers' willingness to pay and the sellers' marginal cost: The inefficiency of monopoly results from underproduction in the same way that a tax leads to underproduction.

## 15-4 Public Policy toward Monopolies

Governments attempt to limit the inefficiency associated with monopoly in a variety of ways. Policies include:

- Making monopolies behave more competitively.
- Regulating monopoly pricing and other behavior.
- Converting monopolies into public enterprises.
- Leaving monopolies alone.

To make monopolies behave more competitively, the government passed a series of antitrust laws, which tend to control monopoly power and promote competition. Under these laws, government can prevent mergers that would lead to monopoly or near-monopoly, it can prevent price fixing and other anticompetitive behavior, and it can even break up large firms in extreme cases, such as the breakup of AT&T in 1984.

Another alternative is to regulate monopoly pricing and other behavior. It is common for the government to regulate the prices charged by natural monopolies such as power companies. However, it is not possible to force them to set price equal to marginal cost, as occurs in perfect competition, without driving them out of business. Natural monopolists have declining average total cost, which means that the marginal cost must be below the average total cost. Forcing them to produce where $MC = P$ would mean $P < ATC$, because $MC < ATC$. This would result in economic losses for the firm, leading them to exit the industry in the long run. Therefore, regulators typically compromise and allow the firm to set its price equal to average total cost, resulting in zero economic profit but positive accounting profit. This guarantees a reasonable rate of return equal to the opportunity cost of using the firm's resources in alternative uses.

The third option, public ownership, is common with natural monopolies in some countries, but not in the U.S. Although it could eliminate the problem of underproduction if taxpayers were willing to make up the difference between price and average total cost, we would lose the advantage of the profit motive to hold down cost.

The final option, doing nothing, is the choice of those who feel that the inefficiency of monopoly underproduction is less than the inefficiency resulting from politically established economic policies, or that the good of society in general is not the proper criterion for establishing economic policy.

## 15-5  Price Discrimination

Many firms engage in price discrimination, which means charging different prices to different customers for the same good. For example, airlines typically offer steeply discounted prices to customers who purchase in advance and stay through a Saturday night. This is a way to discount fares to leisure travelers with highly elastic demand while continuing to charge high fares to business travelers with inelastic demand who are unlikely to want to stay through the weekend. Firms price discriminate in an attempt to get the output effect from cutting price without the price effect that would result if they lowered price to everyone. In the widget case described earlier, if the seller could have sold the 21st unit for $4.80 while continuing to sell the first 20 units for $5.00 each, then marginal revenue would have equaled the $4.80 price.

Interestingly, price discrimination can actually improve economic well-being. Remember that the monopolist underproduces because of the price effect of expanding output and moving down the demand curve. If everyone is charged a different price, then there is no price effect, and $\underline{MR} = \underline{P}$. The monopolist therefore will produce at the socially efficient $\underline{MC} = \underline{P}$, which will be the same as $\underline{MR} = \underline{P}$. The more effectively that the monopolist can discriminate, the closer its output will be to $\underline{MC} = \underline{P}$.

## 15-6  Conclusion: The Prevalence of Monopoly

Although monopoly causes a social welfare loss, its seriousness is limited by the inherent market controls over monopoly power. Total and permanent barriers to entry are rare, and even in the cases of true monopoly, there are usually relatively close substitutes for the product.

## D.  Helpful Hints

1. *No firm, not even a monopoly, can charge whatever it wants (at least not if it cares about the quantity it sells).* Monopolists charge "whatever the market will bear" rather than set price unilaterally. Even monopolists are constrained by the demand curve.

2. *The monopolist must cut price in order to sell more.* If it seems puzzling that price is greater than marginal revenue for monopolists, keep in mind that, unlike the perfect competitor, the monopolist lowers price in order to move along the demand curve and increase sales. Therefore, an extra unit sold adds less than its price to total revenue. Instead, it adds its price minus the loss of revenue caused by cutting price on the earlier units. The net addition to revenue is the marginal revenue. The

only reason that this does not hold for competitive firms is that they can sell all that they want at the market price.

## E. Terms and Definitions

Choose a definition for each key term.

Key terms:

_____Monopoly
_____Natural monopoly
_____Price discrimination
_____Two-part tariff

Definitions:

1. Charging a different price to different customers for the same good.
2. A variation on traditional price discrimination in which the customer pays a fixed amount for the right to buy from the firm and a separate price for each unit.
3. A firm that is the sole seller of a product for which there are no close substitutes.
4. An industry in which one firm can supply a good or service to an entire market at a lower cost than could two or more smaller firms.

## II. Problems and Short-Answer Questions

### A. Practice Problems

1. The chart below provides cost and revenue data for a hypothetical firm:

| Quantity | FC | VC | TC | MC | P | TR | MR | AVC |
|---|---|---|---|---|---|---|---|---|
| 0 | 40 | 0 | | | 25 | | | |
| 1 | | 30 | | | 24 | | | |
| 2 | | 50 | | | 23 | | | |
| 3 | | 58 | | | 22 | | | |
| 4 | | 64 | | | 21 | | | |
| 5 | | 70 | | | 20 | | | |
| 6 | | 80 | | | 19 | | | |
| 7 | | 94 | | | 18 | | | |
| 8 | | 114 | | | 17 | | | |
| 9 | | 144 | | | 16 | | | |

a. Fill in the blanks.

b. Is this firm a competitive firm? How can you tell?_____
_____
_____

c. What price should this firm charge and what output should it produce? What profit or loss will result? Is this a long-run equilibrium? Explain.
_____
_____
_____
_____

## B. Short-Answer Questions

1. Explain why a monopolist produces a lower output than a competitive industry produces even though both maximize profit by producing where $\underline{MC} = \underline{MR}$.

_____

_____

_____

_____

2. What are the advantages and disadvantages of price discrimination for the monopolist and for society as a whole?_____

_____

_____

_____

_____

_____

3. What are antitrust laws and what are their advantages and disadvantages for economic efficiency? _____

_____

_____

_____

_____

_____

4. a. Show equilibrium price and output for the firm in the following graph. Label the profit or loss.

   b. What type of firm is represented in the diagram? How can you tell? Explain.

_____

_____

_____

   c. What would happen if this firm produced where price equals marginal cost? Explain. _____

_____

_____

_____

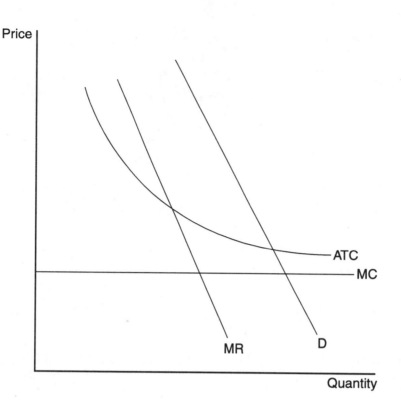

## III. Self-Test

### A. True/False Questions

_____1.     Unlike competitive producers, a monopolist restricts output below the level
at which $\underline{MR} = \underline{MC}$.

_____2.     The efficiency of monopoly is that monopolists tend to overproduce goods
that have little social value.

_____3.     For monopoly, price exceeds marginal revenue.

_____4.     A profit-maximizing monopolist should produce the output at which $\underline{MC} =$
$\underline{P}$.

_____5.     A natural monopoly is a firm with decreasing average total cost throughout
its whole range of production.

_____6.     In the long run, a monopolist is guaranteed a positive economic profit.

_____7.     In the short run, a monopolist would never produce where $\underline{P} < \underline{ATC}$.

_____8.     In the long run, a monopolist earning economic profit would lose its
monopoly position because of new competitors entering the industry.

_____9.     For price discrimination to be effective, a monopolist must be able to
separate consumers into different markets.

_____10.    Price discrimination means charging different prices to different customers
for the same good.

_____11.    A monopolist will always produce in the inelastic range of the demand
curve.

_____12.  A two-part tariff is a pricing scheme that tends to reduce social welfare.

_____13.  Discount coupons are actually irrational behavior by firms because it would be more efficient for them simply to cut price than to incur the added cost of producing coupons.

_____14.  A natural monopolist cannot earn a profit while producing at the competitive output and price levels.

_____15.  To measure the inefficiency of monopoly, simply sum the extra dollars paid by all of the consumers who are charged more than the corresponding competitive price.

## B. Multiple-Choice Questions

1. A monopolist produces where:
   a. $MC = MR$.
   b. $MC = P$.
   c. $P = ATC$.
   d. $P > ATC$.
   e. none of the above.

2. The inefficiency from monopoly results because:
   a. there is no competition to force down cost.
   b. high monopoly prices are not equitable.
   c. monopolies tend to be too big and unwieldy for efficient operation.
   d. monopolists underproduce relative to the ideal, at which society's $MC = MB$.
   e. all of the above.

3. Regulation of monopoly pricing typically leads to price equal to:
   a. $ATC$.
   b. $MC$.
   c. $MR$.
   d. "what the market will bear."
   e. none of the above.

4. A monopolist sets price:
   a. where $MC = MR$.
   b. from the demand curve at the quantity for which $MC = MR$.
   c. where supply = demand.
   d. where marginal revenue = demand.
   e. none of the above.

5. If a monopolist is producing at the point where marginal revenue exceeds marginal cost by the greatest amount, then in order to maximize profit, the monopolist should:
   a. make no change.
   b. increase output and lower price.
   c. decrease output and raise price.
   d. increase both output and price.
   e. decrease both output and price.

6. If a natural monopolist is broken up into several smaller firms, then:
   a. competition will lead to lower prices and costs.
   b. cost of production will rise.
   c. the industry will become more efficient.
   d. price will rise if demand is inelastic but fall if it is elastic.
   e. none of the above.

7. Monopoly results because of:
   a. barriers to entry into the industry.
   b. greed by the seller.
   c. lack of interest by potential competitors.
   d. inadequate regulation by government.
   e. all of the above.

8. A monopoly in long-run equilibrium:
   a. always earns an economic profit.
   b. always earns an accounting profit.
   c. always earns zero economic profit.
   d. will go out of business if it earns a zero economic profit.
   e. none of the above.

9. As the only seller, a monopolist can always:
   a. avoid economic losses.
   b. earn an accounting profit.
   c. earn an economic profit.
   d. earn monopoly profits.
   e. none of the above.

10. Price discrimination by a monopolist tends to:
   a. reduce the deadweight loss.
   b. increase economic efficiency.
   c. lead to output closer to that of the competitive firm.
   d. reduce the gap between marginal revenue and price.
   e. all of the above.

11. Price discrimination is a way for monopolists to:
    a. charge more to people based on personal characteristics rather than differences in demand.
    b. take more of the total surplus than they otherwise would have received.
    c. increase their own welfare at the expense of reduced net social welfare.
    d. lower price when costs of production are lower.
    e. all of the above.

12. The supply curve of the monopolist:
    a. is the whole marginal cost curve.
    b. is the marginal-cost curve above the average variable cost.
    c. is the average-total-cost curve.
    d. is the marginal-revenue curve.
    e. does not exist.

13. Compared with a perfectly competitive industry with the same cost structure, a monopolist would tend toward:
    a. lower price and output.
    b. lower price and higher output.
    c. higher price and lower output.
    d. higher price and output.
    e. lower price and output in the short run, with both rising in the long run.

14. In the short run, a monopolist with a loss of $50, along with marginal revenue of $15 and marginal cost of $10, should:
    a. shut down.
    b. expand output and cut price.
    c. expand output and raise price.
    d. cut output and raise price.
    e. cut output and price.

15. A price-discriminating monopolist would be likely to charge a:
    a. higher price to those with inelastic demand than to those whose demand is elastic.
    b. lower price to those with inelastic demand than to those whose demand is elastic.
    c. high price to those with both elastic and inelastic demand.
    d. higher price than a nondiscriminating monopolist.
    e. higher price in the short run than in the long run.

Use the following graph to answer Questions 16-17.

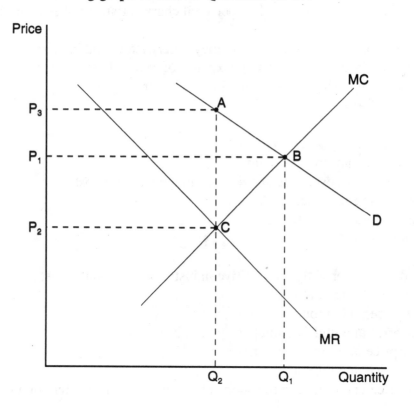

16. The firm shown in the graph would maximize profit by producing output:
   a. $Q_1$ at price $P_1$.
   b. $Q_2$ at price $P_2$.
   c. $Q_2$ at price $P_3$.
   d. $Q_2$ at price $P_1$.
   e. none of the above.

17. The deadweight loss from the monopoly is given by area:
   a. ABC.
   b. $P_3ABCP_2$.
   c. $P_3ACP_2$.
   d. $ABQ_1Q_2$
   e. none of the above.

18. Which of the following could be classified as a natural monopoly?
   a. a patented prescription drug.
   b. the U.S. Postal Service.
   c. a new computer chip that only one company has the technology to produce.
   d. a copyrighted economics textbook.
   e. all of the above.

Use the graph below to answer Questions 19 and 20.

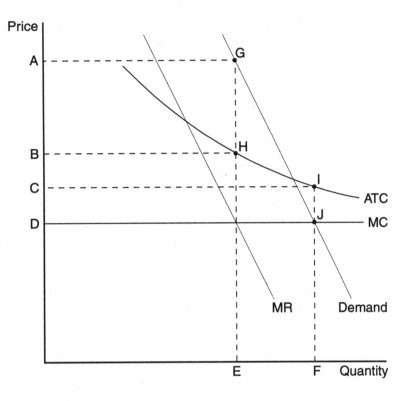

19. The profit-maximizing natural monopolist shown above would earn a profit (loss) of:
    a. AGEO.
    b. AGHB.
    c. (CIJD).
    d. DJFO.
    e. none of the above.

20. If the natural monopolist were forced to produce the competitive output and price, it would earn a profit (loss) of:
    a. AGEO.
    b. AGHB.
    c. (CIJD).
    d. DJFO.
    e. none of the above.

## IV. Advanced Critical Thinking

The production and distribution of electric power traditionally has been treated as a natural monopoly subject to government regulation of pricing.

1. Explain clearly why this is so. Would this industry still be a natural monopoly without regulation?_____

_____

_____

_____

_____

_____

_____

2. Recently there has been a move to deregulate the power industry and allow competition among producers, who could buy and sell electricity through a nationwide power grid similar to the pipelines used to transport petroleum or natural gas. How would this affect the industry's status as a natural monopoly?

_____

_____

_____

_____

_____

_____

_____

## V. Solutions

### Terms and Definitions

__3___Monopoly
__4___Natural monopoly
__1___Price discrimination
__2___Two-part tariff

**Practice Problems**

1. a.

| Quantity | FC | VC | TC | MC | P | TR | MR | AVC |
|---|---|---|---|---|---|---|---|---|
| 0 | 40 | 0 | 40 | 0 | 25 | 0 | 0 | 0 |
| 1 | 40 | 30 | 70 | 30 | 24 | 24 | 24 | 30.00 |
| 2 | 40 | 50 | 90 | 20 | 23 | 46 | 22 | 25.00 |
| 3 | 40 | 58 | 98 | 8 | 22 | 66 | 20 | 19.33 |
| 4 | 40 | 64 | 104 | 6 | 21 | 84 | 18 | 16.00 |
| 5 | 40 | 70 | 110 | 6 | 20 | 100 | 16 | 14.00 |
| 6 | 40 | 80 | 120 | 10 | 19 | 114 | 14 | 13.33 |
| 7 | 40 | 94 | 134 | 14 | 18 | 126 | 12 | 13.43 |
| 8 | 40 | 114 | 154 | 20 | 17 | 136 | 10 | 14.25 |
| 9 | 40 | 144 | 184 | 30 | 16 | 144 | 8 | 16.00 |

b. No, if it were a competitive firm it would be a price taker. This firm faces a downward-sloping demand curve from which it can pick the price–quantity combination that it prefers.

c. The firm should expand output as long as <u>MR</u> exceeds the increasing portion of <u>MC</u> without going beyond the point at which they are equal. This means producing an output of 6 at a price of $19.00. Producing 7 units would be less profitable because the marginal revenue of $12 is less than the marginal cost of $14. The firm would lose $2 on the 7th unit of output. The firm will lose $6 (<u>TR</u> - <u>TC</u> = $114-$120), so this cannot be a long-run equilibrium. In the long run the firm will sell out if business does not improve.

**Short-Answer Questions**

1. Unlike the perfect competitor, the monopolist has an incentive to cut back output to avoid driving down price as it moves along the demand curve (its marginal revenue is less than price). That is, its production decision has a price effect as well as the output effect. The competitive firm, on the other hand, is too small to affect the market price and has no price effect.

2.  The advantage of price discrimination to the monopolist is that it is a means to capture consumer surplus; it is accomplished by charging higher prices to those with low-demand elasticity and lower prices to those with high-demand elasticity. The disadvantage is that it is costly for the monopolist to identify and separate the different groups of consumers. For society, price discrimination can reduce or eliminate the incentive for the monopolist to underproduce because of the price effect of increasing output and moving down the demand curve. Perfect price discrimination would eliminate the deadweight loss from monopoly because marginal revenue would reflect the price paid, leading to output coinciding with society's valuation of the additional product. The discriminating monopolist would be willing to produce whenever the marginal consumer's price is equal to or greater than the cost of producing the additional output.

3.  Antitrust laws are intended to prevent firms or groups of firms from gaining and using monopoly power. For example, they prohibit price fixing by the firms in an industry. They can be useful in promoting competition, but they can also be detrimental when they protect inefficiency rather than competition. Antitrust laws have been used, for example, to prevent large chain stores from undercutting small stores on price, even when the large stores were simply more efficient and passing along savings to the consumer.

4.  a.

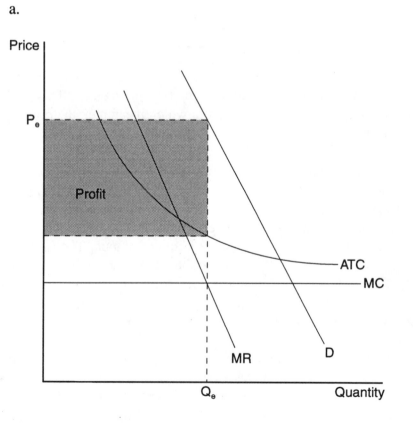

b. The firm is a natural monopoly, as evidenced by the declining average total cost. The declining average total cost occurs because marginal cost is less than average total cost.

c. A competitive firm would produce where $\underline{MC} = \underline{P}$. Because $\underline{MC} < \underline{ATC}$, price would be less than average total cost as well. This means that losses are inevitable, and the firm cannot survive in the long run with marginal-cost pricing.

**True/False Questions**

1. F; monopolists produce at $\underline{MR} = \underline{MC}$, below the competitive output where $\underline{P} = \underline{MC}$.
2. F; the efficiency problem with monopoly is that they underproduce goods that would have social value greater than the cost of producing them.
3. T
4. F; monopolists restrict output below P = $\underline{MC}$; otherwise, they would produce some units with marginal revenue less than the marginal cost due to the price effect of expanding output.
5. T
6. F; monopolists typically earn economic profits, but only if demand is sufficient to charge a price greater than average total cost.
7. F; in the short run, a monopolist might produce at a loss, as long as variable costs are covered, if demand won't support a higher price.
8. F; barriers to entry protect the monopoly position even in the long run.
9. T
10. T
11. F; a monopolist will always produce in the *elastic* range of the demand curve; in the inelastic range, raising price would increase revenues, so it would be rational to raise price until out of the inelastic range.
12. F; a two-part tariff is a variation on price discrimination; as such, it can enhance social welfare by moving the monopolist closer to the competitive output level.
13. F; discount coupons are a form of price discrimination that enables firms to capture part or all of consumer surplus; they are a rational strategy whenever the benefit outweighs the cost of the coupons.
14. T
15. F; from the standpoint of society, the extra dollars paid by consumers are canceled out by the extra dollars received by the monopolist; the inefficiency is the deadweight loss of unproduced benefits that would have been worth more to society than their cost to the monopolist to produce.

## Multiple-Choice Questions

| | | | | | |
|---|---|---|---|---|---|
| 1. | a | 8. | b | 15. | a |
| 2. | d | 9. | e | 16. | c |
| 3. | a | 10. | e | 17. | a |
| 4. | b | 11. | b | 18. | b |
| 5. | b | 12. | e | 19. | b |
| 6. | b | 13. | c | 20. | c |
| 7. | a | 14. | b | | |

## Advanced Critical Thinking

1. The electric power industry traditionally has been characterized by sufficient economies of scale so that one firm has been able to satisfy the market demand at a lower cost than would have been the case with two or more firms. Building more than one power plant for a region would have raised the average total cost. Government regulation of price was a response to natural monopoly, not a cause.

2. Such a nationwide power grid makes it possible for firms to buy and sell electric power between regions. This means that power companies in different regions can compete even though the market demand within a region is not sufficient to justify building more than one plant. This change means that the production of electric power will no longer fit the natural monopoly case, although the transmission lines remain so. It is still inefficient for competing firms to build multiple transmission lines to serve a specific area.

# Chapter 16: Oligopoly

## I. Chapter Overview

### A. Context and Purpose

Previous chapters introduced perfect competition and monopoly. These market structures provide useful information about how markets operate, even though most real-world industries are somewhere between the two extremes.

This chapter and the one that follows introduce imperfect competition, which includes the variety of firms between the two extremes. There are two types of imperfectly competitive firms—oligopolies and monopolistic competitors. This chapter deals with oligopoly, which is the market structure with few firms, each of which has a large impact on price and industry output.

### B. Learning Objectives

In this chapter you will:

1. See what market structures lie between monopoly and competition.
2. Examine what outcomes are possible when a market is an oligopoly.
3. Learn about the prisoners' dilemma and how it applies to oligopoly and other issues.
4. Consider how the antitrust laws try to foster competition in oligopolistic markets.

After accomplishing these goals, you should be able to:

1. List the major characteristics of the two types of imperfect competition, oligopoly and monopolistic competition.
2. Show the relationship between the number of firms in an industry and the equilibrium price and quantity relative to the competitive ideal.
3. Explain how it could be rational for an oligopolist to engage in apparently self-destructive behavior by failing to cooperate with other firms even when it would promote their combined well-being.
4. Evaluate the effectiveness of antitrust laws in promoting competition.

### C. Chapter Review

### 16-1 Between Monopoly and Perfect Competition

Most businesses in the real world fall somewhere between the extremes of perfect competition and monopoly. This market structure with elements of both competition and monopoly is known as *imperfect competition*. Imperfectly competitive firms can be either monopolistic competitors or oligopolists. A monopolistically competitive industry has many firms with some control over price. An oligopolistic industry has few firms, each of which has substantial impact on price and industry output. The major characteristic of oligopoly is interdependence—each firm knows that its decisions will affect decisions by other firms.

## 16-2  Markets with Only a Few Sellers

The simplest type of oligopoly is *duopoly*, which is a market with only two sellers. If the duopolists cooperate to set price and output, they will produce where marginal revenue equals marginal cost and then set price from the demand curve (charging whatever the market will bear). To accomplish this, the duopolists would need to cooperate and form a *cartel*. The problem for the duopolist is reaching an agreement through *collusion* that satisfies each firm and is enforceable. Both firms have an incentive to try to cheat on the agreement and undercut the other firm to gain a larger share of the market. When the duopolists set their production levels and corresponding prices, they choose the best strategy based on the strategies that they expect their competitor to choose. This produces an outcome known as a *Nash equilibrium*. The result is an output greater than the monopoly output but less than the competitive output. As the number of sellers rises, the output approaches the competitive level and price approaches marginal cost.

A good example of the problems inherent in a cartel is the Organization of Petroleum Exporting Countries (OPEC). This cartel of mainly Middle Eastern oil-producing countries was effective in the 1970s in reducing output to near-monopoly level. The energy crisis of 1973 was a result of OPEC efforts to restrict the supply of oil to the West. Again in 1979, with the overthrow of the Shah of Iran, OPEC was able to restrict exports of petroleum and cause another energy crisis. However, members had a tremendous incentive to cheat in order to earn greater profits. The result is that the cartel is no longer effective, and world petroleum production is relatively competitive.

## 16-3  Game Theory and the Economics of Cooperation

*Game theory* is the study of how people behave in strategic situations—situations in which, as decisionmakers, they take into account the possible responses by others. A simple example of game theory is the *prisoners' dilemma*. In its original version, police interrogate two accused criminals separately in order to get a confession. Even though they gain collectively when they refuse to confess, they eventually confess because, if either one caves in and confesses, he will be far better off. If each could have been sure that the other would honor the agreement not to confess, they both would gain by refusing to cooperate with the police. However, each has an incentive individually to confess because his or her individual gain is maximized by confessing regardless of the strategy chosen by the opponent. That is, this is a *dominant strategy*, which is an action that is clearly superior no matter which alternative is chosen by the other person.

Oligopolists face incentives that are similar to those in the prisoners' dilemma. Each seller individually has an incentive to overproduce relative to the monopoly output, even though collectively there is an incentive to restrict output to the monopoly level. Self-interest leads to the eventual breakdown of cooperation.

### 16-4  Public Policy toward Oligopolies

Beginning with the Sherman Antitrust Act of 1890, public policy has treated price fixing and other actions in restraint of trade as criminal conspiracies. Some actions, such as price fixing, are clearly illegal and not in society's interest. Other business actions are less clear-cut in terms of both legality and impact on society. For example, resale price maintenance by producers prohibits retailers from discounting price. As another example, tying agreements are often used to increase sales of supplies or accessories to be used with a piece of equipment. Critics argue that both of these actions restrain trade and limit competition. Supporters argue that both actions are justifiable. They point out that resale price maintenance and tying agreements may be necessary to protect the reputation of the producer.

### 16-5  Conclusion

Competition among oligopolists and antitrust laws prevent the firms from colluding and jointly behaving like a monopolist. Antitrust laws can promote competition, but they can also be used inappropriately, leading to a lessening of competition.

### D.  Helpful Hints

1. *Oligopoly is not a special case with different rules.* All firms maximize profits by producing where marginal revenue equals marginal cost. We can generalize from and extend the oligopoly model to cover most types of firms. The duopoly model with two sellers produces an outcome between competition and monopoly. However, if the two sellers cooperate to maximize their joint profits, the result is the same as the monopoly case. Similarly, as the number of firms increases, the oligopoly case begins to approach the competitive equilibrium.

### E.  Terms and Definitions

Choose a definition for each key term.

Key terms:

\_\_\_\_\_Imperfect competition
\_\_\_\_\_Oligopoly
\_\_\_\_\_Monopolistic competition
\_\_\_\_\_Collusion

_____Cartel
_____Nash equilibrium
_____Game theory
_____Prisoners' dilemma
_____Dominant strategy

Definitions:

1. Strategy that is the best alternative for a player to select regardless of the strategy picked by other players.
2. Market structure in between monopoly and perfect competition; includes both oligopoly and monopolistic competition
3. A group of firms acting in unison to set price and output.
4. An agreement between firms over production and price.
5. A market with many sellers, each of which differentiates its product in order to gain some control over price.
6. A market with few interdependent sellers, each selling an identical or similar product.
7. The study of how people behave in strategic situations.
8. Situation in which economic actors choose their best strategy given the strategies that they expect from others.
9. A game in which each player has as a dominant strategy an alternative that does not maximize the combined gains by both players.

## II. Problems and Short-Answer Questions

### A. Practice Problems

1. The data below apply to the market for widgets, which has only two firms, Will's Widget Works, and Wendell's Widget Wonderland.

**The Market for Widgets**

| Quantity (market) | Price | TR (mkt.) | MR (mkt.) | TR (firm) | Quantity (firm) | ATC (firm) |
|---|---|---|---|---|---|---|
| 1,000 | $500 | _____ | ____ | _____ | _____ | $110 |
| 1,200 | 450 | _____ | ____ | _____ | _____ | 110 |
| 1,400 | 400 | _____ | ____ | _____ | _____ | 110 |
| 1,600 | 350 | _____ | ____ | _____ | _____ | 110 |
| 1,800 | 300 | _____ | ____ | _____ | _____ | 110 |
| 2,560 | 110 | _____ | ____ | _____ | _____ | 110 |

a.  Suppose that the two widget makers divide up the market so that each firm has an equal share. Fill in the missing values in the table. If they jointly set output and price to maximize their combined profit (and they must produce in multiples of 200), how much will they each produce and at what price? How much profit will each firm realize? What will be the industry output, price, and profit? How does this compare with the output, price, and profit with only one firm in the market? Explain. _____

_____

_____

_____

_____

_____

_____

b.  If Will believes that he can cheat on the agreement without Wendell knowing, would he have any incentive to change his level of output? What would happen to his total revenue and profit if he expanded output by 200 and Wendell did not respond? What if he expanded by 400? By 600? What level of output would maximize Will's profit if Wendell does not respond? Is it likely that Wendell would ignore Will's behavior? Explain. If Wendell responds the same way, what would be the new level of output and the resulting price for both firms combined?_____

_____

_____

_____

_____

_____

_____

c.  Does your answer to (b) help to explain the long-term prospects for survival of cartels? What is likely to happen to such agreements in the long run and why? Would the agreement be more likely to survive if the game were run repeatedly with cheating consistently subject to retaliation and cooperation rewarded by the other player?_____

_____

_____

_____

d. Given that the <u>ATC</u> is constant at $110, what is the <u>MC</u> of each additional widget? What would happen to output and price if the number of firms continued to expand until there were many competitors? _____

_____

_____

_____

_____

_____

## B. Short-Answer Questions

1. Suppose that mergers in the auto industry resulted in only two surviving firms, Alpha Automotive Manufacturing and Beta Motor Works. Both firms are considering developing an electric automobile. Each is afraid that the other firm will develop the new automobile first, giving it a competitive edge. Even worse, the firm that fails to develop an electric automobile will lose reputation and sales in other markets as well. However, because the market is quite limited, if both companies develop an electric automobile, they will lose money. Collectively, they would be better off if neither firm develops the new technology. The table below shows the options and profits for Alpha and Beta.

|  | | **Alpha's Decision** | |
|---|---|---|---|
|  |  | Develop | Don't Develop |
|  | Develop | Alpha -$5mil. | Alpha -$30mil. |
| **Beta's** | | Beta -$5mil. | Beta +$20mil. |
| **Decision** | | | |
|  | Don't | Alpha +$20mil. | Alpha +$0 |
|  | Develop | Beta -$30mil. | Beta +$0 |

a. Is there a dominant strategy for Alpha? For Beta? Explain._____

_____

_____

_____

_____

b. If the firms act independently out of individual self-interest, what outcome will result? Is it in their joint interest? Explain._____

_____

_____

_____

_____

c. If the firms cooperate, what outcome is likely? Explain._____

_____

_____

_____

_____

2. What are tying agreements and what is their status under antitrust law? Why would sellers use them? What are the arguments for and against tying agreements? Can you think of a product that you bought subject to a tying agreement? _____

_____

_____

_____

_____

_____

_____

3. Evaluate resale price maintenance laws, or fair trade laws. What are they, and what are the arguments pro and con? _____

_____

_____

_____

_____

_____

_____

4. Oligopolists face a conflict between self-interest and group interest. Self-interest tends to make them compete, even though cooperation would be more beneficial for the group. Which behavior would be more in society's best interest, cooperation or competition, and how does society accomplish this goal? Explain.

_____

_____

_____

_____

_____

_____

## III. Self-Test

### A. True/False Questions

_____1.    The prisoners' dilemma shows that people do not always behave rationally.

_____2.    Oligopoly is characterized by a small number of interdependent firms.

_____3.    Imperfect competition includes all market structures other than perfect competition.

_____4.    Forming a cartel results in output that approaches the competitive ideal.

_____5.     As the number of firms increases in an oligopoly, the price effect diminishes.
_____6.     When a Nash equilibrium is reached, economic actors maximize their self-interest given the strategies others have chosen.
_____7.     Oligopolists maximize profit by holding output below the point at which marginal revenue equals marginal cost.
_____8.     Under oligopoly, price tends to be equal to marginal cost.
_____9.     Although it is not always attainable, a Nash equilibrium maximizes the well-being of the group.
_____10.    A Nash equilibrium leads to a result equivalent to the competitive equilibrium.
_____11.    When an oligopolist sets output to maximize profit, the output effect provides an incentive to produce more.
_____12.    The price effect of an increase in production tends to increase profit.
_____13.    As the number of firms in an oligopoly rises, price approaches marginal cost.
_____14.    Collusion among oligopolists is more likely to be effective in the long run than in the short run.
_____15.    Overutilization of common resources would never occur if people were rational and had full information about resource availability.

## B. Multiple-Choice Questions

1. When the prisoners' dilemma occurs,
   a.  self-interest leads the players to a collectively inferior outcome.
   b.  players ignore their own self-interest.
   c.  players operate out of misguided self-interest.
   d.  the good of the many outweighs the desires of the few.
   e.  players are made worse off, but society's well-being generally is maximized.

The following table shows the possible outcomes if two oil companies drill in the same spot in the Gulf of Mexico. Neither company owns the drilling rights to the entire pool of petroleum, so both have an incentive to drill to extract what is essentially a common resource. However, if both drill, their costs are higher because of the duplication of drilling equipment, but the total amount of oil available is unchanged. Use the data to answer Questions 2-5:

|  |  | **Acme Oil** | |
|---|---|---|---|
|  |  | Drill | Don't Drill |
|  | Drill | Acme: +$5 mil. | Acme: $ 0 mil. |
|  |  | Texas: +$5 mil. | Texas: +$30 mil. |
| **Texas Oil** |  |  |  |
|  | Don't Drill | Acme: +$30 mil. | Acme: $0 mil. |
|  |  | Texas: $0 mil. | Texas: $0 mil. |

2.  The game has a
    a.  dominant strategy for Acme Oil only.
    b.  dominant strategy for Texas Oil only.
    c.  dominant strategy for both Texas Oil and Acme Oil.
    d.  dominant strategy for neither company.
    e.  uncertain without additional information.

3.  The likely outcome from the game is:
    a.  drilling by Texas Oil only.
    b.  drilling by Acme Oil only.
    c.  drilling by either Texas Oil or Acme Oil, but not both.
    d   no drilling by either company.
    e.  drilling by both companies.

4.  The most desirable outcome for the two firms combined would be:
    a.  drilling by Texas Oil only.
    b.  drilling by Acme Oil only.
    c.  drilling by either Texas Oil or Acme Oil, but not both.
    d.  no drilling by either company.
    e.  drilling by both companies.

5.  Cooperation and the optimal joint outcome most likely be the case if:
    a.  both players behaved rationally.
    b.  the game were played only once.
    c.  the game were played repeatedly, with retaliation against noncooperative behavior.
    d.  the players split the proceeds evenly.
    e.  players maximized their self-interest.

6.  Resale price maintenance
    a.  is used by government to maintain price floors.
    b. • is an illegal restraint of trade by retailers acting in collusion.
    c.  establishes a maximum price for resale of items in short supply.
    d.  involves minimum retail prices established by manufacturers to prevent discounting.
    e.  provides a means for setting the rates for service contracts.

7.  Tying agreements are
    a.  a form of price discrimination.
    b.  a means for sellers to force buyers to pay for otherwise worthless products.
    c.  clearly not in the best interest of the general public.
    d.  irrational behavior by sellers who hope in vain to force people to buy products they do not want.
    e.  always legal, unless they result from conspiracies between sellers.

8. Compared with perfect competition, oligopolists tend to:
   a. overproduce and overprice.
   b. underproduce and overprice.
   c. overproduce and underprice.
   d. underproduce and underprice.
   e. underproduce in the short run, then overproduce in the long run.

9. The main reason that cartels such as OPEC tend to fail is that:
   a. self-interest drives individual players to renege on their cooperative agreements.
   b. there are too many producers for coordination to be feasible.
   c. international law prohibits them.
   d. the players fail to behave rationally.
   e. demand is inadequate, resulting in falling prices in spite of the agreement to hold back output.

10. In 1971, Congress banned cigarette advertising on television. Surprisingly, the cigarette companies did not fight the legislation. The most likely reason for this inaction by the cigarette companies is that:
    a. they did not have enough political clout to fight the ban successfully.
    b. the legislation passed quickly, before they could mobilize opposition.
    c. the ban allowed them to concentrate their advertising dollars in more effective media.
    d. the ban helped the companies cooperate to end advertising that they couldn't agree to stop on their own.
    e. each company hoped to be a free rider, letting other companies go to the expense of fighting the legislation.

11. Which of the following statements is true? Oligopolists:
    a. produce more and sell at a lower price than a monopolist when they act independently.
    b. set marginal revenue equal to marginal cost.
    c. tend to produce the monopoly output and sell at the monopoly price when they are able to collude.
    d. behave interdependently.
    e. all of the above.

12. Game theory can help to explain why countries engage in protectionist trade policies because:
    a. when trading partners enact high tariffs, both countries end up better off.
    b. high tariffs represent a dominant strategy for both trading partners.
    c. Nash equilibrium maximizes the two countries' joint welfare.
    d. totally free trade results in one country winning at the expense of another.
    e. none of the above.

13. Game theory is most applicable to markets with:
    a. few firms.
    b. many firms.
    c. cartels.
    d. one firm.
    e. all of the above.

14. Game theory is an appropriate model of firm behavior whenever economic actors are:
    a. motivated mostly by the desire for power, rather than profit.
    b. interdependent.
    c. independent.
    d. motivated by group interest as well as self-interest.
    e. unaffected by the decisions of others.

15. Which of the following would be most likely to result in increased long-run profits for taxicab companies in Gotham City?
    a. tough licensing restrictions limiting the number of new taxis on the streets.
    b. collusion between companies to raise taxi fares 20 percent.
    c. better street maintenance by local government, lowering taxi maintenance costs.
    d. a reduction in the gasoline tax.
    e. $1,000 per month subsidies for each taxi in service.

16. Which of the following may make it difficult for oligopolists to collude to set price?
    a. a large number of firms.
    b. a standardized product.
    c. high barriers to entry.
    d. the tendency for collusion to lower joint profits in the long run.
    e. licensing restrictions by government.

17. The prisoners' dilemma can help to explain:
    a. nuclear arms races.
    b. behavior by oligopolists.
    c. overutilization of common resources.
    d. confessions by criminals who were unlikely to be convicted if they kept quiet.
    e. all of the above.

18. The main factor that could maintain long-run oligopoly profit is:
    a. high demand for the product.
    b. collusion among sellers.
    c. barriers to entry.
    d. favorable tax treatment by government.
    e. inelastic demand for the product.

19. The most important characteristic that would permit short-run monopoly output and pricing by a group of oligopolists is:
    a. a small number of sellers.
    b. a standardized product.
    c. a differentiated product.
    d. government regulation.
    e. inelastic demand.

20. Reaching a cooperative outcome in a prisoners' dilemma game is more likely if:
    a. players realize that the mutual interest is served best by cooperating.
    b. the game is played repeatedly, with the threat of retaliation against those who refuse to cooperate.
    c. the game is played only once, and players know that there will be devastating retaliation if they fail to cooperate.
    d. players realize that if they fail to cooperate, so will others.
    e. none of the above.

## IV. Advanced Critical Thinking

Some economists have argued that antitrust policy has done more harm than good. They believe that monopoly power is more likely to be created by than cured by government action, and that antitrust policy often is aimed toward protecting competitors rather than competition. They believe that the market provides the best protection against inappropriate restraint of trade. Do you agree? Write a short essay in which you give the arguments for and against antitrust laws. Be specific, including at a minimum discussion of resale price maintenance (fair trade laws), tying agreements, and price fixing.

_____
_____
_____
_____
_____
_____
_____
_____
_____
_____
_____

## V. Solutions

### Terms and Definitions

___2___ Imperfect competition
___6___ Oligopoly

___5___Monopolistic competition
___4___Collusion
___3___Cartel
___8___Nash equilibrium
___7___Game theory
___9___Prisoners' dilemma
___1___Dominant strategy

## Practice Problems

1. The data below apply to the market for widgets, which has only two firms, Will's Widget Works, and Wendell's Widget Wonderland.

### The Market for Widgets

| Quantity (market) | Price | TR (mkt.) | MR (mkt.) | TR (firm) | Quantity (firm) | ATC (firm) |
|---|---|---|---|---|---|---|
| 1000 | $500 | $500,000 | — | $250,000 | 500 | $110 |
| 1200 | 450 | 540,000 | $200 | 270,000 | 600 | 110 |
| 1400 | 400 | 560,000 | 100 | 280,000 | 700 | 110 |
| 1600 | 350 | 560,000 | 0 | 280,000 | 800 | 110 |
| 1800 | 300 | 540,000 | -100 | 270,000 | 900 | 110 |
| 2560 | 110 | 281,600 | — | — | — | 110 |

a. If the firms cooperate to maximize joint profit, they jointly will produce the monopoly output and charge the monopoly price (and earn monopoly profit). They will produce as long as marginal revenue exceeds marginal cost for the industry. Output will be 600 each at a price of $450. Each firm will earn a profit of $204,000. Industry output will be 1,200 at a price of $450. Industry profit will be $408,000.

b. Will would earn a greater profit if he could increase output while Wendell continues to produce 600. If he expanded output by 200, his total output would be 800 and industry output would be 1,400 at a price of $400. His revenue would be $320,000 (800 x $400), and his total cost would be $88,000 (800 x $110), for a profit of $232,000. If he increased output to 1,000, his profit would be $240,000 (1,000 x $350 less 1,000 x $110). However, if he increased output to 1,200, his profit would fall to $228,000 (1,200 x 300 less 1,200 x $110). Therefore, Will would maximize profit at output = 1,000. However, Wendell is likely to do the same thing, resulting in combined output of 2,000 at a price of $250. Combined profit would fall to $280,000 (2,000 x $250 less 2,000 x $110).

c. Yes, the answer demonstrates the strong incentive for firms to cheat on their agreements to limit output. Each firm finds it profitable to increase output beyond the agreed-upon amount. If the game is repeated and there is the possibility of rewards for cooperation and penalties for cheating, there is more chance that the agreement will be honored.

d. If <u>ATC</u> is constant at $110, then <u>MC</u> must also be $110. With many competitors, there would be no price effect, and marginal revenue would be the same as price. Output would expand until price equals marginal cost. This occurs at an output of 2,560 and a price of $110.

## Short-Answer Questions

1. Suppose that mergers in the auto industry resulted in only two surviving firms, Alpha Automotive Manufacturing and Beta Motor Works. Both firms are considering developing an electric automobile. Each is afraid that the other firm will develop the new automobile first, giving it a competitive edge that may even spill over into its sales of other automobiles. However, because the market is quite limited, if both companies develop an electric automobile, they will lose money. Collectively, they would be better off if neither firm develops the new technology. The following table shows the options and profit for Alpha and Beta.

|  |  | **Alpha's Decision** | |
|---|---|---|---|
|  |  | Develop | Don't Develop |
| | Develop | Alpha -$5mil.<br>Beta -$5mil. | Alpha -$30mil.<br>Beta +$20mil. |
| **Beta's Decision** | | | |
| | Don't Develop | Alpha +$20mil.<br>Beta -$30mil. | Alpha $0<br>Beta $0 |

a. Yes, both firms have "develop" as a dominant strategy because, whatever choice the competition makes, developing the electric automobile makes the firm better off. For example, if Alpha decides not to develop, then Beta can gain $20 million by developing, but nothing for not developing. If Alpha decides to develop, then Beta loses either way, but the loss is less ($5 million vs. $30 million) if Beta develops.

b. Both firms will develop electric autos because this is a dominant strategy that maximizes each firm's individual gain regardless of the other's choice. It is not in their joint interest, however, because both firms lose $5 million, which they could have avoided if neither developed an electric car.

c. As explained in (b), both firms could cooperate and agree not to produce an electric automobile, resulting in neither a gain nor a loss. This outcome is their best collective choice.

2. Tying agreements are business practices under which sellers bundle two products for sale so that buyers are forced to purchase both if they want either one. Tying agreements have been somewhat restricted by the Supreme Court under the antitrust laws under the argument that they represent restraint of trade. They can be used as a form of price discrimination, making it easier for sellers to capture part of consumer surplus without charging separate prices to different buyers. Manufacturers can also protect against inferior accessories or replacement parts by tying lease agreements to the purchase of original equipment supplies and parts. Although they do restrict consumers' options, they also protect the seller. A good example is the operating system that is bundled with new personal computers—nearly all new machines come with Microsoft DOS and/or Windows software.

3. Fair trade laws allow the manufacturer to set a minimum retail price for the product. Critics argue that they prevent competition and subsidize inefficient, high-cost retailers at the expense of big discount stores. Supporters argue that discounters get a free ride when full-service stores offer product information and advice that the discounters do not offer. Customers get advice from the full-service stores, then buy from a discounter. Also, some manufacturers prefer to avoid having their brand name associated with a discount image.

4. Competition is better for society because it leads to price and output that are closer to the competitive ideal. Antitrust laws are used to limit cooperation by oligopolists in setting price and other production and sales decisions.

**True/False Questions**

1. F; the prisoners' dilemma shows that rational self-interest may not always maximize joint interest.
2. T
3. F; imperfect competition includes the market structures of monopolistic competition and oligopoly.
4. F; forming a cartel results in monopoly output.
5. T
6. T
7. F; oligopolists maximize profit by setting output where marginal revenue equals marginal cost.
8. F; under oligopoly, marginal revenue is equal to marginal cost but less than price.
9. F; a Nash equilibrium often fails to maximize the group's interests.
10. F; a Nash equilibrium may result in increased output relative to the case with cooperation, but it will not move the market all the way to the competitive equilibrium.
11. T
12. F; the price effect decreases profit.
13. T
14. F; collusion tends to be more effective in the short run.

15. F; overutilization of common resources is rational behavior when people are subject to the prisoners' dilemma.

## Multiple-Choice Questions

| | | |
|---|---|---|
| 1. a | 8. b | 15. a |
| 2. c | 9. a | 16. a |
| 3. e | 10. d | 17. e |
| 4. c | 11. e | 18. c |
| 5. c | 12. b | 19. a |
| 6. d | 13. a | 20. b |
| 7. a | 14. b | |

## Advanced Critical Thinking

It is true that results under antitrust policy have been mixed. Some policies have actually restrained competition; for example, resale price maintenance (fair trade) laws that permit the manufacturer to set a minimum retail price. However, without such laws, full-service retailers would be at a disadvantage relative to discount stores that may "free ride" on the full-service stores as providers of production information and service. Similarly, tying agreements can restrict voluntary exchange, but manufacturers may need to protect their reputations by controlling the quality of supplies and accessories used along with their products. Also criticized are restrictions against predatory pricing—selling below cost just long enough to drive competitors out of business, then raising price even higher than before. Critics argue that potential competitors are available to undercut the predatory firm as soon as price rises. Perhaps the strongest case can be made for restrictions on collusion to fix prices.

# Chapter 17: Monopolistic Competition

## I. Chapter Overview

### A. Context and Purpose

Earlier chapters introduced the notion of market structure, which can range from competition, with many buyers and sellers, to monopoly, with a single seller. The extreme cases are useful for analyzing implications of various assumptions about markets, but they may seem unrealistic for the real world, which is rarely that black and white.

We continue our discussion of the gray area between monopoly and competition with Chapter 17, which deals with the market structure of monopolistic competition. This category includes fast-food restaurants, gasoline service stations, corner markets—in short, most of the businesses that we deal with every day. You will see that monopolistic competition shares some of the characteristics of a monopoly and some of a perfectly competitive industry.

### B. Learning Objectives

In this chapter you will:

1. Analyze competition among firms that sell differentiated products.
2. Compare the equilibrium under monopolistic competition and under perfect competition.

After accomplishing these goals, you should be able to:

1. Explain the effect of product differentiation on the pricing and output decisions of firms that have many competitors producing relatively close substitutes—in short, the case of monopolistic competition.
2. Identify the differences between perfect and monopolistic competition, particularly the monopolistic competitor's control over price as a result of differentiating its product, as well as the similarities, notably the lack of long-run profit, because of the ease of entry into the industry.

### C. Chapter Review

Monopolistic competition shares characteristics of both monopoly and perfect competition. There are three major characteristics:

- Many sellers
- Free entry
- Product differentiation

The first two characteristics make monopolistic competition similar to perfect competition. In fact, because of free entry, long-run economic profits are driven to zero, as in the competitive case. The third characteristic is the reason for the monopolistic competitor's control over price. By differentiating its product, the firm is able to control its price within some range.

## 17-1 Competition with Differentiated Products

The ability to differentiate its product allows the monopolistic competitor to act like a monopolist to some extent. In fact, it sets price and quantity in the same manner that a monopolist does: output occurs where $\underline{MC} = \underline{MR}$, and the maximum price it can charge is determined by the demand curve ("what the market will bear"). In the long run, the situation changes. Unlike the monopolist, the monopolistic competitor faces competition from new entrants whenever economic profit is positive. The result is an $\underline{ATC}$ curve that is just tangent to the demand curve in long-run equilibrium. Economic profit is zero, as in the perfectly competitive case. However, unlike the perfect competitor, the monopolistic competitor faces a downward-sloping demand curve; therefore, the tangency is at an output below the efficient scale, and the firm has excess capacity (it could lower $\underline{ATC}$ by increasing output). Also, because $\underline{MR} < \underline{P}$, the firm faces a price effect that discourages production at the socially desirable competitive level. Unlike the perfect competitor, it has no incentive to produce where $\underline{MC} = \underline{P}$.

The monopolistic competitor has mixed effects on efficiency. On the one hand, it adds to the variety of products available for consumers. However, it also produces above minimum $\underline{ATC}$, suggesting that there are too many firms in the industry, each producing below the efficient scale.

## 17-2 Advertising

Just as monopolistic competition has mixed effects on economic efficiency, so does advertising. On the one hand, advertising can impede competition and distort consumers' wants. On the other hand, advertising can be a valuable source of information for consumers. Even emotional advertising can be useful in the sense that a firm that is willing to advertise must believe attracting customers will lead to repeat business. A big advertising campaign provides some evidence that the seller has confidence in its product and will stand behind it.

## D. Helpful Hints

1. *The underproduction of monopolistic competition is a source of inefficiency.* Remember that even though price in monopolistic competition is higher than would be the case in perfect competition, price itself is not the source of inefficiency. Rather, it is the lower quantity that results from the higher price. By itself, the higher price merely redistributes income from buyers to sellers; the efficiency effect occurs because people buy fewer units of the product at the higher price.

## E. Terms and Definitions

Choose a definition for each key term.

Key terms:

_____Monopolistic competition
_____Differentiated product
_____Excess capacity

Definitions:

1. A product with no perfect substitutes; this is a characteristic of monopolistic competition that allows firms to act as price setters.
2. Occurs under monopolistic competition when firms produce on the downward-sloping portion of their ATC curves, resulting in less than the efficient scale of production.
3. A market structure in which many sellers supply somewhat differentiated products in an industry with free entry.

## II. Problems and Short-Answer Questions

### A. Practice Problems

1. The following table lists characteristics of various types of market structure.

**Types of Market Structure**

| Type: | _____ | _____ | _____ | _____ |
|---|---|---|---|---|
| **Characteristics:** | | | | |
| Number of sellers | Very many | Many | One | Few |
| Type of product | Standardized | Differentiated | Standardized or differentiated | Unique |
| Barriers to entry | None | Very low | High | Total |
| Control over price | None | Some | High | Interdependent |
| Long-run profit | Zero | Zero | Typically positive | Typically positive |
| Advertising | None | Yes | Limited; often for public relations | Yes, if differentiated |
| Example | _____ | _____ | _____ | _____ |

a. Fill in the blank for type of market structure and give an example of each.

b. What accounts for the differences in long-run profit between the various market structures? Why is long-run profit listed as "typically positive" rather than simply "positive" for the last two types of market structure listed?

_____

_____

_____

_____

_____

_____

c. Explain why your examples are appropriate._____

_____

_____

_____

d. Why do the different market structures vary in their use of advertising?

_____

_____

_____

_____

## B. Short-Answer Questions

1. Monopolistic competition is criticized for generating wasteful excess capacity.
   Explain what is meant by this charge. Do monopolistic competitors behave
   irrationally, or is it logical behavior? How does this affect the consumer?

_____

_____

_____

_____

_____

_____

2. What does monopolistic competition have in common with perfect competition? In
   what ways does it fall short of the competitive ideal and why? _____

_____

_____

_____

3. What does monopolistic competition have in common with monopoly? In what
   ways are the outcomes in a monopolistically competitive industry preferable to
   those in a monopoly? _____

_____

_____

_____

_____

## III. Self-Test

### A. True/False Questions

_____1.     Advertising is inherently inefficient because it adds an additional layer of cost to the product price.

_____2.     Long-run profit disappears under monopolistic competition because new firms enter the industry and drive down price and profit.

_____3.     Monopolistic competitors in the long run produce at minimum average total cost due to free entry into the industry.

_____4.     With monopolistic competition, production at the efficient scale would require fewer firms, each producing a larger output.

_____5.     Monopolistic competitors set output and price at the point at where marginal revenue equals marginal cost.

_____6.     Brand names can be advantageous to society by providing an incentive for firms to maintain quality.

_____7.     Both monopolistic competition and perfect competition produce at the efficient scale in the long run due to free entry.

_____8.     Both monopolistic competition and monopoly tend to underproduce relative to the competitive ideal of price = marginal cost.

_____9.     Monopolistic competitors are able to differentiate their products enough to maintain modest long-run economic profit.

_____10.    The best example of imperfect competition is monopoly, which is the opposite of perfect competition.

_____11.    Even when it contains little specific information about the product, advertising can provide a signal to consumers about the quality of the product.

_____12.    Bans on advertising of goods such as eyeglasses may be harmful to the seller, but they are useful in protecting the consumer.

_____13.    Most economists agree that because of the problem of excess capacity, monopolistic competition is detrimental to society's well-being.

_____14.    A rational monopolistic competitor would never produce at a loss.

_____15.    Gasoline service stations are not true monopolistic competitors because they do not sell a truly differentiated product:  Gasoline is essentially standardized.

## B. Multiple-Choice Questions

1. Which of the following statements is true regarding monopolistic competition?
   a. Monopolistic competitors produce at the socially efficient level of output, as evidenced by their inability to earn economic profit in the long run.
   b. Monopolistic competitors share entry restrictions with monopoly, although those restrictions are not quite as rigid.
   c. Unlike the oligopolist, the monopolistic competitor sells a product that is different from those of other firms.
   d. Like the perfect competitor, the monopolistic competitor must sell at the prevailing market price.
   e. Like the monopolist, the monopolistic competitor sells at a price that is greater than marginal cost and marginal revenue.

2. The *most important* source of inefficiency under monopolistic competition is:
   a. lack of spending on research and development.
   b. excess capacity, because there are too many firms producing essentially the same product.
   c. failure to capitalize on economies of scale that would make the firm more efficient if it expanded.
   d. the business-stealing externality that results when new firms enter the industry.
   e. the product-variety externality that results from the introduction of a new product.

Use the following information to answer Questions 3 and 4.

A monopolistic competitor is producing an output of 1,000. Marginal cost is $75, marginal revenue is $100, and price is $150. Total cost is $200,000, of which $60,000 is fixed.

3. In the short run, to maximize profit or minimize loss, the firm should:
   a. shut down.
   b. reduce its output and raise price.
   c. keep output at 1,000 but raise price.
   d. keep output and price the same.
   e. expand its output and lower price.

4. In the long run, the firm should:
   a. go out of business unless it can avoid economic losses by increasing output and lowering price.
   b. reduce its output and raise price in order to maximize profit.
   c. keep output at 1,000 but raise price.
   d. keep output and price the same but increase its efficiency in order to maximize profit.
   e. expand its output and maintain price in order to reach a more efficient size and ensure a profit.

Use the information below to answer Questions 5-7:

Suppose that a monopolistic competitor producing an output of 100 units faces the following revenues and costs:   Price = $100; marginal revenue = $50; marginal cost = $75, and average total cost = $90.

5.  In order to maximize profit, the firm should:
    a.  reduce output and raise price.
    b.  increase output and raise price.
    c.  increase output and lower price.
    d.  keep output and price the same.
    e.  keep output the same but raise price.

6.  At its current output of 100 units, the firm:
    a.  realizes a loss of $4,000.
    b.  realizes a loss of $2,500.
    c.  just breaks even.
    d.  earns a profit of $1,000.
    e.  earns a profit of $2,500.

7.  If the firm were a competitive firm with price = $100 and the same cost curves, it should:
    a.  reduce output and raise price.
    b.  increase output and keep price the same.
    c.  increase output and lower price.
    d.  keep output and price the same.
    e.  keep output the same but raise price.

Use the following data for Questions 8 and 9.

A monopolistic competitor is in long-run equilibrium at an output of 5,000.  Price is $50, and marginal revenue is $5.

8.  The marginal cost of the 5,000th unit of output is:
    a.  $5.
    b.  $50.
    c.  $25,000.
    d.  $250,000.
    e.  equal to the ATC.

9. Average total cost is:
   a. at a minimum at $50.
   b. above its minimum point at $50.
   c. at a minimum at $5.
   d. above its minimum at $5.
   e. indeterminate without additional information.

10. The monopolistic competitor differs from the competitive firm in that it:
   a. has no demand curve in the traditional sense.
   b. can earn economic profit for long periods of time.
   c. charges a price greater than marginal cost.
   d. exists in an industry without free entry.
   e. none of the above.

11. Long-run profit is zero for monopolistic competitors because:
   a. new competitors drive profit to zero in the long run.
   b. they are innovative firms that use their economic profit to develop new products.
   c. they produce at an average total cost greater than the minimum.
   d. they fail to operate at the efficient scale.
   e. all of the above.

12. Which of the following statements is true?
   a. Advertising is inherently inefficient because it adds to the cost of production without creating anything of value.
   b. Advertising is inherently valuable because it increases sales and lowers overall average total cost, leading to lower prices.
   c. Advertising is costly, but it also provides benefits in the form of product information.
   d. Brand names add to the price paid by consumers without providing anything of value.
   e. none of the above.

13. Monopolistic competition differs from monopoly in that monopolists:
   a. charge whatever the market will bear.
   b. can earn short-run profit.
   c. can earn long-run profit.
   d. produce where marginal revenue = marginal cost but use the demand curve to set price.
   e. all of the above.

Use the graph below to answer Questions 14-19:

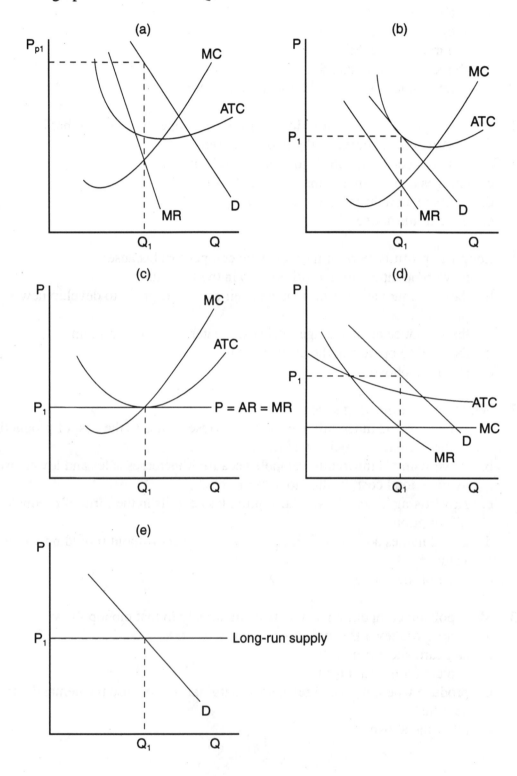

14. A monopolistic competitor in short-run (but not long-run) equilibrium is shown in diagram:
   a. (a).
   b. (b).
   c. (c).
   d. (d).
   e. (e).

15. A monopolistic competitor in long-run equilibrium is shown in diagram:
   a. (a).
   b. (b).
   c. (c).
   d. (d).
   e. (e).

16. A competitive firm in long-run equilibrium is shown in diagram:
   a. (a).
   b. (b).
   c. (c).
   d. (d).
   e. (e).

17. Which of the following diagrams is most likely to represent a monopolist other than a natural monopolist?
   a. (a)
   b. (b)
   c. (c)
   d. (d)
   e. (e)

18. A competitive industry in long-run equilibrium is shown in diagram:
   a. (a).
   b. (b).
   c. (c).
   d. (d).
   e. (e).

19. A natural monopoly in long-run equilibrium is shown in diagram:
   a. (a).
   b. (b).
   c. (c).
   d. (d).
   e. (e).

20. In the short run, a monopolistic competitor that is losing money will:
    a. always shut down, at least until business improves.
    b. continue to produce as long as it is covering its variable cost.
    c. raise price to reduce its losses.
    d. lower price in order to increase sales enough to end the losses.
    e. keep price the same and increase output enough to end the losses.

## IV. Advanced Critical Thinking

A newspaper columnist argued recently that the U.S. economy is much less efficient than it might be because of the large number of virtually identical competing products. He claimed that we would get much more value for our shopping dollars if we had only one brand of toothpaste, for example, rather than the hundreds that now exist. Similarly with automobiles, we could produce a high-quality product at a lower price if we concentrated on producing one or two of the best designs currently available. He argues that one advantage of a command system such as the former Soviet Union is that a central planning board can make such decisions in the public interest.

In the form of a Letter to the Editor, respond to the columnist. Your letter should include an economic interpretation of his argument as well as a critique that explains the extent to which you agree or disagree with his argument. _____

_____
_____
_____
_____
_____
_____
_____
_____
_____
_____
_____
_____
_____
_____
_____
_____

## V. Solutions

### Terms and Definitions

__3___Monopolistic competition
__1___Differentiated product
__2___Excess capacity

**Practice Problems**

1  a.

### Types of Market Structure

| Type: | Perfect Competition | Monopolistic Competition | Monopoly | Oligopoly |
|---|---|---|---|---|
| **Characteristics:** | | | | |
| Number of sellers | Very many | Many | One | Few |
| Type of product | Standardized | Differentiated | Standardized or differentiated | Unique |
| Barriers to entry | None | Very Low | Total | High |
| Control over price | None | Some | High | Interdependent |
| Long-run profit | Zero | Zero | Typically positive | Typically positive |
| Advertising | None | Yes | Limited; often for public relations | Yes, if differentiated |
| Example | Wheat | Convenience marts | Cable television | Automobiles |

b. Freedom of entry accounts for the difference in long-run profitability. Free entry eliminates long-run profits for both competition and monopolistic competition. Both monopoly and oligopoly are characterized by barriers to entry that can permit long-run profit. However, such barriers do not guarantee profit; demand may be insufficient to allow a profit.

c. Wheat is a good example of perfect competition because there are many sellers, each of whom is a price taker who cannot influence the market price. Convenience marts are monopolistic competitors: Each attempts to carve out a market niche in which it has some monopoly power. It can set price within a fairly narrow range. With a government-issued franchise as a single seller, a cable-television company is a good example of monopoly. Automobile companies are classic examples of oligopoly, because there are a few interdependent sellers in an industry with high barriers to entry.

d. Perfect competitors do not advertise because they can already sell all that they produce at the going market price. Monopolistic competitors advertise relatively heavily in order to differentiate their products and gain market share. Monopolists have less incentive to advertise, other than for public relations purposes. Oligopolists with differentiated products tend to advertise heavily in order to build and maintain market share. Those with standardized products, such as the steel industry, are less likely to advertise, other than to provide price information.

## Short-Answer Questions

1. When competition drives the price down to a tangency with average total cost, this tangency occurs above the minimum ATC due to the downward-sloping demand curve faced by monopolistic competitors. This means production is at less than the efficient scale. As a result, if there were fewer firms, each producing a somewhat higher quantity, then ATC would be lower. This is rational profit-maximizing behavior by the firm, which sets quantity where MR = MC. For the consumer, this means higher price but greater variety.

2. Both market structures have free entry, resulting in zero long-run profit. However, because monopolistic competitors have some control over price, their marginal revenue is less than the price and their production where MR = MC results in lower output than the socially optimal marginal-cost pricing used by competitors.

3. Both types of firms produce where MR = MC, which results in less than the socially optimal marginal-cost pricing of perfect competition. This occurs because both are price setters. However, the monopolistic competitor faces enough competition to eliminate long-run monopoly profits.

## True/False Questions

1. F; advertising adds cost, but it also adds benefits by providing information about product quality and price.
2. T
3. F; monopolistic competitors produce at average total cost, but it is above the minimum because of the downward-sloping demand curve.
4. T
5. F; monopolistic competitors set output at the point where marginal revenue equals marginal cost, but price is read from the demand curve.
6. T
7. F; only perfect competitors produce at the efficient scale in the long run.
8. T
9. F; monopolistic competitors achieve zero long-run economic profit.

10. F; imperfect competition includes the cases in between monopoly and perfect competition.
11. T
12. F; bans on advertising of goods such as eyeglasses result in higher prices that hurt the consumer.
13. F; the excess capacity of monopolistic competition must be weighed against the resulting additional variety available to the consumer.
14. F; a rational monopolistic competitor will produce at a loss in the short run, as long as variable costs are covered.
15. F; gasoline service stations are true monopolistic competitors: they are able to set price because they sell a product that is differentiated, at least in the minds of the consumer.

## Multiple-Choice Questions

| | | | |
|---|---|---|---|
| 1. e | 8. a | 15. b | |
| 2. b | 9. b | 16. c | |
| 3. e | 10. c | 17. a | |
| 4. a | 11. a | 18. e | |
| 5. a | 12. c | 19. d | |
| 6. d | 13. c | 20. b | |
| 7. b | 14. a | | |

## Advanced Critical Thinking

The columnist is referring to the well-documented problem of excess capacity under monopolistic competition. Each seller differentiates its product slightly, resulting in a large number of firms, each facing a downward-sloping demand curve. The result is production at less than the efficient scale of output (where ATC is minimized). The alternative may be worse, however, because of the loss of consumer sovereignty. Under the current system, there are more alternatives available to the consumer; the best will survive in the marketplace. The price may actually be lower because of the effect of competition in pushing firms to cut costs and raise quality as much as possible. A single seller, perhaps operated by the government, would have little incentive to innovate and increase productivity. Without competition, the producers in the former Soviet Union produced products that were less innovative and of lower quality than would have been the case in the presence of competition. If we were to adopt this plan, who would make the decision regarding which toothpaste or which automobile would be produced? Who would push the seller to be more innovative or to increase productivity? Even in the former Soviet Union, sellers were encouraged to use brand names in order to promote accountability for product quality.

# Chapter 18: The Markets for the Factors of Production

## I. Chapter Overview

### A. Context and Purpose

Previous chapters provided a framework for analysis of product markets. This chapter and the following chapter analyze the operation of input markets—markets for the factors of production. Chapter 18 explains the behavior of labor markets, followed in Chapter 19 by an indepth look at how wages are determined in the U.S. economic system.

### B. Learning Objectives

In this chapter you will:

1. Analyze the labor demand of competitive, profit-maximizing firms.
2. Learn why equilibrium wages equal the value of the marginal product of labor.
3. Consider how the other factors of production—land and capital—are compensated.
4. Examine how a change in the supply of one factor alters the earnings of all the factors.

After accomplishing these goals, you should be able to:

1. Explain how the demand for labor is derived from the demand for labor's product and why the demand curve for labor is downward sloping.
2. Apply to the firm's hiring decision the general rule for decisionmaking—do anything as long as the marginal benefit is at least equal to the marginal cost, recognizing that the value of marginal product and wages represent marginal benefit and marginal cost, respectively.
3. Extend marginal productivity theory to other inputs as well, showing that the demand for land and capital is also the value of the marginal product and that supply and demand jointly determine the return to any factor of production.
4. Demonstrate that a change in the supply of a factor of production affects the value of the marginal product of other factors, thereby changing the demand for those factors; for example, access to additional capital makes labor more productive, leading to higher demand (and higher wages).

### C. Chapter Review

The demand for a factor of production is a *derived demand*; that is, it is derived from the demand for its product. This chapter analyzes factor demand by competitive, profit-maximizing firms.

## 18-1 A Firm's Demand for Labor

Labor markets differ from product markets because labor is a derived demand. Firms value labor not for itself, but for what it can produce. Nevertheless, the basic principle still applies that rational people think at the margin. Employers deciding how much labor to hire must weigh the additional cost of another worker against the additional benefit received by selling the output produced by an additional worker. The general rule for decisionmaking still applies: Do anything as long as the marginal benefit is at least equal to the marginal cost. In the case of the labor market, this means hiring additional workers as long as they add less to cost than they add to revenue.

In a competitive environment, the added cost of another worker is simply the wage. The added revenue is the dollar value of the extra worker's output. This added revenue is known as the *value of the marginal product*. Specifically, the value of the marginal product is the marginal product times the price of the product. The value of the marginal product begins to decline when the marginal product itself begins to decline. Because the profit-maximizing firm is willing to hire workers up to the point at which the wage (the price of labor) equals the value of the marginal product, the value of the marginal product is the firm's demand curve for labor.

## 18-2 Labor-Market Equilibrium

For the overall labor market, the wage is the price of labor, and it adjusts to bring supply and demand into balance. In addition, the wage must always equal the value of the marginal product. Therefore, any change in supply and demand that affects the wage must also change the value of the marginal product by the same amount. For example, if the supply of labor falls, the wage rises. The intersection of the old demand and new supply curves will be at a point on the demand curve with a higher value of the marginal product. Similarly, if the value of the marginal product of labor increases, either because of an increase in productivity or an increase in product price, the rightward shift in labor demand will increase equilibrium wages and employment. Again, the value of the marginal product and the wage rate increase together.

Because wages equal productivity (value of the marginal product), it should not be surprising that higher productivity leads to a higher standard of living. Countries with more physical capital, human capital, and technological knowledge tend to have higher productivity and wages, providing a higher standard of living.

## 18-3 The Other Factors of Production: Land and Capital

The analysis of wage determination in labor markets has a parallel in the markets for land and capital. However, it is important to separate the purchase price of land and capital from the rental price. Just as the price of labor—the wage—is essentially a rental price, the prices of land and capital are rental prices for the use of the resources. Producers essentially rent, or buy the services of, land, labor and capital when they buy productive resources. The demand for capital is the value of the marginal product of capital. The same is true for land. Producers will use any resource as long as an additional unit adds at least as much to revenues as it adds to cost.

The value of the marginal product of any factor of production is related to the supply of other factors of production. Labor productivity is affected by the amount of capital and land that are available, just as land productivity and capital productivity are affected by availability of the other factors. As a result, an increase in the supply of a factor of production will reduce the value of its marginal product while raising the value of the marginal product of other factors of production.

## 18-4 Conclusion

According to the *neoclassical theory of distribution* presented in this chapter, each factor of production in a competitive market earns the value of the marginal product. If one worker or other factor of production earns more than another, it is because it has a higher value of the marginal product.

## D. Helpful Hints

1. *The profit-maximizing firm hires additional workers until it breaks even on the last worker hired.* If it seems counterintuitive that employers would hire workers until they just break even on the last worker hired, remember that this is a *marginal* decision. They are not breaking even on the *average* worker. By hiring every worker who can produce more than enough to pay his or her wage, the firm is maximizing its net gain or profit. It breaks even on the marginal worker, but it keeps the gains from all of the workers who were hired before.

## E. Terms and Definitions

Choose a definition for each key term.

Key terms:

_____Factors of Production
_____Derived Demand
_____Production Function
_____Marginal Product of Labor
_____Diminishing Marginal Product
_____Value of the Marginal Product
_____Capital

Definitions:

1. The relationship between the quantity of inputs used in production and the resulting quantity of output.
2. The inputs used to produce goods and services; land, labor, and capital.
3. The stock of equipment and structures used for production.
4. Marginal product of an input multiplied by the product price.
5. Demand that is derived from the demand for the product itself, such as the demand for labor.
6. The point at which marginal product begins to decline; total output continues to increase, but at a decreasing rate.
7. The increase in total output from an additional unit of labor.

## II. Problems and Short-Answer Questions

### A. Practice Problems

1. The data below show the relationship between number of workers hired and costs and revenues for a small Italian restaurant in East Poughkeepsie, Eddie's Eggplant Emporium.

| Quantity of Labor | Output | Marginal Product | Price | Value of the Marginal Product | Wage | Marginal Profit |
|---|---|---|---|---|---|---|
| L | Q | $MP_{labor}$ | P | $VMP_{labor}$ | w | $\Delta_{profit}$ |
| 0 | 0 | _____ | $10 | _____ | $11 | _____ |
| 1 | 5 | _____ | $10 | _____ | $11 | _____ |
| 2 | 10 | _____ | $10 | _____ | $11 | _____ |
| 3 | 14 | _____ | $10 | _____ | $11 | _____ |
| 4 | 17 | _____ | $10 | _____ | $11 | _____ |
| 5 | 19 | _____ | $10 | _____ | $11 | _____ |
| 6 | 20 | _____ | $10 | _____ | $11 | _____ |
| 7 | 20 | _____ | $10 | _____ | $11 | _____ |
| 8 | 19 | _____ | $10 | _____ | $11 | _____ |

a. Fill in the blanks in the table.

b. At what point do diminishing returns set in? Explain._____

_____

_____

c. How many workers should be hired? Explain._____

_____

_____

d.  If the fixed cost is $100 and labor is the only variable factor, what is the firm's profit? Explain._____

_____

_____

_____

e.  If the price of the product increases to $12, how many workers should be hired? Explain. If the wage increases to $15 after the price hike, how many workers should be hired? Explain._____

_____

_____

_____

_____

2.  A case study in the text describes the economic effects of the Black Death in 14th Century Europe.

a.  Show graphically below the effects of the plague that destroyed about one-third of the population within a few years. Indicate clearly which curves shift and in which direction, as well as the direction of the changes in factor prices and equilibrium quantities.

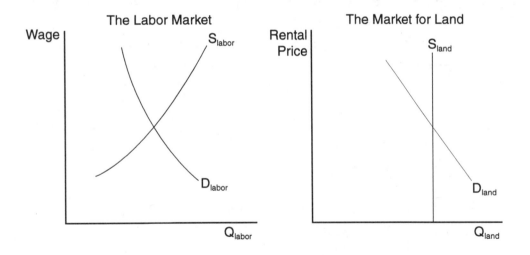

b.  Explain the unusual shape of the supply curve for land. Is this reasonable? Can you think of any way that the supply curve might have a positive slope?

_____

_____

_____

_____

c. Explain the shifts that you identified in part (a), including discussion of the effects on value of the marginal product of each of the factors of production.

_____

_____

_____

_____

## B. Short-Answer Questions

1. How is marginal cost related to marginal product?_____

_____

_____

_____

2. Among the owners of the factors of production, who would win and who would lose from increasing the restrictions on immigration into the United States? Explain in terms of marginal productivity theory._____

_____

_____

_____

_____

3. Explain the relationship between the equilibrium wage and the value of the marginal product._____

_____

_____

_____

## III. Self-Test

### A. True/False Questions

_____1. The demand for labor is derived from the demand for capital and land.

_____2. An increase in the demand for oranges will cause an increase in the value of the marginal product of orange pickers.

_____3. A technological breakthrough that raises the productivity of apple pickers will have no effect on the value of the marginal product of apple pickers, although it will raise the value of the marginal product of capital.

_____4. The demand for a factor of production by a competitive firm is the value of its marginal product.

_____5. When a firm hires labor up to the point at which the wage equals the value of the marginal revenue product, it is producing up to the point at which price exceeds marginal cost by the greatest amount.

_____6. The demand curve for a resource tends to be perfectly inelastic.
_____7. The derived demand for labor means that it is derived from the marginal product of labor.
_____8. An increase in the supply of electricians will lead to a decrease in the value of the marginal product of electricians.
_____9. Diminishing marginal product causes a decline in the value of the marginal product.
_____10. An increase in capital leads to an increase in the value of the marginal product of both capital and labor.
_____11. The demand for labor is independent of the price of the product.
_____12. A profit-maximizing employer will hire labor up to the point that maximizes the difference between the value of the marginal product and the wage rate.
_____13. The supply of labor is determined by the value of the marginal product.
_____14. The production function is the relationship between quantity of input and profit.
_____15. The value of the marginal product of labor is the wage times the quantity of labor hired.

## B. Multiple-Choice Questions

1. Diminishing marginal product means that hiring an additional worker will:
   a. cause total output to diminish.
   b. result in negative marginal product.
   c. cause marginal product to increase, but at a decreasing rate.
   d. cause a reduction in marginal product.
   e. none of the above.

2. Which of the following would increase (shift to the right) the demand for a factor of production?
   a. an increase in its supply, causing a decrease in its price.
   b. a decrease in the demand for the product.
   c. a reduction in the price of a substitute factor of production.
   d. an increase in the price of a substitute product.
   e. an increase in the price of a complementary factor of production.

3. An increase in the supply of labor in a competitive market will:
   a. increase labor productivity.
   b. increase the wage rate and the value of the marginal product.
   c. increase the wage rate and decrease the value of the marginal product.
   d. decrease the wage rate and the value of the marginal product.
   e. decrease the wage rate and increase the value of the marginal product.

4. An increase in the demand for apples will cause:
   a. an increase in apple pickers' wages.
   b. an increase in the value of the marginal product of apple pickers.
   c. higher short-run profits for apple growers.
   d. an increase in the number of apple pickers employed.
   e. all of the above.

5. An increase in the demand for labor means that:
   a. employers are willing to buy more capital and land as well.
   b. the supply of labor will also increase.
   c. the supply of labor must have decreased.
   d. employers are willing to hire more workers at every wage.
   e. none of the above.

6. As the wage rate increases due to a decrease in labor supply,
   a. the value of the marginal product will fall.
   b. the value of the marginal product will rise.
   c. a shortage of labor will result.
   d. a surplus of labor will result.
   e. none of the above.

7. Which of the following is *not* an example of a factor of production?
   a. steelworkers used to produce sheet metal.
   b. foundries used to produce steel.
   c. iron ore used to produce steel.
   d. share of stock in a steel company.
   e. all of the above are examples of factors of production.

8. Which of the following statements about factors of production is correct?
   a. capital includes factories, machines, and the money necessary to start a business.
   b. natural resources include land, raw materials, and human resources.
   c. money is the most basic factor of production.
   d. the basic factors of production are land, labor and capital.
   e. all of the above are true.

9. An increase in the supply of labor will:
   a. increase the value of the marginal product of capital.
   b. increase the value of the marginal product of land.
   c. decrease the value of the marginal product of labor.
   d. lead to increased output.
   e. all of the above.

Ken's Kamera Kiosk sells film in small booths in shopping centers. Ken must decide how many people to hire, based on the data below. Use the following table to answer Questions 10-14.

| Labor Hired | Output | Marginal Product | Product Price |
|---|---|---|---|
| 0 | 0 | — | — |
| 1 | 5 | ___ | $5 |
| 2 | 12 | ___ | $5 |
| 3 | 17 | ___ | $5 |
| 4 | 19 | ___ | $5 |
| 5 | 20 | ___ | $5 |
| 6 | 19 | ___ | $5 |

10. What is the marginal product of the 4th unit of labor hired?
    a. 2
    b. 4.75
    c. 5
    d. 19
    e. none of the above

11. What is the value of the marginal product of the 3rd unit of labor hired?
    a. $5.00
    b. $8.67
    c. $25.00
    d. $85.00
    e. none of the above

12. If Ken wants to maximize profit, up to how many workers should he hire if the wage is $5.00?
    a. 1
    b. 2
    c. 3
    d. 4
    e. 5

13. How many workers should Ken hire if the wage rises to $5.50?
    a. 1
    b. 2
    c. 3
    d. 4
    e. 5

14. At what quantity of labor does diminishing returns set in?
    a. 2
    b. 3
    c. 4
    d. 5
    e. 6

15. Suppose that a terrible epidemic destroyed most of the earth's population. The most likely economic effect on the survivors would be the following:
    a. wages would rise, and the return to capital and land would fall.
    b. returns to all factors of production would fall.
    c. returns to all factors of production would rise.
    d. wages would fall, but the returns to capital and land would rise.
    e. only wages would change; the returns to other factors of production would not change.

16. The people in the U.S. most likely to support immigration restrictions to reduce the supply of labor are:
    a. U.S. workers.
    b. employers.
    c. landlords.
    d. owners of capital.
    e. all of the above are likely to support restrictions.

Use the following information to answer questions 17-20. Suppose that Bob's Burger Box is maximizing profit hiring workers at $6.00/hour. Bob sells hamburgers in a competitive market for $2.00 each. He currently employs 18 people.

17. The value of the marginal product of the 18th worker is:
    a. $0.11
    b. $0.33
    c. $3.00
    d. $6.00
    e. $12.00

18. The marginal product of the 18th worker is:
    a. 1
    b. 2
    c. 3
    d. 4
    e. 5

19. If the price of hamburgers rises to $3.00, the value of the marginal product will _____ and the number of workers hired will _____.
    a. rise to $9.00; increase
    b. rise to $18.00; increase
    c. fall to $6.00; decrease
    d. fall to $3.00; decrease
    e. remain unchanged; remain unchanged

20. Suppose that Congress raises the minimum wage to $7.00/hour. As a result, Bob would _____ wages and _____the number of workers hired.
    a. raise wages; increase
    b. raise wages; decrease
    c. raise wages; keep unchanged
    d. lower wages; increase
    e. not change; keep unchanged

## IV. Advanced Critical Thinking

Critics of the minimum wage argue that it causes unemployment by putting a floor under the price of labor in competitive labor markets, and that it hurts those whom it is designed to help—workers with the least amount of experience and job skills. Supporters of the minimum wage argue that the minimum wage has little or no negative impact on employment, because it has been kept at a very low level, typically less than half of the average wage paid by manufacturing firms. In addition, they claim that labor markets do not behave competitively; rather, they assert that big employers set wages with little regard for supply and demand. They argue further that even if the minimum wage reduces employment, the lost jobs would be the least productive, lowest paid jobs in the economy, so that society wouldn't gain much by keeping them anyway.

1. Evaluate the opposing arguments. What are the advantages and disadvantages of the minimum wage? Who gains and who loses under a minimum wage?

   _____
   _____
   _____
   _____
   _____
   _____
   _____

2. If you wanted to measure the negative impact of the minimum wage on employment, why would it be a bad idea to look at the overall level of employment in the economy before and after a change in the minimum wage? Can you think of any specific groups of workers whose employment experience before and after a minimum wage change might be a better indicator of the effects of the minimum wage? Explain._____

_____

_____

_____

_____

_____

_____

## V. Solutions

### Terms and Definitions

__2___Factors of Production
__5___Derived Demand
__1___Production Function
__7___Marginal Product of Labor
__6___Diminishing Marginal Product
__4___Value of the Marginal Product
__3___Capital

### Practice Problems

1 a.  Fill in the blanks in the table.

| Quantity of Labor | Output | Marginal Product | Price | Value of the Marginal Product | Wage | Marginal Profit |
|---|---|---|---|---|---|---|
| L | Q | $MP_{labor}$ | P | $VMP_{labor}$ | w | $\Delta_{profit}$ |
| 0 | 0 | — | $10 | — | $11 | — |
| 1 | 5 | 5 | $10 | $50 | $11 | $39 |
| 2 | 10 | 5 | $10 | $50 | $11 | $39 |
| 3 | 14 | 4 | $10 | $40 | $11 | $29 |
| 4 | 17 | 3 | $10 | $30 | $11 | $19 |
| 5 | 19 | 2 | $10 | $20 | $11 | $ 9 |
| 6 | 20 | 1 | $10 | $10 | $11 | ($1) |
| 7 | 20 | 0 | $10 | 0 | $11 | ($11) |
| 8 | 19 | (1) | $10 | ($10) | $11 | ($21) |

b. The third unit of labor hired results in diminishing returns; the marginal product of the third worker is only 4, down from the marginal product of 5 for the second worker.

c. The firm should hire five workers, following the marginal rule that they should add workers as long as additional workers add more to revenue than they add to cost. The fifth worker has a <u>VMP</u> of $20, but costs the firm a wage of only $11, for a marginal profit of $9 on that worker. Another worker would cost the firm $11 but add only $10 to revenues for a marginal loss of $1.

d. The firm will earn a profit of $35. The variable cost is the wage bill of $55 (5 workers @ $11). Total cost is $155 (fixed cost of $100 plus variable cost of $55). Total revenue is $190 (19 units @ $10). The difference (<u>TR</u> - <u>TC</u>) is $35.

e. At a price of $12, the firm should hire a sixth worker. The <u>VMP</u> will be $12 (<u>MP</u> x <u>P</u> = 1 x $12). The wage is still $11, so the firm makes a $1 marginal profit on the sixth worker. However, if the wage increases to $15, the sixth worker is not worth the cost ($15 > $12). The fifth worker, however, costs $15 and adds $24 (2 x $12), and therefore should be hired.

2. A case study in the text describes the economic effects of the Black Death in 14th Century Europe.

a. Show graphically the effects of the plague that destroyed about one-third of the population within a few years. Indicate clearly which curves shift and in which direction, as well as the direction of the changes in factor prices and equilibrium quantities.

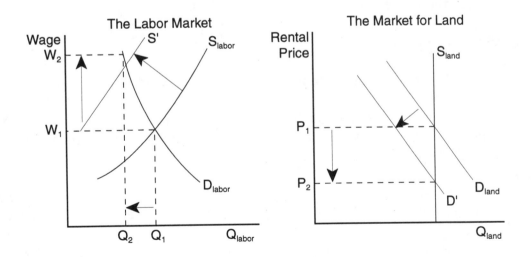

b. The vertical slope of the supply curve for land suggests that it is totally inelastic, because it is in fixed supply. This is reasonable, unless it is possible to respond to higher land rental prices by retrieving unusable land such as swamps or land that had been under water. In the latter case, the supply curve would have a positive slope.

c. The supply of labor shifts to the left because of the high death rate. The wage increases because of the decreased supply. The value of the marginal product of labor rises until it is equal to the new wage rate, because in equilibrium, employment will adjust until the last worker hired has a VMP just equal to his or her wage. The drop in the number of workers will reduce the productivity of land, causing a shift to the left in its VMP curve. The rental price of land will drop as a result of the drop in demand.

## Short-Answer Questions

1. Marginal cost is inversely related to marginal product. Specifically, $MC = w/MP$. As a result, the point at which diminishing returns sets in corresponds to the point at which MC begins to rise.

2. The reduction in the supply of labor would raise the wage and value of the marginal product for current workers. With less labor available, the value of the marginal product of capital and land would fall because of a fall in the marginal product of both capital and land. As a result, the rental price of both capital and land would fall. Owners of capital and landlords would lose, although workers would gain.

3. The equilibrium wage must equal the value of the marginal product in competitive markets. This occurs because employers will hire additional workers as long as the wage exceeds the value of the marginal product.

## True/False Questions

1. F; the demand for labor is derived from the product demand.
2. T
3. F; a technological breakthrough that raises the productivity of apple pickers will raise the value of the marginal product of apple pickers and raise the value of the marginal product of capital.
4. T
5. F; when a firm hires labor up to the point at which the wage equals the value of the marginal revenue product, it is producing up to the point at which price equals marginal cost.
6. F; the demand curve for a resource is downward sloping, due to diminishing marginal product.
7. F; the derived demand for labor means that it is derived from the demand for the product.

8. T
9. T
10. F; an increase in capital leads to an increase in the value of the marginal product of labor, but a decrease in the value of the marginal product of capital.
11. F; the demand for labor is dependent on the price of the product and the marginal product of labor.
12. F; a profit-maximizing employer will hire labor up to the point that the value of the marginal product equals the wage rate.
13. F; the supply of labor is determined independently from the value of the marginal product.
14. F; the production function is the relationship between quantity of input and quantity of output.
15. F; the value of the marginal product of labor is the product price multiplied by the marginal product of labor.

**Multiple-Choice Questions**

| | | |
|---|---|---|
| 1. d | 8. d | 15. a |
| 2. d | 9. e | 16. a |
| 3. d | 10. a | 17. d |
| 4. e | 11. c | 18. c |
| 5. d | 12. e | 19. a |
| 6. b | 13. d | 20. b |
| 7. d | 14. b | |

**Advanced Critical Thinking**

1. The minimum wage can put a floor under income for the working poor. It can provide more dignity than welfare for those who need assistance. However, it can lead to unemployment, particular among groups with few job skills and little experience. Teenagers just entering the labor force are particularly susceptible to the negative impact of the minimum wage on their employability. An employer who might have hired an untested young worker for $4.00/hour may decline to take a chance at $6.00/hour. The winners are those who keep their jobs and realize higher wages. The losers are those who lose their jobs or fail to get hired as a result of the minimum wage

2. The overall level of employment would probably hide the effect of the minimum wage on employment among the relatively hard-to-employ, such as teenagers or those with relatively low education levels. A better measure of the impact of the minimum wage would be to look at employment among teenagers, especially minorities, and others who may be at a disadvantage in the labor market. With a few exceptions, those studies generally have shown a negative effect on employment due to the minimum wage.

# Chapter 19: Earnings and Discrimination

## I. Chapter Overview

### A. Context and Purpose

The previous chapter introduced markets for the factors of production, with an emphasis on the labor market. Chapter 19 explores wage patterns in the United States, looking at the factors that explain differences in wages. It extends the supply and demand analysis of Chapter 18 to investigate in more depth the factors that affect the supply of and demand for labor. This chapter provides the background for a discussion of the distribution of income in Chapter 20. Understanding the factors that determine wages will help to explain why some people are rich and some are poor.

### B. Learning Objectives

In this chapter you will:

1. Examine how wages compensate for differences in job characteristics.
2. Learn and compare the human-capital and signaling theories of education.
3. Examine why in some occupations a few superstars earn tremendous incomes.
4. Consider why it is difficult to measure the impact of discrimination on wages.
5. See when market forces can and cannot provide a natural remedy for discrimination.
6. Consider the debate over comparable worth as a system for setting wages.

After accomplishing these goals, you should be able to:

1. Explain how compensating wage differentials can make up for unattractive non-monetary characteristics of jobs.
2. Compare and contrast the view that education raises wages by making workers more productive with the view that education simply provides a signal to employers that the job seeker has more ability.
3. Identify the distinguishing characteristics of an occupation in which superstars can earn tremendous incomes—specifically, the ability for the best producer (the superstar) to supply every customer at low cost (for example through televised performances).
4. Explain the difficulty in identifying separately the effects of discrimination, human capital and job characteristics on wage differentials.
5. Distinguish employers' tastes for discrimination, which a competitive market can suppress, from discrimination by customers or government, which the market may not eliminate and may even actually encourage.
6. Distinguish the well-intended goal of comparable worth of eliminating discrimination from its unintended side-effect of distorting labor markets that previously provided an incentive for those in lower-paying jobs to shift to jobs with higher wages (and value of the marginal product).

## C. Chapter Review

### 19-1 Some Determinants of Equilibrium Wages

Equilibrium wages are determined by labor supply and demand, which in turn are determined by the many differing characteristics of workers and jobs. Some jobs are more desirable than others; these typically need not pay as much as less attractive jobs in order to attract the same number of workers. As a result, wages tend to be higher the less attractive the job is, all other factors (such as education and skills) constant. Economists refer to wage differentials that arise from such non-monetary characteristics of different jobs as *compensating differentials*.

Wages also tend to be higher for workers who have invested more in human capital. *Human capital* is the accumulation of investments in people, for example, in the form of education or health care. The return to investment in education has grown in recent decades, as the earnings gap between workers with high and low skills has grown. Other factors that affect earnings are natural ability, amount of effort, and luck.

An alternative explanation of the positive correlation between education and earnings is that education provides a signal of high ability to employers. Thus, a college degree can serve as a screening device to weed out less able job applicants.

### 19-2 The Economics of Discrimination

Discrimination results when labor market opportunities vary for individuals who differ only by personal characteristics—such as race, sex or age—that are irrelevant to job performance. Wage differentials exist between males and females, and between blacks and whites; however, it is not easy to measure how much of the differential is due to discrimination, rather than differences in human capital or job characteristics. Competition among employers can eliminate discrimination by employers, because those who hire anyone other than the best person for the job will be at a competitive disadvantage. It is more difficult to eliminate discrimination by customers. Employers who discriminate because their customers demand it will have a competitive advantage over those who do not.

One reason that women earn less than men is that traditional male occupations pay more than traditionally female occupations. Advocates of *comparable worth* argue that jobs should be evaluated, and those that are judged comparable should offer the same pay. The problem is that the market already evaluates jobs through supply and demand. Women who are the primary care-givers for their children may choose occupations that offer flexible hours, even though the pay is low. The pay gap may be a compensating differential. Without that differential, there will be surpluses of labor in the pleasant occupation and shortages in the less desirable occupation. Equalizing the pay artificially takes away the labor market's signal for more people to enter the higher paying job.

### 19-3 Conclusion

In competitive markets, workers receive a wage equal to the value of their marginal product, which is determined by many factors, such as workers' training, ability and experience, as well as the demand for their product. As a result, some workers earn more than others. Whether or not that is fair goes beyond economics.

### D. Helpful Hints

1. *Shaquille O'Neill may be worth $17 million.* People often react in horror to high salaries by superstars. Upon learning that Shaquille O'Neill earns a salary of $17 million playing basketball for Los Angeles, a common reaction is that he is overpaid, that "nobody deserves that much." Marginal productivity theory tells another story: If O'Neill is paid $17 million, it is because he is worth at least that much to the team. Suppose that he brings in $34 million in additional ticket sales and advertising revenues to the Lakers. Is he overpaid or underpaid? There is no easy answer, but remember that in this case, he would be earning only half of the value of his marginal product! Superstars can earn super salaries to a large extent because they can provide a service to many fans simultaneously through television. They earn a lot because we have made them valuable productive factors.

2. *Different pay for different people does not necessarily mean that discrimination exists.* Different jobs and different people have different characteristics that affect the supply of and demand for labor. What seems to be a discriminatory wage differential may actually be a compensating differential that offsets a non-monetary aspect of the job.

### E. Terms and Definitions

Choose a definition for each key term.

Key terms:

_____ Compensating differential
_____ Human capital
_____ Discrimination
_____ Comparable worth

Definitions:

1. Differences in opportunity facing similar individuals who differ only by personal characteristics such as race or sex.

2. The accumulation of investments in people, such as education and on-the-job training.
3. A view that jobs should be classified according to factors such as difficulty, skill requirements, and risk, in order to assign equal wages for comparable jobs.
4. A difference in wages arising to offset non-monetary characteristics of different jobs.

## II. Problems and Short-Answer Questions

### A. Practice Problems

1. A positive relationship exists between education (or training) and earnings. Workers with higher educational attainment earn more than those with lesser amounts of education or training. In fact, this wage gap has grown in recent years.

   a. In economic terms, how do you explain the relationship between education and earnings? What are the two theories that might help to explain the relationship, and why is it difficult to determine which view is correct? Why is the wage gap growing between the educated and the less educated?

   _____
   _____
   _____
   _____
   _____
   _____
   _____
   _____
   _____
   _____
   _____

   b. Why is experience also correlated with earnings?

   _____
   _____
   _____
   _____

### B. Short-Answer Questions

1. According to a letter to the *New York Times* several years ago, garbage collectors in New York City earned more than assistant professors at Yale University. The letter writer attributed this to powerful unions in New York City. Do you think that the letter writer was correct about the cause, or could there be other reasons for the garbage collectors to earn more?

_____

_____

_____

_____

2. Debate continues over whether or not the free market can cure labor market discrimination without government intervention. What do you think? To what extent can the market solve problems of discrimination without government intervention? What problem areas are likely to remain without intervention?

_____

_____

_____

_____

## III. Self-Test

### A. True/False Questions

_____1. The rate of return to higher education has fallen since 1960.

_____2. Employer discrimination is hard to eliminate, because if one employer discriminates, competition forces others to follow suit.

_____3. Signaling refers to the role of a college degree as an indicator of ability, rather than its function as a measure of actual human capital.

_____4. The best evidence of continuing discrimination against women by employers is the wage gap in the market: Women still earn roughly three-fourths of what men earn.

_____5. The signaling theory helps to explain why wages have risen over time in the U.S. as the average educational level has risen.

_____6. The wage gap between men and women has actually increased in recent years, although this appears to be due mostly to changing job characteristics, rather than discrimination.

_____7. Even if employers do not discriminate, the wage gap between men and women will not disappear as long as women carry most of the child rearing responsibilities.

_____8. The pay gap between men and women is narrower for younger women than for women nearing retirement.

_____9. The return to investments in human capital has increased over the past decade.

_____10. Differences in earnings can be explained completely by differences in investment in human capital.

## B. Multiple-Choice Questions

1. The earnings gap between college-educated and less educated workers has:
   a. disappeared in recent decades.
   b. increased in recent decades.
   c. decreased in recent years.
   d. decreased in the '90s, after increasing for two decades.
   e. increased in the '90s, after decreasing for two decades.

2. Two jobs require the same amount of knowledge, skills and experience. The lower paying of the two jobs is likely to be more:
   a. pleasant.
   b. unpleasant.
   c. risky.
   d. inconvenient.
   e. routine.

3. Which of the following is an example of human capital?
   a. basic education.
   b. on-the-job training.
   c. higher education.
   d. health care.
   e. all of the above.

4. Which of the following would provide evidence favoring human-capital theory over the signaling theory regarding the effect of education on earnings?
   a. High school dropouts earn less than high school graduates.
   b. College graduates earn more than high school graduates.
   c. Earnings are higher for students who stayed in school longer because of compulsory attendance laws.
   d. Technical school graduates earn more than workers who did not attend technical school.
   e. All of the above demonstrate that human-capital theory is correct.

5. Mandating fringe benefits for all workers in a job would be most likely to:
   a. increase both labor supply and demand.
   b. decrease both labor supply and demand.
   c. increase labor supply and decrease labor demand.
   d. decrease labor supply and increase labor demand.
   e. have no effect on labor supply or demand.

6. The labor market is most likely to cure which of the following types of discrimination?
   a. employer discrimination
   b. discrimination by customers
   c. discrimination caused by government mandates
   d. all of the above
   e. none of the above

7. Employer discrimination against blacks is likely to raise the incomes of which of the following groups?
   a. white employees
   b. employers
   c. employees as a group, although not all employees individually.
   d. black employees working for other firms that do not discriminate.
   e. all of the above

8. Which groups would be *hurt* by the employer discrimination described in the previous question?
   a. employers
   b. black employees
   c. black employees of other firms that do not discriminate
   d. society overall, in the form of a net social welfare loss
   e. all of the above

9. Which of the following is *not* a form of discrimination?
   a. employers' preferences for employees with certain characteristics
   b. customers who prefer to deal only with certain racial or ethnic groups
   c. government mandates that some jobs are not available to people with certain characteristics
   d. lower demand for the labor of certain groups with lower value of marginal product
   e. all of the above are forms of discrimination

The following graph shows the markets for auto workers and steel workers. Workers in the two markets have similar skills, so they can move freely between the two. In both markets the initial equilibrium is at the intersection of $S_1$ and $D_1$. Use the graph to answer questions 10-13.

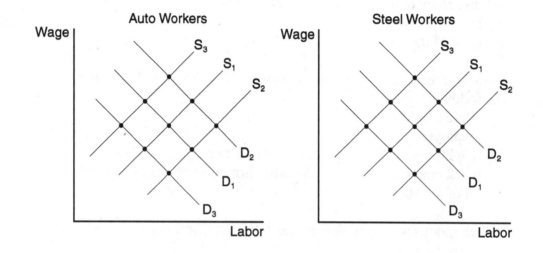

10. What is the likely result in the market for steel workers of a new study showing that steel workers are much more at risk of injury on the job than was previously thought to be the case:
    a. Demand will increase and supply will fall, raising wages and employment.
    b. Demand will increase, leading to higher wages and higher employment.
    c. Supply will decrease, leading to higher wages and lower employment.
    d. Supply will increase, leading to lower wages and higher employment.
    e. Demand and supply will decrease, lowering employment.

11. Referring back to the previous question, what will the change in the market for steel workers do to the market for auto workers?
    a. Demand will increase and supply will fall, increasing the wage rate and employment.
    b. Demand will increase, increasing the wage rate and employment.
    c. Supply will decrease, increasing the wage rate and reducing employment.
    d. Supply will increase, decreasing the wage rate and increasing employment.
    e. Demand and supply will decrease, reducing employment.

12. Suppose that U.S. automakers hire Canadian auto workers who work in the United States but live (and spend their incomes) in Canada. What will happen to the markets for auto workers in the U.S.?
   a. Both the supply of and the demand for auto workers will increase in the same proportion, leaving the wage rate unchanged.
   b. The supply of auto workers will rise, leading to higher employment but a lower wage rate; demand will not change.
   c. The demand for auto workers will increase, driving up the wage rate and employment; supply will not change.
   d. The demand for auto workers will decrease, driving down the wage rate and employment; supply will not change.
   e. Both the supply of and the demand for auto workers will decrease in the same proportion, leaving the wage rate unchanged.

13. Assuming that workers can easily change jobs between the auto industry and the steel industry, what impact will the changes in the auto industry described in the previous question have on the market for steel workers in the United States?
   a. The supply of steel workers would increase to $S_2$, demand would not change, employment would rise and the wage rate would fall.
   b. The supply of steel workers would decrease to $S_2$, demand would not change, and employment and the wage rate would decrease.
   c. The demand for steel workers will fall to $D_3$, and employment and the wage rate will fall.
   d. The demand for steel workers will rise to $D_2$, and employment and the wage rate will rise.
   e. Both the supply of and the demand for steel workers will increase, employment will rise, and the wage rate will remain unchanged.

14. Which of the following results in a wage differential between males and females?
   a. discrimination against females by employers
   b. differences in job choice by males and females
   c. discrimination against females by consumers
   d. clustering by females into certain traditionally low-paying occupations
   e. all of the above

Use the following graph to answer questions 15 and 16.

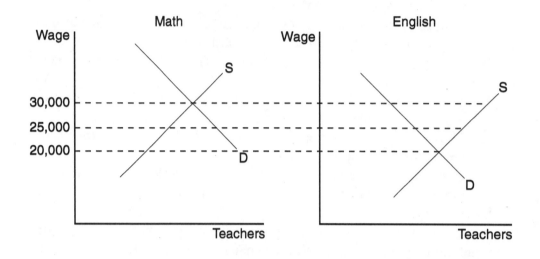

15. If the government passes a law that all teachers with the same seniority must receive the same pay, and the salaries were set at $25,000 for both math and English teachers, the result would be:
    a. a surplus of math teachers and a shortage of English teachers.
    b. a shortage of math teachers and a surplus of English teachers.
    c. just enough teachers, because on average the wage is at equilibrium.
    d. an incentive for more teachers to become math teachers, because of the shortage.
    e. none of the above.

16. The most likely outcome of equalizing salaries in the previous question would be:
    a. a reduction in the quality of teachers in both math and English.
    b. an increase in the quality of teachers in both math and English.
    c. the hiring of English teachers with better credentials than those hired in math.
    d. the hiring of math teachers with better credentials than those hired in English.
    e. greater efficiency, by maximizing net social welfare.

17. The immediate effect of immigration is to:
    a. increase the supply of labor.
    b. decrease the supply of labor.
    c. decrease the demand for labor.
    d. increase the number of workers who cannot find jobs at any wage.
    e. none of the above.

18. Over time, immigration is likely to:
    a. decrease the supply of labor.
    b. decrease the demand for labor.
    c. increase the demand for labor.
    d. make it increasingly difficult for U.S. citizens to find work.
    e. increase the wage rate of skilled workers.

19. Differences in wages that compensate for unpleasant working conditions, or riskiness of certain jobs are known as:
    a. wage premiums.
    b. employer discrimination.
    c. compensating wage differentials
    d. signaling wage differentials.
    e. none of the above.

20. Which of the following groups of workers is likely to receive the highest pay as a result of a compensating wage differential?
    a. garbage collectors
    b. waiters at ski resorts
    c. dish washers
    d. maids
    e. ticket takers at rock concerts

## IV. Advanced Critical Thinking

According to a columnist for the *Harper Valley Times*:

"Comparable worth legislation is long overdue. Women are paid less than 80% of the wages paid to men, and improvement is coming at a glacially slow pace. Until the law recognizes that women are equal to men and should receive equal pay for equal work, there will be no justice in the workplace. Female English teachers, for example, earn less than male economics teachers with the same training. A simple act of Congress could solve this problem by requiring job evaluation and comparable pay for comparable occupations."

Write a letter to the editor critiquing this column, explaining why you agree or disagree. Whether you agree or disagree, acknowledge the arguments on both sides of the issue and then explain your position.

_____
_____
_____
_____
_____
_____
_____
_____
_____
_____
_____

## V. Solutions

### Terms and Definitions

___4____Compensating differential
___2____Human capital
___1____Discrimination
___3____Comparable worth

### Practice Problems

1 a. Education or training raises the value of the marginal product of the worker. It represents an increase in human capital that makes the worker more productive, just as a piece of physical capital increases workers' productivity. An alternative to the human capital theory is the signaling theory, which states that additional educational attainment tells the employer something about the ability and effort of the potential employee. Even if the education does not increase the value of the marginal product to the employer, it suggests that the employee is somehow superior to those who did not receive comparable education. This helps to explain why college graduates may find good-paying jobs outside of their areas of academic expertise: the degree itself signals something to potential employers. Both theories lead to similar conclusions, namely that better educated workers earn more. This makes it hard to distinguish the signaling effect from the human capital effect. The education wage gap has grown as the demand for skilled workers has increased relative to the demand for unskilled workers in an increasingly technological society.

b.  Experience is a form of human capital. Workers can gain skills through training or through on-the-job experience and training. Therefore, with experience, the value of the marginal product of the worker rises, at least up to a certain point. As a result, earnings tend to rise with age, and then peak and fall somewhat as the worker nears retirement, when productivity may be slowing down.

## Short-Answer Questions

1.  Although the unions could help to explain such a wage differential, it is more likely that New York garbage collectors receive a compensating wage differential that more than offsets the effect of their lower human capital. Even for a higher wage, it is doubtful that Yale's assistant professors would quit their jobs in order to collect garbage in New York City. In fact, a position at Yale is so desirable that lesser universities may even have to pay compensating wage differentials to compete with the non-monetary aspects of a position at Yale.

2.  The labor market is likely to deal effectively with employer discrimination. Those employers with tastes for discrimination will be at a competitive disadvantage relative to employers who hire the best person for the job without regard for irrelevant personal characteristics. At least under competition, long-run profit is zero; there is no room for an employer to hire anyone other than the best person for the position without losing money. In the case of discrimination by customers, however, the employer may find it profitable to discriminate. If customers do not like to deal with certain ethnic groups, for example, a profit-maximizing employer will respond accordingly. Until attitudes change, the problem may well require government intervention to ban such discrimination, because the market will not take care of it.

## True/False Questions

1.  F; the rate of return to higher education has risen in recent decades.
2.  F; employer discrimination puts the employer at a competitive disadvantage, because other competitors who hire the best person for the job will have lower costs of production and be able to undercut the discriminator on price.
3.  T
4.  F; even though women still earn less than men, it is difficult to determine how much of the differential is due to discrimination.
5.  F; signaling theory works only to explain *relative* wages, because relatively more education by one person suggests relatively more ability or effort; if everyone has more education, then higher earnings must be due to increased productivity.
6.  F; the wage gap between men and women continues to narrow.
7.  T
8.  T

9.  T
10. F; not entirely: differences in earnings are also attributable to luck, ability, effort, and discrimination.

## Multiple-Choice Questions

| | | |
|---|---|---|
| 1. b | 8. e | 15. b |
| 2. a | 9. d | 16. c |
| 3. e | 10. c | 17. a |
| 4. c | 11. d | 18. c |
| 5. c | 12. b | 19. c |
| 6. a | 13. a | 20. a |
| 7. a | 14. e | |

## Advanced Critical Thinking

On the positive side, comparable worth is an attempt to deal with discrimination that the free market has been unable to eliminate. Competitive labor markets can stop employer discrimination, but not all labor markets behave competitively. Employers with preferences for discrimination may be able to indulge those tastes if they can afford somewhat higher costs. Comparable worth laws can stop such discrimination without waiting generations for attitudes to change.

Unfortunately, comparable worth laws often have unintended consequences. At first glance, it seems desirable: Women are paid less then men when they cluster into occupations that pay less. However, those wage differentials reflect differences in relative supply and demand. Some occupations may seem more demanding, or less appealing in some other non-monetary aspect. Without a financial incentive to go into that industry, not enough people will choose that occupation. As a result, there will be shortages. Also bad is the loss of the incentives for little girls and little boys to reach for non-stereotypical jobs. Those pay differentials between traditionally male and traditionally female jobs have helped to break down the cultural barriers. More girls are growing up to become doctors, economists, and computer programmers today, rather than nurses, English teachers, and elementary school teachers, thanks in part to salaries that have encouraged them to take the chance. The irony of comparable worth legislation is that however well-meaning it is, it actually would slow down this change and perpetuate the inefficiency of people clustering into occupations that may not be those most in demand by society.

# Chapter 20: The Distribution of Income

## I. Chapter Overview

### A. Context and Purpose

The previous chapter analyzed wage patterns in the United States, describing the factors that explain differences in wages. It extended the supply and demand analysis of Chapter 18 to investigate in more depth the factors that affect the labor market. Chapter 20 explores the resulting distribution of income in the United States and evaluates our efforts at curing poverty.

### B. Learning Objectives

In this chapter you will:

1. Examine the degree of economic inequality in our society.
2. Consider some problems that arise when measuring economic inequality.
3. See how political philosophers view the government's role in redistributing income.
4. Consider the various policies aimed at helping poor families escape poverty.

After accomplishing these goals, you should be able to:

1. Track the patterns of income inequality in the U.S. over time and identify the groups most likely to fall below the poverty line.
2. Explain the shortcomings of our measures of inequality, particularly the exclusion of progressive taxes and in-kind transfers in tempering the inequality of incomes.
3. Compare and contrast the views of utilitarians, liberals, and libertarians in terms of the role of government in altering the distribution of income.
4. Evaluate minimum wages, traditional welfare, in-kind transfers, and cash transfers through a negative income tax as alternatives for redistributing income.

### C. Chapter Review

Previous chapters have considered the role of government in improving the efficiency of the market. This chapter describes the patterns of poverty in the United States and analyzes government's role in altering the distribution of income.

## 20-1 The Measurement of Inequality

Before we can analyze income redistribution policy, it is necessary to measure the degree of income inequality, identify those who live below the poverty line, explore how often people move among income classes, and evaluate the measurement problems that make it difficult to measure inequality.

The degree of income inequality, is measured most commonly by calculating the percentage of income earned by each quintile, or one-fifth, of families. The distribution of pretax income is not much different than it was 60 years ago. The top 20% earn roughly 50% of the income (51.7% in 1935; 46.9% in 1994), and the bottom 20% earn just over 4% (4.1% in 1935; 4.2% in 1994). However, this comparison disguises the patterns over time. Income inequality fell dramatically from 1935 to 1970 and then increased from 1970 until the present. Actual disposable (spendable) income is more equally distributed than these numbers suggest, because these comparisons are before taxes and transfer payments such as welfare.

Of course, knowing the income patterns by quintile does not tell us whether the outcome is fair. Whether incomes should be more or less equal cannot be settled by economists. It is interesting, however, to compare the U.S. with other countries. When compared with other countries, the U.S. is roughly in the middle in terms of the degree of income inequality. Family incomes are more nearly equal in Japan, for example, but more unequal in Brazil.

Another measure of the distribution of income is the *poverty rate*—the percentage of the population whose income falls below an absolute level known as the *poverty line*. The federal government defines the poverty line as three times the cost of a providing a family with an adequate diet. The poverty line varies with family size and is adjusted each year for inflation. In the mid-1990s, the poverty line was roughly $15,000 for a family of four. Those who are at the greatest risk of being poor are the very young or the very old, blacks or Hispanics, and people in single-parent households headed by a female.

The poverty rate fell in the 1960s, during a period of economic growth and during President Johnson's War on Poverty. It has risen since the 1970s low of 11 percent to 14.5 percent in 1994. Although economic growth has continued, the growth has benefitted primarily those with the education and training increasingly demanded by the market.

### Problems in Measuring Inequality

Measuring the patterns of income distribution and the incidence of poverty is difficult for the following reasons:

- **In-Kind Transfers**: transfers to the poor in the form of goods and services, rather than cash, are not included in measuring inequality.

- **Economic Life-Cycle** Income varies naturally over a person's lifetime, exaggerating the income differences between people at a given point in time.

- **Transitory versus permanent income** Random, temporary changes in income increase the measured degree of income inequality, even though families can adjust to such temporary factors and base their standard of living on *permanent income*, which is their normal, or average income.

## Economic Mobility

Economic mobility in the United States is quite high. It is relatively common for people to move from one income bracket to another. Even though poverty becomes a vicious cycle for some families, this is not as common as is usually thought: less than 3 percent of families are poor for eight or more years, compared with nearly 15 percent of all families who qualify as poor. It is important to keep in mind in designing poverty programs that no more than roughly 20 percent of the poor are permanently poor.

## 20-2 The Political Philosophy of Redistributing Income

Three views of economic justice play heavily in our policy decisions regarding the appropriate level of income redistribution by government:

- **Utilitarianism** Utilitarians argue for the greatest good for the greatest number of people. That is, we should maximize sum of the utility, or well-being, of everyone in society. Because of diminishing marginal utility, utilitarianism argues that redistributing from a rich person to a poor person increases the social good (the marginal dollars are worth more to the poor person).

- **Liberalism** Philosopher John Rawls argues that a just system is one that we would devise if we set up the rules of the economic game before we knew what part we would play—if we could vote on the economic system before we were even born. According to Rawls, we would act to maximize the utility of the least fortunate member of society—*the maximin criterion*—because we might end up being that person. This would not mean total redistribution, however, because that would destroy incentives and make everyone worse off.

- **Libertarianism** Libertarians believe that society does not earn income, individuals earn income. Society therefore has no right to take from some to give to others. Philosopher Robert Nozick believes that the only role for government is to enforce individual rights so that everyone has equality of opportunity, but not outcome.

According to Nozick, it is inappropriate even to ask what level of inequality is acceptable. He believes that the actual level of inequality is determined by individuals' actions operating through free will. As long as the process is fair, the outcome is fair.

## 20-3 Policies to Reduce Poverty

Policies designed to reduce poverty include the following:

- **Minimum-Wage Laws**   Although it raises wages for some workers, the minimum wage also reduces employment opportunities for those with the lowest value of the marginal product, making it unsatisfactory as a cure for poverty.

- **Welfare**   Welfare provides cash assistance based on certain "need" tests. The problem is that existing programs create incentives for people to change their behavior in undesirable ways in order to qualify. For example, traditional welfare programs often encourage families to break up by cutting benefits if both parents are present. They also often penalize work by reducing benefits dollar-for-dollar whenever a welfare recipient earns income. This is like a 100% income tax! Obviously, it will discourage people from working.

- **Negative Income Tax**   Under this tax, families below a certain income level would receive a "negative" tax, or a transfer payment, from government. This negative tax would be equal to a given percentage of the gap between earned income and a specified level. The only requirement for the program is that families have incomes below a specified level. A disadvantage is that society would lose control over behavior; even people who are simply lazy could receive benefits. An advantage is that there would be more of a financial incentive to work, because work would always lead to higher income: recipients would never pay a 100% tax rate on their earnings.

- **In-Kind Transfers**   It is politically popular to help the poor by providing them directly with goods and services, but it is not usually efficient. Individuals know what they most desire. If our goal is to raise their total utility as much as possible for a given amount of public spending, then cash transfers are more effective. Supporters of in-kind transfers argue that cash would help to support alcoholism and drug addiction. Critics respond that in-kind transfers do not really control recipients' spending—most have other cash that they can spend as they please.

## 20-4 Conclusion

Perhaps the most basic tradeoff in economic policy making is equity versus efficiency. Nowhere is this seen more clearly than in our attempts to use government to alter the distribution of income without causing serious distortions in behavior that reduce productivity and output.  We might prefer a more nearly equal distribution of income, but we do not know how to accomplish this goal without lowering the overall level of incomes.  Some inequality can make everyone better off: as John Kennedy said, "A rising tide lifts all boats."  Our problem is deciding how much inequality is desirable.

## D.  Helpful Hints

1.  *Equity and equality are not necessarily synonymous.*  For some people, equity means moving toward greater equality of incomes.  For others, equity may require only equal opportunity, even if the outcomes are dramatically unequal.

## E.  Terms and Definitions

Choose a definition for each key term.

Key terms:

_____Poverty Rate
_____Poverty Line
_____In-Kind Transfers
_____Life Cycle
_____Permanent Income
_____Utilitarianism
_____Utility
_____Liberalism
_____Maximin Criterion
_____Libertarianism
_____Welfare
_____Negative Income Tax

Definitions:

1.  The claim that the government should aim to maximize the well-being of the worst-off person in society.
2.  An absolute level of income set by the federal government for each family size below which a family is deemed to be in poverty.
3.  A person's normal or average income.
4.  A tax system that below a specified income level converts to a negative tax, or transfer, equal to a percentage of the gap between the family's actual income and the specified income level.
5.  The percentage of people whose family income falls below an absolute level called the poverty line.
6.  Government programs that supplement the incomes of the needy.

7. Transfers to the poor given in the form of goods and services rather than cash.
8. The regular pattern of income variation over a person's life.
9. The political philosophy according to which the government should punish crimes and enforce voluntary agreements but not redistribute income.
10. The political philosophy according to which the government should choose policies deemed to be just as evaluated by impartial observers behind a "veil of ignorance."
11. The political philosophy according to which the government should choose policies to maximize the total utility of everyone in society.
12. A measure of happiness or satisfaction.

## II. Problems and Short-Answer Questions

### A. Practice Problems

1. The Negative Income Tax has been discussed for decades as an alternative to traditional welfare. The following table shows a hypothetical negative income tax for the United States:

A Negative Income Tax Option:
Tax Paid = 1/3 of Income, less $15,000

| Earned Income | Tax Paid | Disposable (after-tax) Income (= Earned income less tax) |
|---|---|---|
| 0 | $_____ | $_____ |
| $15,000 | $_____ | $_____ |
| $30,000 | $_____ | $_____ |
| $45,000 | $_____ | $_____ |
| $60,000 | $_____ | $_____ |

a. Fill in the table above.

b. If the goal is to eliminate poverty in the U.S. without a major distortion of work incentives, why is it important to keep the tax formula as it is stated at the top of the table? Could we lower the $15,000 deductible and still cure poverty? What would happen if we change the fraction, currently 1/3, that is taxed away?

_____
_____
_____
_____
_____
_____

c. What do you think the political repercussions would be from using the formula above, considering that most families in the U.S. would fall into the negative tax range? (Hint: what is the average family income in the U.S., and at what income level does the negative tax switch over to a traditional positive income tax?) Would it help politically to raise the negative tax rate from $1/3$ to $1/2$? How would the critics respond?_____

_____

_____

_____

_____

_____

_____

_____

_____

_____

## B. Short-Answer Questions

1. Utilitarians would like to maximize society's total utility or well-being. How would they accomplish this, and what is the limitation on government's ability to achieve the goal? How is this limitation like a "leaky bucket?"_____

_____

_____

_____

_____

2. The richest families in the U.S. earn about ten times as much as the poorest families. How do we decide if this is the most desirable ratio? How would a utilitarian, a Rawlsian, and a libertarian respond?_____

_____

_____

_____

_____

_____

## III. Self-Test

### A. True/False Questions

_____1.　The poorest fifth of the U.S. population earns about 10 percent of the total income.

_____2.　Roughly 25 percent of the U.S. population lived below the official poverty line in 1994.

_____3.　Most children born into families in the top income bracket stay in that income bracket.

_____4.　The high overall standard of living in the U.S. hides an income distribution that is among the most unequal in the world.

_____5.　The average family income in 1994 was roughly $39,000.

_____6.　Utilitarians tend to support only those income redistribution policies that increase work incentives.

_____7.　A major problem with traditional income redistribution programs is the large reduction in benefits for each dollar of income the recipient earns.

_____8.　The 1996 welfare reform legislation abolishes the AFDC program over a two-year period, because the program has caused many distortions of work incentives.

_____9.　A Negative Income Tax would eliminate all adverse effects of income redistribution on work incentives.

_____10.　The maximin criterion is John Rawls' proposal for economic justice, which would maximize the utility of the least-advantaged member of society.

### B. Multiple-Choice Questions

1. The Earned Income Credit:
   a. allows businesses an income tax credit for hiring minorities.
   b. is a kind of a Negative Income Tax for the working poor.
   c. has replaced much of traditional welfare in the U.S.
   d. helps to redistribute income but discourages people from working.
   e. all of the above.

2. Eliminating welfare in order to encourage people to become more self-reliant and ultimately more productive, increasing everyone's well-being, would be tied most closely to a philosophy of:
   a. utilitarianism.
   b. Rawlsian Theory of Justice.
   c. democratic socialism.
   d. libertarianism.
   e. none of the above.

3.  The Aid to Families with Dependent Children (AFDC) Program:
    a.  has virtually eliminated poverty.
    b.  has been increasing in size relative to other programs in recent years.
    c   minimizes the disincentive to work by focusing on children who wouldn't be working anyway.
    d.  encourages the breakup of the family.
    e   all of the above.

4.  The "veil of ignorance" refers to:
    a   liberals' unwillingness to consider the incentive effects of redistribution policies.
    b   libertarians' unwillingness to consider the inequities generated by the unrestrained free market.
    c   government's inability to make decisions for people that maximize their utility.
    d   Rawls' view that justice requires we make the rules for the system before we know the part we will play in that system.
    e   according to utilitarians, the lack of information about individuals' utility that prevents us from adopting policies that would maximize everyone's combined utility.

5.  If the poverty level is $15,000, then a minimum-wage law high enough to generate income of $15,000 for a full-time worker would:
    a.  eliminate poverty.
    b.  more than eliminate poverty, because many families have two incomes.
    c.  make some workers better off and others worse off.
    d.  raise everyone's income, because even those above the minimum would have their wages pushed up by the higher minimums.
    e.  none of the above.

6.  Under the 1996 Welfare Reform, Congress:
    a.  raised AFDC and other welfare benefits to keep up with inflation.
    b.  cut current welfare benefits sharply.
    c.  forced states to increase their spending on welfare to replace federal programs.
    d.  required recipients to begin work within two years or lose most welfare benefits.
    e.  established a Negative Income Tax.

7. Current welfare programs discourage work because they:
   a   make people so comfortable that they have no incentive to work—welfare benefits are so high today that recipients earn more than most people in the middle class.
   b   provide benefits that effectively are taxed away at a high rate—often 100 percent or more— when recipients earn income.
   c.  have no allowance for retraining in order to increase productivity and earnings.
   d   provide no in-kind support, such as benefits for day care and other vital goods and services that recipients need.
   e.  all of the above.

8. Under AFDC, a welfare recipient who scrimps and is able to save most of the welfare benefit each month:
   a.  is rewarded with higher benefits.
   b.  may lose his or her welfare benefits.
   c.  will receive preferential treatment for government-sponsored training programs.
   d.  will be penalized unless the savings are used eventually for goods or services that benefit the children.
   e.  none of the above.

9. Why is it difficult to determine the true degree of income inequality in the U.S.?
   a.  Our measures of inequality look at the differences after taxes, rather than before.
   b.  We count in-kind transfers at their market value, even though they may be worth far less to the recipient.
   c.  Income inequality is measured over a lifetime, which ignores serious fluctuations during that lifetime.
   d.  Our measures of inequality do not reflect the fact that many people are permanently part of the hard-core unemployed and stuck in a poverty trap.
   e.  Most of our inequality measures fail to include the effects of tax and transfer policies designed to redistribute incomes.

10. In which of the following countries is family income more nearly equally distributed than it is in the United States?
   a.  Japan
   b.  Mexico
   c.  United Kingdom
   d.  Brazil
   e.  none of the above: The U.S. is closer to income equality than any of these countries

11. The degree of income inequality in the U.S.
    a. decreased from the 1930s to the 1970s, then began rising again.
    b. increased from the 1930s to the 1970s, then began falling again.
    c. has increased steadily since the 1930s, with the exception of the war years in the 1940s.
    d. has decreased steadily since the 1930s, due to increased anti-poverty programs.
    e. has been virtually unchanged over the past 60 years.

12. The family income distribution—measured as percent received by each fifth of the population:
    a. has remained virtually unchanged since the Great Depression.
    b. became more equal from the Great Depression until after the 1960's War on Poverty; since then it has become less equal.
    c. has become steadily more equal as taxes have become more progressive.
    d. has become steadily less equal over the past 60 years as the rich have become richer and the poor have become poorer.
    e. has become more equal over the past 60 years, with the exception of the Reagan years.

13. Which of the following statements is true regarding the inequality of family incomes in the U.S.?
    a. annual income is more unequal than is lifetime income.
    b. income after taxes and transfers is more unequal than is income before taxes.
    c. income including in-kind payments is more unequal than income without such payments.
    d. since the 1970s, income inequality has been reduced.
    e. all of the above.

14. The official poverty level for a family of four in the U.S.:
    a. was roughly $10,000 in 1994.
    b. was roughly $15,000 in 1994.
    c. varies according to the region of the country.
    d. has not changed since the 1960s.
    e. none of the above.

15. If the official poverty level had been set at $5000 at the beginning of the year, and prices went up by 10 percent during the year while the overall standard of living rose by 2 percent, then next year's poverty level would be:
    a. $ 500.
    b. $5000.
    c. $5200.
    d. $5500.
    e. $5600.

Use the following information to answer questions 16-18: Suppose that a small island with 100 residents has an income distribution such that 99 people have incomes of $25,000 and one has nothing.

16. The utilitarian argument for redistributing income to the poor resident is that:
    a. it would be more efficient, because total consumption would rise, creating jobs and raising the standard of living.
    b. it would benefit the least advantaged member of society.
    c. it would increase the total well-being of the society as a whole.
    d. it would satisfy the criterion "from each according to his ability; to each according to his need."
    e. it is consistent with a "rising tide lifting all boats."

17. In the preceding question, John Rawls would respond that redistribution would be desirable because:
    a. it would be more efficient, because total consumption would rise, creating jobs and raising the standard of living.
    b. it would benefit the least advantaged member of society.
    c. it would increase the total well-being of the society as a whole.
    d. it would satisfy the criterion "from each according to his ability; to each according to his need."
    e. it is consistent with a "rising tide lifting all boats."

18. According to the libertarian view, the existing distribution of income is unfair if:
    a. the more affluent residents gained their position by cheating.
    b. the less affluent resident was a hard worker but simply unlucky.
    c. the initial distribution of income hurt the poor resident more than it benefited the others.
    d. it fails to increase the well-being of society as a whole.
    e. all of the above.

19. The major advantage of the Negative Income Tax over current welfare programs is that it would:
    a. cure poverty.
    b. reduce the work disincentives associated with existing programs.
    c. minimize the risk of welfare checks being spent on alcohol or drugs.
    d. not cost the taxpayers anything.
    e. all of the above are major advantages.

20. What is the best measure of a family's standard of living?
    a. annual income.
    b. transitory income.
    c. permanent income.
    d. non-monetary income.
    e. consumption.

## IV. Advanced Critical Thinking

In a guest column recently in a weekly news magazine, a U.S. Senator argued for drastic welfare reform. According to the Senator,

"Welfare is not working. When we give people cash, they blow it on frivolous expenditures, or even alcohol and drugs. We can eliminate this problem by giving them the basic commodities that they need to survive and cutting out all cash payments. Let's provide minimal food and housing and clothing, and nothing else. That will make the system a lot more efficient, cutting out the waste and fraud."

Write a response to this column, as you think an economist would have written it. To what extent is the Senator right? What is incorrect? You may want to present an alternative, if you believe that another policy would make more sense. _____

_____

_____

_____

_____

_____

_____

_____

_____

_____

_____

_____

_____

_____

## V. Solutions

### Terms and Definitions

__5___Poverty Rate
__2___Poverty Line

\_\_7\_\_\_In-Kind Transfers
\_\_8\_\_\_Life Cycle
\_\_3\_\_\_Permanent Income
\_\_1\_\_\_Utilitarianism
\_\_12\_\_Utility
\_\_10\_\_Liberalism
\_\_1\_\_\_Maximin Criterion
\_\_9\_\_\_Libertarianism
\_\_6\_\_\_Welfare
\_\_4\_\_\_Negative Income Tax

## Practice Problems

1   a.   The Negative Income Tax has been discussed for decades as an alternative to traditional welfare. The following table shows a hypothetical negative income tax for the United States:

A Negative Income Tax Option:
Tax Paid = 1/3 of Income, less $15,000

| Earned Income | Tax Paid | Disposable (after-tax) Income (= Earned income less tax) |
|---|---|---|
| 0 | ($15,000) | $15,000 |
| $15,000 | ($10,000) | $25,000 |
| $30,000 | ($5,000) | $35,000 |
| $45,000 | 0 | $45,000 |
| $60,000 | $ 5,000 | $55,000 |

a.   Fill in the table above.

b.   The formula balances the effective tax rate on earned income against the break-even point—the income at which a family neither receives nor owes money.  If we increase to ½ the fraction that is taxed away, we reduce the "break-even" or zero-tax income level from $45,000 to $30,000, but we also discourage recipients from working.  However, if we don't increase the fraction, then every family with an income less than $45,000 will receive a check from the government.   If we lower the deductible to reduce this break-even income level, then the deductible will be below the poverty level of $15,000, and poverty will be reduced but not eliminated.

c.   As explained above, there is no practical way to use the Negative Income Tax to eliminate poverty completely.  With a fraction low enough to maintain decent work incentives, and with a deductible at the poverty line, the "break-even" level of income is $45,000, which is well above the $39,000 average family income. The result would be that most people would receive "welfare" payments from the government. The Negative Income Tax certainly can reduce poverty, using less ambitious but politically more acceptable values for the deductible and the fraction to be taxed away.

## Short-Answer Questions

1. Utilitarians would adopt policies that maximize the sum of all individuals' utility, thereby maximizing society's overall well-being. Because of diminishing marginal utility, they would do this largely by redistributing income from the rich to the poor, whose marginal utility of income is higher (because they have less income). They would make an exception, however, if the act of transferring income caused a loss of utility greater than the possible gain. This is where the analogy with the "leaky bucket" comes from. Transferring income is like transferring water to a better use: transfer if and only if the gain exceeds the loss of water from the leaky bucket. Government transfers can enhance social welfare, but they also cause losses due to administrative costs and distortion of work incentives.

2. There is no "correct" ratio. The U.S. is roughly in the middle internationally, although that still does not make it correct. There is a trade-off between equity and efficiency. We may believe that less inequality would be more fair, but that this inequality provides incentives that make people work harder and produce more. A utilitarian would look at the "greatest good for the greatest number," arguing that redistribution would shift the income to those for whom it has the highest value. A Rawlsian would agree up to a point, arguing that we should redistribute if we can make the least advantaged better off. A libertarian would argue that as long as everyone had a fair chance to compete in the marketplace, the equality of the outcome is irrelevant.

## True/False Questions

1. F; the poorest fifth of the U.S. population earns less than 5 percent of the total income.
2. F; roughly 15 percent of the U.S. population lived below the official poverty line in 1994.
3. F; there is tremendous mobility between income brackets. Most people do not stay in their parents' income brackets.
4. F; the U.S. is about average in income inequality.
5. T
6. F; utilitarians tend to support income redistribution policies favoring the poor, because they value the additional dollars more than the rich do.
7. T

8. F; AFDC has not been eliminated, although welfare recipients must find work within two years.
9. F; a Negative Income Tax would reduce but not eliminate the adverse effects on work incentives—the actual effect would depend on the rates chosen.
10. T

## Multiple-Choice Questions

| | | |
|---|---|---|
| 1. b | 8. b | 15. d |
| 2. d | 9. e | 16. c |
| 3. d | 10. a | 17. b |
| 4. d | 11. a | 18. a |
| 5. c | 12. b | 19. b |
| 6. d | 13. a | 20. c |
| 7. b | 14. b | |

## Advanced Critical Thinking

You are correct in pointing out that there are flaws in the current welfare system. In many ways welfare has distorted behavior. It has penalized work by effectively taxing at a 100%+ rate welfare recipients who choose to work. It breaks up families by excluding families with both parents in the home, even when they cannot find work. However, in-kind transfers add additional problems. It is less efficient to provide goods and services, for several reasons. First, people know best what they want. If our goal is to maximize their utility for a given level of welfare spending, then, cash allows them to maximize utility at the least cost to the taxpayers. Giving them goods and services involves the same problem that we have with holiday gift exchanges with friends: we hope that we have picked the gifts that they really want, because otherwise, we could have spent our money more productively. At least with family, we can rationalize a poor choice of gifts by arguing that "it's the thought that counts." Second, providing goods and services is more costly administratively than simply writing checks. Third, the additional costs of in-kind transfers may be futile: if society provides certain basic commodities as in-kind support, it frees the recipients' own money for other uses, even those that society had hoped to prevent. Providing free food does not keep people from spending money on alcohol or drugs; in fact, it makes it easier. The most efficient approach to income redistribution would be cash grants without the extreme work disincentives that exist under traditional welfare.

# Chapter 21: The Theory of Consumer Choice

## I. Chapter Overview

### A. Context and Purpose

The previous chapters analyzed the supply of and demand for productive resources and explored the resulting distribution of income in the United States. The section concluded with a critique of U.S. anti-poverty programs. This chapter returns to the earlier discussion of consumer choice, using indifference curve analysis to analyze consumer maximization of utility and its implications for demand.

### B. Learning Objectives

In this chapter you will:

1. See how a budget constraint represents the choices a consumer can afford.
2. Learn how indifference curves can be used to represent a consumer's preferences.
3. Analyze how a consumer's optimal choices are determined.
4. See how a consumer responds to changes in income and changes in prices.
5. Decompose the impact of a price change into an income effect and a substitution effect.
6. Apply the theory of consumer choice to four questions about household behavior.

After accomplishing these goals, you should be able to:

1. Draw a budget constraint showing the different bundles of goods that a consumer can afford to purchase and interpret the slope as the ratio of the prices of the two goods.
2. Draw an indifference curve showing a consumer's preferences toward two goods and interpret the slope of the curve as the consumer's willingness to trade one good for the other.
3. Demonstrate that the consumer maximizes utility when the indifference curve is just tangent to a budget constraint, so that the marginal rate of substitution equals the relative price (the ratio of the two prices).
4. Show graphically and explain the effects of changes in income or prices on the budget constraint and its tangency with an indifference curve.
5. Illustrate on an indifference curve diagram and explain in your own words the income effect and the substitution effect of a change in the price of a good.
6. Use indifference curve analysis to explore four applications: downward sloping demand, wages and labor supply, interest rates and savings, and cash vs. in-kind transfers to help the poor.

## C. Chapter Review

People make decisions based on the marginal costs and marginal benefits of their actions. This chapter returns to the topic of consumer choice to look at how people make consumption decisions.

### 21-1  The Budget Constraint: What Consumers Can Afford

People generally would like to have more of the things they consume, but they are limited by their incomes. The *budget constraint* shows the different combinations of goods and services that are affordable. The opportunity cost of consuming more of one good is the reduced amount of the other good that can be purchased. For example, suppose that Bob has $200/month to spend on nights out and groceries. If an average night out costs $20, then he could have 10 nights out if he spends his whole budget on his social life. Alternatively, if groceries cost $10 per average small bag, he could have 20 small bags of groceries if uses all of his income for groceries. Of course, he could also pick any of the in-between points, such as 5 nights out for $100, plus 10 bags of groceries for $100. In this example, the opportunity cost one additional night out is the 2 bags of groceries that he could have bought with the $20. All of these examples assume that Bob has spent all of his money on the two goods. He could purchase less of the two goods and save the rest of the money. But it is not possible for him to spend more than the limits set by his budget constraint.

### 21-2  Preferences: What the Consumer Wants

The preceding section discussed the cost of making a choice; however, it did not deal with the benefit of that choice, which depends on the consumer's preferences. Therefore, we still cannot tell how Bob should divide his income between groceries and partying. We use a tool known as the *indifference curve* to measure consumers' relative preferences between two goods. The indifference curve shows the bundles of consumption that make a consumer equally happy. In Bob's case, an indifference curve would show different combinations of nights out and groceries that would leave him equally satisfied (that is, his total utility would be unchanged). Because more is always preferred to less, Bob would also like to reach a higher indifference curve.

Indifference curves have four properties:

- **Higher indifference curves are preferred to lower**, because more is always preferred to less.
- **Indifference curves are downward sloping,** showing the tradeoff between two goods: more of one good can compensate for having less of another.
- **Indifference curves do not cross**; otherwise, the results would be inconsistent: the consumer would be indifferent between two combinations and yet would prefer one to the other, because more is preferred to less.

- **Indifference curves are bowed inward**, because of diminishing marginal utility: as consumers get more of a good, they are willing to give up more of it to get some of the other good.

## 21-3 Optimization: What the Consumer Chooses

Bob likes to party, but within reason (he knows when to say when). Also, he would like to have something left from his $200 budget to spend on groceries. He went out 6 times last month and bought 8 small bags of groceries. His friends are complaining that he is becoming boring and that he should go out twice a week (or 8 times a month). As much as he values his social life, two more nights out next month would force him to give up four bags of groceries, and he is not willing to bear that cost. Bob doesn't need an economics course to figure out that if a night out costs twice as much as a bag of groceries, he should pick the bundle of nights out and groceries for which the night out is worth twice as much as a bag of groceries. The graph below shows Bob's initial indifference curve $I_2$ and his budget constraint for nights out and groceries, with a $200 budget, and with nights out and groceries priced at $20 and $10, respectively.

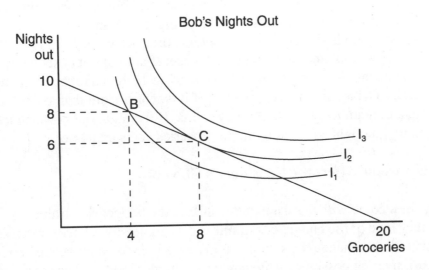

Note that Bob's original indifference curve $I_2$ is just tangent to the budget constraint at his current consumption bundle, point C (6 nights out and 8 bags of groceries). This suggests that he is maximizing utility, because he clearly has reached the highest possible indifference curve given his budget constraint. If he followed his friends' advice and partied more, he would end up on a lower indifference curve—at point B on $I_1$. Even though he may like a night out more than he likes a bag of groceries, he doesn't like it twice as much (which is what it costs). Bob certainly can afford to purchase 8 nights out and 4 bags of groceries. But by purchasing a few more bags of groceries and spending fewer nights partying, Bob is able to move from $I_1$ to $I_2$.

We can also use the slopes of the indifference curve and the budget constraint to see that Bob would not be maximizing utility with 8 nights out and 4 bags of groceries. The slope of the indifference curve equals the rate of which the consumer is willing to substitute one good for another, or the *marginal rate of substitution* (MRS). Suppose that at point B, the MRS is equal to one—that is, in Bob's mind, one more night out is equivalent to one bag of groceries. However, the price ratio, which is the slope of the budget constraint, is equal to ½ (groceries cost half as much as a night out). Clearly, he will get more for his money buying the good that gives him the same utility for half the price. He should buy more groceries and fewer nights out.

The general rule is that utility-maximizing consumers should rearrange their consumption patterns until the following rule is satisfied:

**MRS = Relative Price**

or, indifference curve slope = budget constraint slope

This means consuming at the tangency of the budget constraint with an indifference curve, in order to reach the highest possible indifference curve. For Bob, maximizing utility means rearranging consumption of nights out and groceries until the marginal rate of substitution is just equal to 2, which is the relative price of nights out versus groceries. This is consistent with common sense: If a night out costs twice as much as a bag of groceries, and you are buying some of each, then a night out should be worth twice as much as a bag of groceries to you. If it is worth more than twice as much, then nights out are a bargain and you should buy more. If the night out is worth less than twice as much, then you might as well buy more groceries and stay home.

## How Changes in Income Affect the Consumer's Choices

A change in income will cause a parallel shift in the budget constraint. Remember that the slope of the budget constraint is determined by relative price, so a change in income will not change the slope. An increase in income moves the budget constraint outward, making possible a tangency with a higher indifference curve. A decrease in income has the reverse effect, lowering the budget constraint in a parallel shift. If the consumption of a good increases as income increases, the good is a *normal good*. If consumption decreases as income increases, the good is an *inferior good*.

## How Changes in Price Affect the Consumer's Choice

When the price of one good changes, this causes the budget constraint to pivot, changing slope to reflect the change in the possible consumption of the good that has changed in price. The following graph shows the effect of an increase in the price of groceries for Bob. The budget constraint becomes steeper, and therefore Bob can no longer afford his original bundle of nights out and groceries. If Bob spends all of his

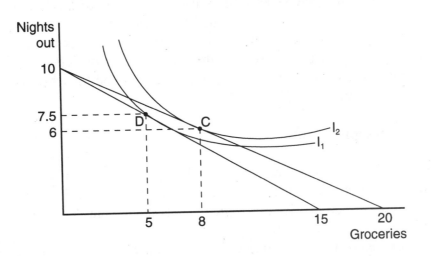

money on nights out, the increase in the price of groceries has no impact on his purchases. But once he starts purchasing groceries, the higher price per bag will leave him with less money to spend on nights out. In other words, if he wants to continue to purchase 8 bags of groceries, Bob will have to consume fewer than 6 nights out per month. The new equlibrium for Bob is on a lower indifference curve, $I_1$, and it is at a marginal rate of substitution of 2/3. He will now buy fewer bags of groceries, cutting his consumption from 8 bags to 5. There are two reasons for this decrease in consumption of groceries when the price rises. First, he feels poorer, because his dollars do not buy as much as they used to buy. This drop in his "real" income due to a price increase is known as the *income effect*. Second, the relative price of groceries has risen, making nights out a better buy. This is known as the *substitution effect*.

## Deriving the Demand Curve

The information shown in the graph is the basis for Bob's demand curve for groceries. Remember that the demand curve shows the relationship between price and quantity demanded, holding all other factors constant. The increase in price from $10 to $13.33 results in a drop in quantity demanded from 8 to 5, holding income and other prices constant. This can be plotted as two points on a demand curve for groceries.

## 21-4  Four Applications

### Downward Sloping Demand

According to the law of demand, demand curves have a negative slope. However, it is at least theoretically possible to have an upward sloping demand curve. Remember that the slope of the demand curve is due to the combined income and substitution effects. For normal goods, the income and substitution effects reinforce each other. At higher prices people cut back consumption because other goods are a relatively better buy and because they feel poorer. However, in the case of inferior goods, an increase in price that makes the consumer feel poorer could actually increase quantity demanded. If this effect is strong enough to dominate the negative substitution effect, then quantity demanded will increase as price increases, resulting in a positively sloped demand curve. Such a case is known as a *Giffen Good*, which is an inferior good for which the income effect dominates the substitution effect.

## Wages and Labor Supply

Indifference curves can also be used to analyze the work-leisure tradeoff. As wages increase, there are two conflicting pressures on the quantity of labor supplied. The higher wage raises the effective price of leisure, because each hour of leisure means giving up an hour's wages. This causes a substitution effect away from leisure and in favor of more work. However, the higher wage also makes the worker feel richer. Because leisure is a normal good the demand for which rises with income, there is an income effect that discourages work. Whether the labor supply is upward sloping depends on the relative income and substitution effects. If the income effect is greater, work effort decreases as wages rise; if the substitution effect is greater, work effort rises as wages rise.

The evidence on labor supply suggests that the income effect is very strong and can dominate the substitution effect at higher income levels. For example, over time, as wages have risen, the average workweek has fallen, suggesting that people prefer to buy more leisure time as their incomes rise, in spite of the higher opportunity cost of forgoing work.

## Interest Rates and Household Saving

The interest rate represents the relative price of present versus future consumption. As the interest rate rises, the relative price of present consumption rises. This should discourage present consumption. However, the higher interest rate also makes the saver feel richer, encouraging more present and future consumption. Thus, the income effect has the opposite effect from the substitution effect of a change in the interest rate. It is not clear, therefore, whether higher interest rates will encourage or discourage savings.

## Cash Versus In-Kind Transfers for the Poor

Policymakers often attempt to exercise control by providing in-kind transfers rather than cash grants to help the poor. However, indifference curve analysis can be used to show that in general, cash grants can provide the same increase in utility at a lower cost to the taxpayer than in-kind transfers. The common sense interpretation is that imposing someone else's consumption preferences on the recipient means that the recipient's total utility for a given level of expenditure will be lower, unless by coincidence the policymaker's preferences are the same as the recipient's.

## 21-5 Conclusion: Do People Really Think This Way?

Obviously, people do not calculate indifference curves each time they buy groceries or have a night out. However, this model does describe how they behave when they simply act in their self-interest in maximizing utility. Stated simply, people respond to economic incentives.

### D. Helpful Hints

1. *It is easy to get tripped up on the slopes of the curves.* The slope of the budget constraint is the $P_x/P_y$, where x is on the horizontal axis and y on the vertical. This may seem backwards, because slope is normally $\Delta y / \Delta x$. Remember, however, that the formula uses the *price* of x, not the quantity. The higher the price, the lower the quantity that can be purchased.

2. *Be careful when measuring indifference curve slopes not to compare two equilibrium points.* For example, the previous graph showed a change in equilibrium from 8 bags of groceries to 5 and from 6 nights out to 7.5 (don't ask me how you can have half a night out!). These numbers have nothing to do with the slope, however. The slope of the budget constraint (and the indifference curve at its tangency) is either ½ or $^2/_3$, depending on whether it is measured before or after the price change.

### E. Terms and Definitions

Choose a definition for each key term.

Key terms:

_____Budget Constraint
_____Indifference Curves
_____Marginal Rate of Substitution
_____Perfect Substitutes
_____Perfect Complements
_____Normal Good
_____Inferior Good
_____Income Effect
_____Substitution Effect
_____Giffen Good

Definitions:

1. Two goods with right-angle indifference curves.
2. A good for which an increase in income reduces the quantity demanded.
3. Curves that show consumption bundles that give the consumer the same level of satisfaction.
4. A good for which an increase in price raises the quantity demanded.
5. The limit on the consumption bundles that a consumer can afford.
6. The change in consumption that results when a price change moves the consumer to a new indifference curve.
7. The rate at which a consumer is willing to trade one good for another.
8. The change in consumption that results when a price change moves the consumer to a new marginal rate of substitution.
9. Two goods with straight-line indifference curves.
10. A good for which an increase in income raises the quantity demanded.

## II. Problems and Short-Answer Questions

### A. Practice Problems

1. The indifference curve diagram below shows the tradeoff between ice cream and brownies for Ben.

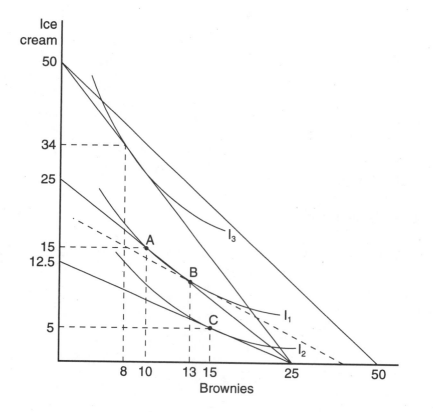

a.  The prices of ice cream and brownies are initially $1 each, and Ben can buy 25 brownies if he spends his entire budget on brownies. How much ice cream and how many brownies will Ben buy? Explain. What will happen if the price of ice cream doubles? What is his new indifference curve? How much ice cream will Ben buy now? How many brownies will he buy?_____

_____

_____

_____

_____

_____

b.  Separate the effect of raising the price of ice cream into a substitution and an income effect. Illustrate on the diagram and explain in your own words.

_____

_____

_____

_____

_____

_____

c.  Can you tell what Ben's income is? Show the effect of a 100 percent increase in income from the original budget constraint, due to a fabulous new job. Label the new curve(s) with'. What will happen to his consumption of ice cream? Of brownies? Label the new equilibrium as E'. Can you tell from the diagram if brownies are a normal or an inferior good? How can you tell? _____

_____

_____

_____

_____

_____

## B. Short-Answer Questions

1.  Joe has a marginal rate of substitution of beer for soda of 1/5. Beer costs $10/case, and soda costs $5/case. What should Joe do, and why? Can you tell how much beer Joe should buy? How much soda? What will his MRS be in equilibrium? Why? _____

_____

_____

_____

_____

2. Explain what could make a labor supply curve backward bending.

_____

_____

_____

_____

_____

## III. Self-Test

### A. True/False Questions

_____1.   For a demand curve to slope upward, the substitution effect must outweigh the income effect.

_____2.   The budget constraint is independent of consumer preferences.

_____3.   The main problem with indifference curve analysis is that people don't actually calculate utility in making choices.

_____4.   The marginal rate of substitution (MRS) of good x for good y is the relative price of good x versus good y.

_____5.   A Giffen good must be an inferior good, but not all inferior goods are Giffen goods.

_____6.   Assuming that people maximize utility, a higher interest rate will always lead to more savings.

_____7.   For a normal good, the income effect of an increase in price leads to decreased consumption.

_____8.   The substitution effect of a price increase always leads to lower consumption.

_____9.   An inferior good is one of lesser quality than those produced by the competition.

_____10.  The indifference curve between Budweiser and Miller beer is likely to straighter than the indifference curve between Budweiser and Coca-Cola.

_____11.  It is not possible for every good to be an inferior good for a consumer.

_____12.  If all prices double and money income also doubles, the budget constraint will also double.

_____13.  The substitution effect of a price change is the change in consumption that results from a change in the marginal rate of substitution.

_____14.  The income effect of a price change is the change in consumption that results from movement to a higher or lower indifference curve without any change in relative price.

_____15.  An increase in the price of a good shifts the budget constraint out for that good.

## B. Multiple-Choice Questions

1. For a demand curve to slope upward,
   a. consumers must be irrational.
   b. the good must be a normal good with a substitution effect that dominates the income effect.
   c. the good must be an inferior good with a substitution effect that dominates the income effect.
   d. the good must be a normal good with an income effect that dominates the income effect.
   e. the good must be an inferior good with an income effect that dominates the substitution effect.

2. A rational consumer who likes cranberry juice twice as much as he likes orange juice would:
   a. buy only cranberry juice.
   b. buy cranberry juice until at the margin, he is indifferent between the two juices.
   c. buy twice as much cranberry juice as orange juice.
   d. buy whichever juice gives him the most utility per dollar spent.
   e. none of the above.

3. The indifference curves for two goods that are perfect substitutes will be:
   a. straight lines.
   b. right angles.
   c. bowed inward.
   d. bowed outward.
   e. upward sloping.

4. The indifference curves for two goods that are perfect complements will be:
   a. straight lines.
   b. right angles.
   c. bowed inward.
   d. bowed outward.
   e. upward sloping.

5. A consumer maximizes utility by choosing consumption bundles that:
   a. maximize the marginal rate of substitution (MRS).
   b. maximize the gap between the MRS and the relative price.
   c. sets the MRS equal to the relative price.
   d. maximizes consumption of the lower-priced good.
   e. maximizes consumption of the higher-valued good.

6. Suppose a consumer decreases her consumption of good x when the price of good y rises. Which of the following is the most likely explanation for this behavior?
   a. Goods x and y are substitutes.
   b. Good x is an inferior good.
   c. Good y is an inferior good.
   d. the income effect dominates the substitution effect for good x.
   e. the substitution effect dominates the income effect for good x.

7. A backward-bending labor supply curve would mean that:
   a. workers are behaving irrationally.
   b. the income effect dominates the substitution effect.
   c. the substitution effect dominates the income effect.
   d. both income and substitution effects are quite weak.
   e. none of the above.

8. Leisure is:
   a. a normal good.
   b. an inferior good.
   c. a Giffen good.
   d. not an economic good.
   e. a complement for hours of work.

9. The bowed shape of the typical indifference curve is due to:
   a. people typically preferring one good to another.
   b. diminishing marginal utility.
   c. increased average utility.
   d. diminishing relative utility.
   e. all of the above.

10. If two indifference curves intersected, this would suggest that:
    a. consumers were inconsistent or irrational.
    b. one of the goods must be inferior.
    c. both goods must be inferior.
    d. at least one of the goods must be normal.
    e. people prefer more to less.

11. When winners of large prizes in state lotteries quit their jobs in response, this is evidence of:
    a. short-sightedness.
    b. irrational behavior.
    c. a strong income effect.
    d. a strong substitution effect.
    e. leisure as an inferior good.

12. In the labor market, when wages increase, the
    a. substitution effect encourages more work, but the income effect discourages work.
    b. income and substitution effects both encourage more work.
    c. income and substitution effects both discourage work.
    d. income effect encourages more work, but the substitution effect discourages work.
    e. income and substitution effects are irrelevant.

13. Suppose that Bill prefers pizza to fried chicken 2:1. If pizza costs $9.00 and chicken costs $3.00, then Bill should:
    a. buy more chicken and less pizza, until the prices are equal and the marginal utilities are equal.
    b. buy more pizza and less chicken, until the marginal utilities are equal to the relative price.
    c. buy more chicken and less pizza, until another pizza is worth three times as much as another order of chicken is worth to him.
    d. continue to buy the same quantities of pizza and chicken.
    e. switch to hamburgers.

14. Which of the following combinations is likely to have the closest to a straight-line indifference curve?
    a. left shoes and right shoes
    b. gasoline and automobiles
    c. Shell gasoline and Amoco gasoline
    d. pizza and beer
    e. Braun electric shavers and Braun electric coffee makers

Use the graph below to answer questions 15-19. The diagram shows the equilibrium for goods x and y, starting at an equilibrium at point A. The consumer's income is $60.

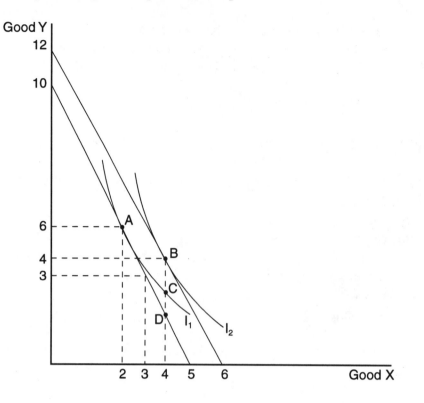

15. What is the price of good x in the graph?
    a. $2
    b. $5
    c. $12
    d. $30
    e. none of the above

16. Which of the following statements is true?
    a. Both x and y are normal goods.
    b. Both x and y are inferior goods.
    c. Good x is inferior and y is normal.
    d. Good x is normal and y is inferior.
    e. uncertain without additional information

17. What is the equilibrium MRS?
   a. ½
   b. 2
   c. 3
   d. $^1/_3$
   e. uncertain without additional information

18. The consumer is indifferent between points:
   a. A and B
   b. A and C
   c. A and D
   d. C and D
   e. A, B, C, and D

19. If income is cut in half, then the:
   a. marginal rate of substitution will be cut in half.
   b. indifference curve will shift down by half.
   c. budget constraint will shift down by half.
   d. budget constraint will increase by 50 percent.
   e. indifference curve will increase by 50 percent.

20. An increase in men's wages will be most likely to:
   a. cause an increase in labor force participation by married women due to the substitution effect.
   b. cause a decrease in labor force participation by married women due to the income effect.
   c. cause no effect on the labor force participation by married women, although the substitution effect will increase the participation of married men.
   d. cause an increase in labor force participation by married men, due to the income effect.
   e. none of the above.


## IV. Solutions

### Terms and Definitions

__5___Budget Constraint
__3___Indifference Curves
__7___Marginal Rate of Substitution
__8___Perfect Substitutes
__1___Perfect Complements
__4___Normal Good
__2___Inferior Good
__6___Income Effect

## Practice Problems

1. The indifference curve diagram below shows the tradeoff between ice cream and brownies for Ben.

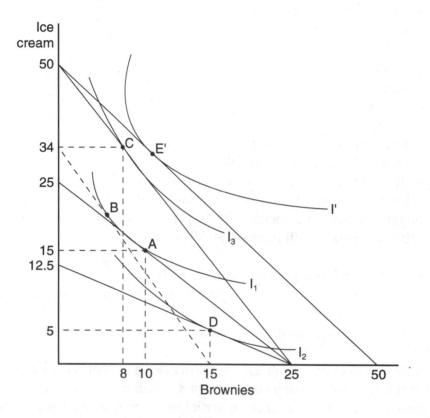

a. Ben will buy 15 servings of ice cream and 10 brownies. This maximizes his utility at the current prices of $1 each. He must be on indifference curve $I_1$, because this is the only indifference curve that is tangent to a budget line with a relative price of 1 ice cream to one brownie. If the price of ice cream doubles, then the budget constraint will pivot around its intercept point with the brownie axis: Maximum possible brownie consumption will not change, but potential ice cream consumption will be halved, from 25 to 12.5. At this new equilibrium on $I_2$, Ben will buy 15 brownies and only 5 ice creams.

b. When the price of ice cream increases from $1 to $2, the budget constraint pivots from 25 to 12.5 ice creams. Ben cuts back on ice cream consumption for two reasons: First, brownies have become a better buy (the budget constraint slope has decreased), and second, his income has fallen in real terms (he feels poorer because of the price hike). The first effect, the substitution effect, is the movement along $I_1$ from A to B, reflecting only a change in relative price. The second effect, the income effect, is the movement from B to C, which is a parallel shift in the budget constraint showing a drop in real income. The dashed line tangent to $I_1$ at point B is a hypothetical budget constraint reflecting the change in relative price while holding real income constant (utility has not changed from $I_1$). The combined effect is A to C.

c. Ben's income must be $25, because his initial budget constraint allowed him to purchase either 25 ice creams or 25 brownies when the price was $1 for either. A 100 percent increase in income would double his budget constraint. The new equilibrium would be at E', on indifference curve I'. If both ice-cream and brownie consumption rise relative to his old equilibrium at point A, (as shown on the graph at E'), this shows that both goods are normal goods (consumption rises as income rises).

## Short-Answer Questions

1. Buy more beer! Joe should cut back on soda and buy more beer, because beer is worth five times as much as soda to him, but it costs only twice as much. He can get more utility per dollar by buying more beer, until the marginal utility of beer falls and the marginal utility of soda rises enough to change the MRS of beer for soda to ½, which equals the relative price. We do not know, however, how much beer and soda he will actually purchase when he reaches that equilibrium, without knowing the exact shape of his indifference curve as well as his income.

2. As wages rise, the substitution effect encourages more work effort. At the same time, the higher wages make the worker feel richer, causing an income effect. Because people demand more leisure at higher incomes (leisure is a normal good), the income effect of a wage increase discourages work effort. If this effect is stronger than the substitution encouraging work, the net effect will be less labor supplied at higher wages: a backward-bending supply curve.

## True/False Questions

1. F; for a demand curve to slope upward, the income effect must be dominant, (and the good must be inferior).
2. T
3. F; people don't need to calculate utility in making choices for the model to predict behavior and describe the outcome accurately.
4. F; the marginal rate of substitution (MRS) of good x for good y is rate at which the consumer is willing to trade x for y; in equilibrium only it is equal to the relative price of good y versus good x, not good x versus good y.
5. T
6. F; utility-maximizing people may save less in response to a higher interest rate if the income effect is dominant.
7. T

8. T
9. F; an inferior good is one with negative income elasticity.
10. T
11. T
12. F; if all prices double and money income also doubles, the budget constraint will be unchanged, because real income has not changed.
13. T
14. T
15. F; an increase in the price of a good *pivots* the budget constraint *inward* for that good.

## Multiple-Choice Questions

| | | | | | |
|---|---|---|---|---|---|
| 1. | e | 8. | a | 15. | c |
| 2. | d | 9. | b | 16. | d |
| 3. | a | 10. | a | 17. | b |
| 4. | b | 11. | c | 18. | b |
| 5. | c | 12. | a | 19. | c |
| 6. | d | 13. | c | 20. | b |
| 7. | b | 14. | c | | |